THE GOLDEN
DAWN

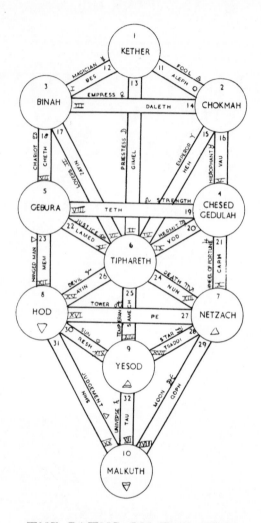

THE PATHS ON THE TREE

(see Chapter 17)

R. G. TORRENS

THE GOLDEN DAWN

DAWN

The Inner Teachings

SAMUEL WEISER
New York

First Published in Great Britain 1969
First American Paperback Edition 1973
Second Impression 1977

© R. G. Torrens 1969

Library of Congress Catalogue Card No. 73-83721
ISBN 0-87728-239-0

Samuel Weiser, Inc.
734 Broadway
New York, N.Y. 10003

Printed in U.S.A. by
NOBLE OFFSET PRINTERS, INC.
NEW YORK, N.Y. 10003

Contents

Introduction

The intention of this book is to present material which is not ordinarily available even to the serious student of esotericism. Theory and practice alike are based on a true understanding of natural fundamental forces and a serious study of this book will lead to a degree of enhanced consciousness at which the student will be enabled to live in healthy harmony with both the visible and invisible worlds.

Many approaches to occult science fail because the personal nature of the teacher intrudes. Herein, the material is so presented that the student is obliged to extend his researches in such a way as to ensure that he tests and proves all things at every stage.

The self-cancelling effects of dogma and of a teacher's personality are thus both removed at source.

The material presented ranges over the whole field of occult study. The reader will find information about the mysteries, true astrology, alchemy, the chakras and tattwas, the Quabala and the realities dealt with in many branches of the ancient wisdom— all presented in such a way as to provide the essential ground upon which genuine and *safe* practice may proceed.

Although the techniques given in the pages that follow derives from The Golden Dawn, the theory is universal and can be verified and extended from many sources.

Relevant works are quoted at the end of each chapter and the reader may be assured that the sources quoted are valid, being authenticated by experience.

Chapter 1. Knowledge

St. Paul in 1. Thessalonians V. 21 said: "Prove all things, hold fast that which is good". A curious, critical mind is necessary for research into the mysteries of nature and science. Dogma is detrimental to progress. Therefore, consider all ideas presented to you. Prove them by trial before you finally accept them. Dogma and disbelief will prevent your approach to new ideas. Truth should stand up to any trial, so do not be afraid to apply the test of reason to all ideas presented to you.

Have you really thought what Occult Science is? Over the temple door of the Grecian mysteries was written "Man, Know Thyself". Occult science is the basic knowledge of the true man. Our working life is illusion; our inner life is truth. To those familiar only with external conscious impressions this may seem fantastic. The microscope shows details that the eye cannot see unaided and atomic science has proved that matter is not solid as our senses tell us. Therefore, what we see is an illusion created by the impact of light vibrations on our senses and the interpretation of our nervous mechanism. In fact, all sensations are caused by various vibrations and our personal interpretation is an illusion created by our senses. These are useful for living, but useless if we try to find the truth.

The real truth lies within and it is the peace which passeth all understanding. This is the real object of the search. What follows is designed to present a brief yet reasoned account of the various techniques which have been employed in the past to enable a seeker to find the truth. Only the facts can be presented; it is for the seeker to apply them. We can only show the door; you must yourself open it and find the way.

Exercises will be given at intervals throughout the exposition that follows, designed to create mental states in which you can experiment; but first and always you must endeavour to create peace within yourself.

Get into a comfortable position where no interruptions are likely to occur and try to still your thoughts. To begin, fix your thoughts on a simple object by making a dot on a clean sheet of white paper. After a few trials you will be able to dispense with the paper and imagine a point. At first, extraneous thoughts will intrude but with practice you should be able to still your mind without effort. A few minutes daily will soon enable you to achieve a definite result and prepare you for later developments.

This is the beginning of practical work, the first step towards knowledge as distinct from information.

The modern world values information very highly and does not understand that information separate from knowledge leads nowhere.

Even though a man understood the material forces of the Universe, the phenomena of the heavens and the composition of the distant suns, in the eyes of Ancient Egypt that was not sufficient. In the days of her glory no man was able to participate in the Hidden Wisdom of the Divine Nature until he had prepared himself by contemplation. To the candidate thus prepared, however, there were three methods of receiving knowledge—by simple instruction, by inner vision and most important by personal participation. These techniques required release from the dominion of the senses and a temporary death to the flesh. Final initiation was the result of a carefully organized approach, clues to which can be discerned in the landmarks that remain in stone, papyrus and ritual. So much can be taken as a working hypothesis. Do the facts substantiate this?

The huge pyramids and magnificent temples whose ruins still lie in the sandy tomb of the Nile valley presuppose a very high degree of skill in architecture. The Zodiacs found at Dendyra and many passages in the written records indicate an advanced knowledge of astronomy. An examination of many of the plans of Egypt's temples in search of a common denominator reveals a surprising fact. Each and every one is arranged like some gigantic telescope with cunningly arranged diaphragms instead of lenses. The narrow portals are too high in relation to their width for mere architectural symmetry. Windows in the main body of the building are conspicuous by their absence, and if present at all are of small dimensions. In some cases, notably the rock-cut temples, there could be no possible way of incorporating windows. Herein lies a clue to solve the mystery.

Sir J. Norman Lockyer calculated the orientation of a large number of the temples. Allowing for the height of the distant hills and in some cases artificially constructed mounds in a direct line with the long axis of the building, he showed that the temples are built to focus light from one of the heavenly bodies, direct and unpolluted, into the Holy of Holies over the heads of the assembled congregation. Anyone who has knowledge of Masonic working in the higher degrees, will mark a part of one ceremony which maintains a record of this in its ritual.

Some temples were orientated to the setting or rising sun, others were aligned to receive the light from certain stars. Often these formed part of, or were adjacent to, sun or other temples. The orientation of the smaller temple was to warn of the exact time of approach by observing the rising or setting of a star which preceeded the major event. In many cases there is evidence of a change of orientation by building over an old site, or blocking the view of an older temple. The reason for this is that the continuous variation in the star's position rendered the instrument obsolete after a time, owing to the precession of the pole. A temple was therefore useful for perhaps some two hundred years and then became redundant, and a new cult later sprang up dedicated to another star personification. This explains in some degree the curious arrangement of the axis of many of the temples at Karnak and other places.

Professor Smyth has pointed out that the descending passage of the Great Pyramid at Giseh was orientated to the Pole Star, Alpha Draconis, about 2170 B.C. Marsham Adams has suggested that this monument was used for ceremonies of the higher initiation. The postulant going through the symbolic ritual of the *Book of the Dead*, finally lying in the tomb of transgression in the Inner Chamber, correctly orientated to the magnetic points, experienced the darkness visible and understood the secret wisdom by direct and personal participation. There is a record of as much as was lawful to be told in the *Golden Asse*, where Apuleius uses the words "I approached to the confines of death and having trod on the threshold of Proserpine, I returned from it, being carried through all the elements. At midnight I saw the sun shining with splendid light and I manifestly drew nearer to the gods beneath and the gods above and proximately adored them".

The statues of the gods placed in the temples were most probably used as concentrators or receptors of the specialized light or energy. Heredotus II, 44, speaking of a similar type of temple dedicated to Hercules, says, "in it were two pillars, one of fine gold, the other of emerald stone, both shining exceedingly at night".

Maspero describes the Sa as a mysterious fluid and carrier of health, vigour and life. He details how the transfusion of this fluid was performed in the temples. The god was first charged with the vital fluid, then— "the King, or any ordinary men who wished to be thus impregnated, presented himself before the statue of the god, and squatted at its feet with his back towards it. The statue then placed its right hand on the nape of his neck, and by making passes, caused the fluid to flow from it and to accumulate in him as a receiver". The odic fluid of Von Reichenbach was known and used some 5,000 years ago.

The heavy stone walls and pillars used in the construction of the massive temple buildings complete the picture. These would form a perfect insulating medium for the exclusion of unwanted vibratory influences. It would scarcely be possible to create a more suitable setting to obtain perfect conditions within a carefully constructed instrument for the fulfilment of the initiatory processes. In such beautifully designed lodges with the elimination of non-harmonious vibrations, the contact with and the investigation of the universal knowledge was comprehensive and complete.

The answer to the question is now clear and the working hypothesis is set upon a logical basis of reason. The architecture of the temples and the astronomical knowledge have a definite link. The records of Egypt indicate that the intellectual standard of the initiated priests was of no mean order. Therefore, it does not require a great stretch of the imagination to credit these men with experience of supreme wisdom by direct and personal participation. This knowledge was on a different plane to our modern kind. In those days minds sought essential qualities, whereas now minds are only satisfied with a quantitative approach based on mathematical formulae. The two types of understanding are complementary and it is hoped that in the not too distant future the rational thought of scientists will be mellowed with the true intuitive touch. The two factors wedded would lead to the expansion of human understanding and eliminate the errors or over-organization.

Sir J. Norman Lockyer. *The Dawn of Astronomy*. 1894 Cassell.
Marsham Adams. *The House of the Hidden Places*. 1895 Murray.
Marsham Adams. *The Book of the Master*. 1895 Murray.
C. Maspero. *Dawn of Civilisation*. 1894 S.P.C.K.

Chapter 2. Thinking

"The Universe of Magic is in the mind of man, the setting is but Illusion even to the thinker" stated Aleister Crowley. The tendency of modern teaching is to cram the student's mind with information, most of which is of little importance compared with the true function of the mind. To *use* the mind is its proper function and for that purpose the basic principles can be found in their purest form in the Buddhist doctrines.

Buddhism is an ethico-philosophical system. Its aim is to obtain deliverance from suffering, which characterizes all phenomenal existence. By causing no harm to living creatures, by cultivating intelligence and by reasoning from cause to effect, intuitive thinking can be awakened. This is the path along which free investigation and reason will guide the student through the jungle of ignorance.

Following the law of causality step by step the cessation of inferior states of consciousness will lead to the creation of superior states. Each being is the result of his own thoughts in the past, and present thoughts will condition future lives. A deed is only a manifestation of a thought. A true peaceful thought cannot give birth to a deed of violence.

It is possible to control and purify thought through proper training in meditation. When the mind has been sufficiently perfected it will perceive the difference between real and false values and when the senses and the mind are tranquillized, the disciple will be able to free himself from his prejudices and personal point of view. The habit of thinking "self" in opposition to "others" prevents impersonal thinking. To obtain true knowledge it is absolutely essential to think impersonally. The student must follow a definite system of mind training, he must plan and practise certain exercises frequently in order to acquire concentration. With repeated practice of concentration he will create a habit of mind which will facilitate meditation.

There are eight steps on the Noble Path to Enlightenment.

13

1. Right Knowledge   2. Right Aims
3. Right Speech   4. Right Conduct
5. Right Means of Liveli-   6. Right Effort
hood
7. Right Attention   8. Right Concentration

1. *Right Knowledge.* This is the understanding of the impermanence of all external of physical phenomena and in all the constituents of one's own personality. Eliminate prejudice, be intelligent and tolerant. Ideas will change as the comprehension develops, ordinary ideas will be shed like dead leaves and superior ideas will replace them.

2. *Right Aims.* The immediate aim is to live the truth that one has ascertained, the final goal is liberation from the limitation of personality and from suffering. Determine to become free from all attachments to wordly ties.

3. *Right Speech.* Be truthful, honest and kindly.

4. *Right Conduct.* Be peaceful, upright and benevolent.

5. *Right Means of Livelihood.* Follow an occupation that brings no harm to any living being. This helps one to recognise the Unity of Life beneath the diversity of all its forms. Only he who is free of violence is capable of right meditation.

6. *Right Effort.* Persistent effort to control thoughts and deeds will destroy all that which is harmful. To overcome ignorance and desire is to progress along the path.

7. *Right Attention.* Keen observation of life and personal thoughts, acts, intentions and their causes. Observe the functions of body and mind, recollect experiences, cultivate awareness of the present and be thoughtful of the future. This habit facilitates analysis and reflection which are necessary for meditation.

8. *Right Concentration.* Think one object or idea at a time to the exclusion of all others. This is practised to obtain supreme knowledge not for oneself alone but for the benefit of all beings. Since all life is interdependent this helps all humanity. The power of pure concentrated thought is inestimable.

Such are the fundamentals of the Buddhist teachings as exemplified to the students of the Yogic method of enlightenment. In the system there are many ways of gaining mental control, most of which first depend on gaining mastery over body and thought process. Evans-Wentz gives the various parts in the following table:

The Part	Giving Mastery of	Leading to yogic control of
I Hatha yoga	Breath	physical body and vitality
II Laya yoga	will	powers of mind
(1) Bhakti yoga	love	powers of divine love
(2) Shakti yoga	energy	energizing powers of nature
(3) Mantra yoga	Sound	powers of sound vibrations
(4) Yantra yoga	form	powers of geometric forms
III Dhyana yoga	thought	powers of thought processes
IV Raja yoga	method	powers of discrimination
(1) Jnana yoga	knowledge	powers of intellect
(2) Karma yoga	activity	powers of action
(3) Kundalini yoga	kundalini	powers of psychic nerve force
(4) Samadhi yoga	self	powers of ecstasy

Extend your point exercise to thinking colour. Choose a colour harmonious to yourself. Close your eyes and see that colour. It is helpful to do this exercise on retiring.

About 1780 C. F. Volney journeyed to visit the ruined cities of the Middle East. He arrived at Hamsa on the borders of the Ordontes at no great distance from the city of Palmyra, resolved to examine its boasted monuments. While so doing he relates:

"In the meantime a noise struck my ear like to the agitation of a flowing robe and the slow steps of a foot, upon the dry and rustling grass. Alarmed, I drew my mantle from my head and casting around me a timid glance, suddenly, by the obscure light of the moon, through the pillars of a ruined temple, I thought I saw, at my left, a pale apparition, enveloped by immense drapery, similar to what spectres are painted by issuing out of the tombs. I shuddered and while, in this troubled state, I was hesitating whether to fly, or ascertain the reality of the vision, in grave and solemn accents, this addressed me:

'How long will man importune the heavens with unjust complaint. How long, with vain clamours, will he accuse Fate as the author of his calamities? Will he then never open his eyes to the light, and his heart to the insinuations of truth and reason? This truth everywhere presents itself in radiant brightness, and he does not see it. The voice of reason strikes his ear, and he does not hear it. Unjust man! If you can for a moment suspend the delusion which fascinates your senses, if your heart be capable of comprehending the language of argumentation, interrogate these

15

Ruins! read the lessons which they present to you, and your sacred temples, venerable tombs, walls once glorious, the witnesses of twenty different ages, appear in the cause of nature herself. Come to the tribunal of sound understanding, to bear testimony against an unjust accusation to confound the declamation of false wisdom, or hypocritical piety, and avenge the heavens and the earth of man, who culminates them."

Within this passage lies the key to mental development, true magic, alchemy of the mind, call it what you will. The starting point is clearly defined : Suspend the delusion which fascinates your senses. That is the aim of Yogic training. It must be positive controlled action of mental effort. A negative uncontrolled state will however lead to delusion and possible mental illness, or possession by demons. Therefore, at all times be cautious and have a positive end in view in all mental exercises.

To get the best out of these lectures it is essential that you keep a Magical Note Book for records and drawings. To be scientific the effects of your exercises should be recorded. It will only be possible to calculate your progress if you so do. Furthermore you will in your researches acquire various notes, tables of correspondences, diagrams, etc. The Tarot and Quabala will require at least 34 lines per page, so it is advised that you procure a foolscap size ($9'' \times 12\frac{3}{4}''$) loose leaf notebook. The English National 939 is quite suitable with a four-pin easily worked clip. Get also 100 lined sheets (with 36 lines standard).

C. P. Smyth. *Our Inheritance*. London.
Herodotus. *Euterpe*. 1865 Bohn.
Aleister Crowley. *Equinox* Vol. 1. No. 1. 1909 London.
W. Y. Evans-Wentz. *Tibetan Yoga and Secret Doctrines*. 1935 O.U.P.
Felix Guyot. *Yoga for the West*. Rider.
C. C. Lounsbury. *Buddhist Meditation*. 1935 Kegan Paul.
C. F. Volney. *The Ruins*. 1819 Davidson.
Charles Wase. *The Inner Teachings of Yoga*. 1931 Watkins.

Chapter 3. Symbols

The Ancients used a large number of symbols to illustrate many abstract ideas. This is simple statement of fact, but the difficulty is that different schools used the same symbols to express varying ideas. That is why a student finds symbols surrounded by a veritable chaos of thought. Yet any student who applies himself to a new subject must familiarize himself with a new terminology, so too must the student of Occultism master the specialized meaning of any particular teaching and its symbols before he can hope to gain even a spark of illumination therefrom.

Living on the material plane and working generally in the three dimensions and being conscious of phenomena interpreted through the five senses alone, we have a very limited capacity for understanding. This veritable Saturn influence might be called a "ring-pass-not", and thus the senses of the masses are so little developed that they verge almost on the unconscious. By concentration and meditation some senses can be extended and others developed; by applying them in the correct direction the searchlight of the mental forces can be utilized to unveil the Secrets of Nature. This is the starting point which can lead towards truth or illumination via extension of consciousness.

This form of thought is unknown to the average man because his thought is unformed or in chaos. Project a formed thought to the centre, or from the centre (depending on the point of view) and the result can be two emanations with opposite yet balanced forces. Control the balance, maintain the characteristics of the seventh Zodiac Sign Libra and thought can become creative.

The Quaballa symbolises this principle in the dual emanations of Chokmah and Binah derived from Kether. The Indian gods, Brahma, Vishnu and Shiva, illustrate the same ideas—Life is a balanced mixture of the builder and destroyer, active and passive, male and female, centrifugal and centripetal, positive and negative.

In chemistry a simple compound is formed by the combination of a negative and positive radicle. Here science has a parallel

17

in ancient doctrines. The great difficulty in understanding and co-relating these points is the assortment of meaning in the terminology.

The words positive and negative applied to modern electron physics are used with the opposite meanings to those applied to the same two words in other contexts. The Halogens at the right side of the Mendelieff table are acid formers; they lack an electron in the outer ring and are on this account deficient in energy (i.e. adsorb or attract an electron). The metals or alkali formers on the left side are able to donate one external electron from the outside orbit, and thus have energy or electrons to spare. Chemistry uses these terms, positive and negative respectively, to denote these two types of activities.

Thus by an understanding of symbolism or terminology, ancient truths can be used to expand and understand scientific findings. A knowledge of symbolism does not mean illumination, rather can it lead to confusion, but by using symbolism to formulate thought, an insight into the inner meaning or quality is obtained and the power of experience is extended into other dimensions. The Secret Doctrine is only secret to those who will not make the effort. It is the effort and method of Knowing that alone leads to the pot of gold at the end of the rainbow with its seven vibratory frequencies.

The prolonged contemplation of the Three Mothers as basic qualities cannot fail to lead to a study of seven doubles or active vibratory scales. These seven rates are parallelled in various ranges. A knowledge of one scale can be used as a symbol in helping to understand the others by means of the Hermetic rule, "as above—so below". The *modus operandi* is *pari passu* with the periodic arrangement in the Mendelieff table. It was by this rule that he predicted some then unknown elements which have since been discovered.

If to the above three and seven are added a further twelve external forces, similar in comparative value to the Zodiac qualities, there is a total of twenty-two. Thus, the letters of the Hebrew alphabet interpreted according to the ancient teachings can be used to symbolize the three creative forces or primary divine activities, the seven planetary forces indicated by the basic metals used by the alchemists for transmutation while the twelve external forces suggest the mould or cauldron to affect this sublimation.

Thus the traveller in the foreign land of sublimation has a

system of signposts and maps to assist his journey. The maps are useless unless he knows how to co-relate symbols with reality.

> There are Three Mystical Fountains,
> And over these Twelve Trees bend,
> Making music like sweet harps
> When they tremble to the silver touch.
> And out of their depth Dawn arises;
> The Dawn of the primary beam;
> Light rushes over their depths;
> The Eagles cried, the Serpents rose,
> Like the flames of fire into the Sun,
> And I saw the Gleam of the Most Ancient;
> WORSHIP GOD ALONE.
>
> Enoch. Chap. XXIX.

As in the course of our researches symbolism is a necessary basis it is important that the student learns the signs which have been used from time immemorial to denote various thought patterns. Basically, the Elements of the Ancients, frequently misrepresented by modern chemists, indicate certain basic characteristic qualities of matter. They were designated as follows by the Alchemists of old.

Fire; Water; Air; Earth.

All bodies comprised varying proportions of these elements or qualities. The basis of alchemy was that by changing the proportions of the elements present the transmutation could be performed. As the alchemists believed that all matter was a form of thought they may well have had something which our modern scientists have not. The relationship of the four elements can be explained by the following diagram:

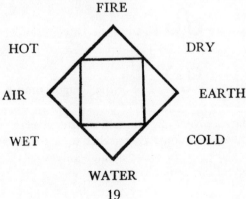

FIRE

HOT   DRY

AIR   EARTH

WET   COLD

WATER

19

Thus, the four Elements of the Ancients are dual conditions of :

Heat and Dryness	Fire	△
Heat and Moisture	Air	△
Cold and Moisture	Water	▽
Cold and Dryness	Earth	▽

The ancients knew but six planets. The sun, which had a similar astrological effect was classified as a planet, making seven in all. Their symbols are given as,

Saturn ♄ Jupiter ♃ Mars ♂ Sun ☉

Venus ♀ Mercury ☿ Moon ☽

They also assigned two planetary values to the north and south nodes of the Moon. These points were where her orbit touched the Ecliptic.

Caput Draconis ☊ Head of the Dragon similar to Neptune.

Cauda Draconis ☋ Tail of the Dragon similar to Uranus.

Since the discovery of two more distant planets, Neptune and Uranus (otherwise known as Herschel) these two terms have been partially replaced by the new planetary values.

The Signs of the Zodiac are twelve :

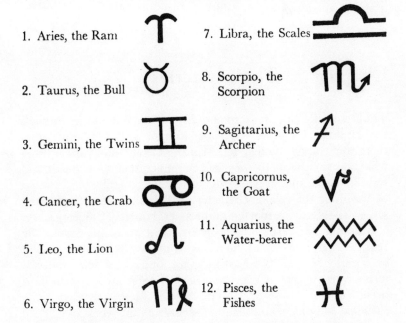

1. Aries, the Ram

2. Taurus, the Bull

3. Gemini, the Twins

4. Cancer, the Crab

5. Leo, the Lion

6. Virgo, the Virgin

7. Libra, the Scales

8. Scorpio, the Scorpion

9. Sagittarius, the Archer

10. Capricornus, the Goat

11. Aquarius, the Water-bearer

12. Pisces, the Fishes

The student should familiarize himself with these symbols which will form the basis of future studies. Frequent drawing and using these signs will assist memorizing.

E. V. Kenealy. *Enoch, second messenger of God.* 1870 Trubner.
Manley Hall. *Codex Rosae Crucis.* 1938 Los Angeles.
John Read. *Prelude to Chemistry.* 1939 Bell.
E. J. Holmyard. *Alchemy.* 1957 Pelican.
C. Aq. Libra. *Astrology, its technics and ethics.* 1917 Holland.

Chapter 4. The Mysteries

Tradition tells us that from the days of Atlantis down through the Druidic, Egyptian, Grecian, Roman and Medieval times there were many mystery schools. The Ceremonies varied somewhat, but in the main they had a similar theme—a death and resurrection drama in which the candidate generally participated by assuming the role or character of the slain victim. Today the same basic drama is enacted in the several orders of Freemasonry.

Masonry has become to no little extent an empty form. The result is that today many men regard the ancient craft as a club or friendly society. Consequently, the inner meaning—the real secret of masonry—is never unveiled. The genuine secrets have been lost until time or circumstance shall restore them. The so-called Masonic secrets can be learnt from the works of Carlisle and others; they are therefore not truly secret if they are available to the outside world. The real secret of Masonry can only be obtained, like those other secrets of the occult, by one means only. The fundamental necessity is a sincere and genuine desire on the part of the candidate to partake of that knowledge which gives power over darkness. It is not dependent on creed or sectarian monopoly.

To a mind thus modelled by virtue and science, nature presents one more great and useful lesson, for which the candidate must prepare himself by hard work and contemplation. When the apprentice has proved his ability and sincerity, he becomes a craftsman. The secrets of the ancient and modern mysteries can not be communicated indiscriminately, but are conferred on candidates according to merit and ability.

A curious mind will always question conventional custom and destructive dogma. Thus an inquisitive nature will tend along a line of research on the true nature of life itself. This investigation will result in a continuous path from purely chemical arguments to the conclusion, now generally accepted by science, that all life and material substances are just a matter of vibration. Students of the ancient wisdom have cherished the same view for many thousands of years. Ritual and ceremony based on occult teachings should offer to the seeker after knowledge of himself much more than the mere form of the ceremony can give. Therefore, seek to extend your researches into the hidden mysteries of nature and science. The ancient Egyptian mysteries are a fruitful field for study. The Lesser Mysteries of Isis consisted briefly in preparatory instruction, followed by meditation within the temple and introduction to the sanctuary for participation in a performance of a drama of death and resurrection.

The Greater Mysteries were an amplification of these rituals and as Brunton suggests included a journey of the astral body into that region which to the average man is hidden by that mysterious veil, which the eye of human reason cannot penetrate unless assisted by that light which is from above.

It is indeed probable that after many trials and purifications of the body, the minds of the candidates were prepared for the lesson that death had no terrors. The priest, by a process akin to hypnotism, caused the neophyte to undergo a temporary dissociation of mind and body. His astral or spirit body was conducted through a kind of fourth dimension and, guided by his conductor, he was able to see from without his physical body lying horizontally, as if dead. His true ego was then shown the forms which exist on a plane not far from his own. After he had proved his unshaken fidelity, he was in a later phase given power to control this dissociation himself. As an adept he could communicate and unite with other adepts in distant parts of the world. This astral communication of spirit with spirit is taught in Yoga schools.

By reading between the lines, the study of the ancient mysteries helps to expand the knowledge of ourselves and proves that occult teachings are founded on the purest principles of truth. By a comparison of the points of ceremony with the ancient beliefs, one learns the real secret of Masonry. This is no empty form but a true and sincere knowledge of the type that enables martyrs to meet their trials and tortures without flinching.

Leadbeater gives the correspondences of the lodge officers to the principles and planes of man's nature as follows:

Officers (Co-Masonry)	Principles	Planes
Right Worshipful Master	Spiritual Will	Spiritual

Worshipful Senior Warden	Intuitional Love	Intuitional
Worshipful Junior Warden	Higher Intelligence	Higher Mental
Senior Deacon	Lower Mind	Lower Mental
Junior Deacon	Lower Emotions	Astral
Inner Guard	Etheric Double	Higher Physical
Tyler	Dense Physical Body	Lower Physical

In the Lodge opening ceremony the procession is in the reverse order to that given above. In all occult exercises this indicates the withdrawal of the various principles in the search for inner consciousness. The Tyler or Physical Body is left outside on guard and the other or inner parts are free to seek enlightenment at that particular level on which the ceremony is to be worked.

The three ceremonies in craft masonry roughly correspond to the lesser mysteries of old. They were used to prepare the candidate's mind by familiarizing him with repeated ceremonial. The greater mysteries were open only to a few chosen candidates and then only after severe trials and privations. These have some parallel with Royal Arch or Chapter Masonry and are more aptly demonstrated in the Golden Dawn ceremonies. Many of the so-called higher degrees worked are of comparatively recent origin and have little place in the ancient workings. They are for the most part founded on the Christian tradition and story. These, therefore, have little attraction for the seeker after the truth in the Ancient Wisdom.

The more advanced occult ceremonial teachings were probably contained in the Rosicrucian teachings, although this cannot be claimed for many of the orders using that title as a cloak for their lack of omniscience. The purest form of these ceremonies is given in the Golden Dawn, founded by McGregor Mathers, Wynn Westcott and others in 1877.

Aleister Crowley joined this order but shortly afterwards broke away and formed his own organization known as the A. . A. . (The Argentium Astrum), or the Order of the Silver Star. He published a number of private papers in his various works but these are difficult to find and not always as pure as the original. These works are so full of claptrap and leg-pulling that it is difficult to obtain a clear picture of the essentials.

The Golden Dawn ceremonies and instructions were not published; the various papers were loaned to the student to copy and then had to be returned. The result is that the original working is almost impossible to obtain. All over the world men and women ground down by the cultural systems of today are crying out for the banished age of beauty and enlightenment—for something practical in the highest sense of the word. A few are beginning to realize that so-called civilization in its present form is at the vanishing point; that coldness, heartless commercialism and material efficiency are impractical, and only that which offers opportunity for the expression of love and ideality is truly worth while. All the world is seeking happiness but knows not in what direction to search. Men must learn that happiness crowns the soul's quest for understanding. Only through the realization of goodness and infinite accomplishment can the peace of inner self be assured.

The great philosophical institutions of the past must rise again, for these alone can rend the veil which divides the world of causes from that of effect, only the Mysteries—those sacred Colleges of Wisdom—can reveal to struggling humanity that greater and more glorious universe which is the true home of the spiritual being called man. Modern philosophy has failed in that.it has come to regard thinking as simply an intellectual process. Materialistic thought is as hopeless a code of life as commercialism itself. The power to think is the saviour of humanity.

Paul Brunton. *In Search of Secret Egypt*. London.
E. A. W. Budge. *The Book of the Dead*. 1933 Brit. Museum.
Richard Carlisle. *Manual of Freemasonry*. 1855 Vickers.
C. W. Leadbeater. *Glimpses of Masonic History*. 1927 T.P.S.
C. W. Leadbeater. *Hidden Life of Freemasonry*. 1926 T.P.S.
Douglas Howell. *Secret Signs of a Million Men*. 19/6/52 Daily Mirror.
Lewis Spence. *The Mysteries of Egypt*. Rider.

Chapter 5. Fundamentals

What is it all about? If that question had an answer, and if you had that answer, these lectures would be quite unnecessary; but before our examination of interesting material becomes too complex it is advisable to consider some fundamental principles. These may see axiomatic and their truth self-evident. Nevertheless, it is essential in our extension of knowledge to find out what makes life "tick".

Material phenomena and non-material noumena are based on at least five fundamental or basic principles, i.e. mentalism, correspondence, vibration, polarity, cause and effect. The possession of knowledge, unless accompanied by a manifestation in action, is like the hoarding of precious metals—a vain and foolish thing. Knowledge, like wealth, is intended for use. The Law of Use is universal and he who violates it suffers by reason of his conflict with material forces. Therefore, consider well these principles and examine how they can be applied to expand the knowledge both of yourself and your function in life.

I. *The Principle of Mentalism*
The All is Mind, the Universe is Mental. Everything you see around you is the form of thought : every man-made object is the result of a thought. The house, aeroplane, engineering works great and small originated on a drawing board and before that they were in the form of a thought in someone's brain. Thought is now being considered as an electrical impulse. Matter and energy are probably different forms of the same thing—one manifest, the other unmanifest. For many years the occult schools have taught this and it is the basis of the Quabala. So too the vegetable and mineral systems might be understood as a manifestation of universal life, or mind, each in its particular sphere.

II. *The Principle of Correspondence*
The ancient occult adage is well-known—as above, so below. This does not mean that heaven and earth are equal, but it means

26

that if one sequence is known, another sequence of a similar type in a parallel sphere bears a proportional resemblance to it. For example, consider the periodic table of the elements. Mendelieff when he arranged the known chemical elements according to their various characteristics, found that there were certain gaps. These gaps he predicted and so described the characteristics of many then unknown elements which have since been found.

For another example consider the octaves of the musical scale, since each note bears a similar relationship in its own particular octave to those in another octave. The Quabala and the cards in the Tarot pack form a series of symbols illustrating this principle— so that knowing one sequence, other sequences can be inferred. When the Greek Mystery Schools instructed the student "Man know Thyself" they realized that man was a microcosm, a study of which leads to a knowledge of the macrocosm.

III. *The Principle of Vibration or Rhythm*

Nothing rests; everything moves; everything vibrates; everything flows in and out; everything has its tides; all things rise and fall; the pendulum swing manifests in everything; the measure of the swing to the right is the measure of the swing to the left and rhythm compensates. The atom is a vibration and the plant is a cycle of pulsation. Thought, too, is a vibration. Thus, to change your mood or mental state—change your vibration— change your thought.

IV. *The Principle of Polarity*

Everything is dual; everything has its poles; everything has its pair of opposites; likes and unlikes are the same—opposites are identical in nature but different in degree; extremes meet; all truths are but half-truths and all paradoxes may be reconciled. Gender is in everything; everything has its masculine and feminine principles; gender manifests on all planes. To destroy an undesirable rate of mental vibration, put into operation the Principle of Polarity and concentrate on the opposite pole to that which you desire to suppress. Kill off the undesirable by changing its polarity. Rhythm may be neutralized by an application of the same idea.

V. *The Principle of Cause and Effect*

Every cause has its effect; every effect has its causes; everything happens according to the Law; chance is but a name for a Law not recognized; there are many planes of causation, but nothing escapes the Law. Nothing escapes the Principle of Cause and Effect, but there are many planes of causation and one may use the laws of the higher to overcome the laws of the lower. True Hermetic Transmutation is a Mental Art.

These precepts may be indicated in the Smaragdine Table of Hermes. Tradition relates that this tablet was found on the body of Hermes at Hebron, by an Isarim, an initiate. It contains the essence of Hermetic wisdom and forms an ideal exercise for meditation. To those who read it with bodily eyes it will suggest nothing extraordinary. Study it carefully and read between the lines.

The Smaragdine Tablet of Hermes

"True, without error, certain and most true; that which is above is as that which is below, and that which is below is as that which is above, for performing the miracle of the One Thing; and as all things were from one, by the meditation of one, so all things arose from this one thing by adoption; the father of it is the sun, the mother of it is the moon; the wind carries it in its belly; the nurse thereof is the earth. This is the father of all perfection, or the consummation of the whole world. The power of it is integral if it be turned into earth. Thou shalt separate the earth from the fire, the subtle from the gross, gently with much sagacity; it ascends from earth to heaven, and again descends to earth : and receives the strength of the superiors and of the inferiors—so thou hast the glory of the whole world; therefore let all obscurity flee before thee. This is the strong fortitude of all fortitudes, overcoming every subtle and penetrating every solid thing. So the world was created. Hence were all wonderful adaptions of which this is the manner. Therefore am I called Thrice Greatest Hermes, having the three parts of the philosophy of the whole world. That which I have written is consummated concerning the operation of the sun."

This mysterious thing is the universal magical agent, astral light, the alkahest, the Philosopher's Stone and the Elixir of Life. Hermetic Philosophy calls it Azoth, the soul of the world, the celestial virgin, *magnum opus*. Physical science knows it as heat, light, electricity and magnetism. It explains and depicts the crystalline forms of the snowflake and their modification of an hexagonal prism, which shoots out an infinity of delicate needles, which diverge from each other at an angle of 60°. It forms the atom in its many forms, which constitutes all that we know in the material world around us and it groups these atoms as proteins—the chemical foundation of all living creatures. It forms the sugars and cellulose, which are the basis of the vegetable kingdom. It forms the urge by which all forms of life are attracted and repelled. It forms the vehicle of life itself and its knowledge and utilization, gives power to the initiated to fulfil his destiny and guide his footsteps to his ultimate goal. It forms a shower of messages snowed by spiritual hands from the world above for spiritual eyes below to read.

At a later stage the characteristics of the Zodiac will be needed and it will be well to memorize them at this stage. The twelve signs given in lesson 3 may be distributed in groups of three. Each of these sets is attributed to one of the Four Elements and represents the operation of the element in the Zodiac as follows :

Fire belong to Aries, Leo, Sagittarius, which are spiritual and impulsive.

Earth belongs to Taurus, Virgo, Capricornus, which are material and restrained.

Air belongs to Gemini, Libra, Aquarius, which are intellectually active.

Water belongs to Cancer, Scorpio, Pisces, which are emotional and intuitive.

They may also be arranged in groups of four or Quadruplicities or qualities as follows :

Cardinal : Aries, Cancer, Libra, Capricornus which are Enter-prising.

Fixed : Taurus, Leo, Scorpio, Aquarius which are intense or steadfast.

Mutable : Gemini, Virgo, Saggittarius, Pisces which are adaptable or variable.

Each sign traditionally refers to a part of the body and also causes a planet to function through it in a certain manner.

Aries	Head	objectively
Taurus	Throat and Neck	productively
Gemini	Chest	adaptively
Cancer	Stomach	defensively
Leo	Heart	powerfully
Virgo	Intestines	analytically

Libra	Kidneys	harmoniously
Scorpio	Genitalia	penetratingly
Sagittarius	Thighs	freely
Capricornus	Knees	prudently
Aquarius	Calves	detachedly
Pisces	Feet	impressionably

The signs represent the static forces which colour and modify the influence of the planets. The planets represent the driving forces of life. Their key-words are represented as below :

Sun	Self integration, individuality
Moon	Rhythm, personality
Mercury	Communicative, reason
Venus	Uniting, social activities
Mars	Activity, dynamic energy
Jupiter	Expansion, vision, idealism
Saturn	Formative through restriction
Uranus	Deviation through invention
Neptune	Refining, occultism
Pluto	Transforming

A knowledge of these key-words will be very helpful when we come to the study of the Quabala. These basic qualities may be modified by context and positioning. This is explained in the field of astrology, which is well worth serious investigation by those who are interested. Here however, we are mainly concerned with the basic qualities.

Rudolph Steiner. *An Outline of Occult Science*. 1914 New York.
Three Initiates. *The Kyballion*. 1908 Chicago.
H. P. Blavatsky. *Isis Unveiled*. 1908 Rider.
S. Laing. *A Modern Zoroastrian*. 1898 Chapman Hall.
Alan Leo. *Symbolism and Astrology*. 1914 Fowler.
H. S. Green. *Reason Why in Astrology*. 1914 Fowler.
C. Jinarajadasa. *First Principles of Theosophy*. 1928 T.P.S.
Jeff Mayo. *Teach Yourself Astrology*. 1964 E.U.P.

Chapter 6. Dowsing

To increase one's sensitivity to certain vibrations it may some-times be necessary to utilize some kind of instrument. Whether this be a divining-rod, pendulum, or de la Warr's "Black Box", is immaterial. The simplest and most convenient for the average person is the pendulum. This is very popular in France, where many medical men carry one and use it as an aid in diagnosis.

There are many forms and shapes of pendulums for specific purposes, but almost any object varying in size from a hazel nut to a walnut will prove effective. A glass bead or a gold ring—even a lump of wood—will do for a start. It is tied to a short length of thin string about eight inches long. The free end of the string is held between the thumb and first finger, the other fingers being straight and parallel with the table on which lies the object to be tested. The hand is held firmly with the arm slightly away from the body so that the pendulum is about half an inch above the object and free to move as it will. Keep the hand steady and allow the pendulum to gyrate or swing without attempting to correct it or restrain it in any way. It may require some patience before the movement becomes definite. Nevertheless, it is surprising what reactions can be obtained from different objects.

In the main there are two gyrations : an anti-clockwise move-ment and a clockwise one; the former usually denotes positive or masculine characterization and the latter negative or female vibrations. Generally the pendulum will rotate in a circular direction, but under certain circumstances an elliptical path, or a swing from one point to another may occur. As an introduction to the fascinating art of dowsing try two coins, one of copper and one of silver—remember that the newer British coins are mostly nickel. When reactions to these two metals are strongly developed, try two photographs, one male and the other female and note the differing directions of gyration. When proficient at this exercise turn the photographs face downwards and try to tell the sex of the person without looking at the photograph side.

If reactions are slow to develop and are also weak, obtain a powerful magnet. With a bar magnet you should get a powerful swing at the centre and two opposing gyrations at each end. The north pole gives an anti-clockwise gyration to most people. Usually the power of a good magnet is such that its forces can be felt easily and the zones of magnetism can be ascertained without difficulty as the pendulum is moved about in and out of the varying fields of force.

There is no historical evidence about who invented either the divining rod or the pendulum. Certain objects have been found amongst Egyptian antiquities which resemble both these Instruments and tradition suggests that Moses may have used a divining rod to discover the spring on Mount Horeb. It has been alleged that the first use of the rod was by the Chinese Emperor Yu, who reigned from 2205 to 2197 B.C. and he is credited with its use in finding underground springs and hidden treasures.

It has also been suggested that the Roman legions had dowsers who preceded the troops in their expeditions into Gaul and Germany. In one of the earliest books on Satanism, published in 1521, entitled *Dragon Rouge*, written by Ammanius Marcelinus, is it stated that in A.D. 370 the pendulum was used for finding not only water, but also for obtaining oracles. Other books about the middle of the sixteenth century described the use of the rod for finding minerals.

During the next century, the Benedictine monks became well-known as experts in the art of dowsing and there are many references in works of that time. A number of authors attributed the action of the rod to the work of the Devil, but in spite of its evil reputation dowsing must have maintained its fascination with many research workers. Towards the end of the nineteenth century the pendulum and rod had an enthusiastic following.

The somewhat less bigoted attitude of the present era has allowed many developments in the use of the rod and pendulum. There is today quite an extensive literature on the subject. In 1933 the British Society of Dowsers was formed—a body which is still active with several hundred members. It has however become a little too fascinated by the de la Warr box to the almost complete exclusion of its original interest : the rod and pendulum.

In 1943 the Royal Engineers established a course of instruction with the object of having soldier water-diviners to operate with the Army, using as indicators, not scientific instruments, but hazel and willow twigs, there being no instrument in existence of equal efficiency. The R.A.F. in the desert found that water supplies were often a problem. One light bomber squadron found that it had a diviner in its ranks, and at a camp in Tripolitania he went to work and found a plentiful supply of water at a depth of 20 feet. In the *Illustrated London News* for March 20, 1943 appeared four photographs of this exercise and moreover the forked twig and the technique for holding it are well shown therein.

To dowse with the rod, a suitable twig preferably of hazel or willow must be found. This should be in the shape of an inverted Y and roughly about half an inch in diameter and about a foot long. The two ends of the Y are held in the hands with an equal tension on both sides. The hands are held palm upwards with the twig held firmly by the clenched fists. The single end of the twig is held to point forward and parallel with the ground; this position bends the two arms of the fork and create a tension. As the operator moves forward the twig will move up or down as water is reached.

In the latter part of the last century, Dr. Abrams of America invented his famous box. This was a somewhat complicated electrical apparatus based on the principle of the Wheatstone Bridge. He used this to diagnose disease but it was never accepted generally by the medical profession and was the subject of fierce controversy.

In 1941 George de la Warr of Oxford perfected a complicated diagnostic treatment apparatus. Briefly, this consisted of a box a little more than twelve by fifteen inches. There are 9 numbered dials with a rubber pad in one corner and according to the setting of these dials, each one being connected to a variable "ariel", a reaction in the form of a "stick" on the rubber pad was produced, when the operator rubbed his finger on it. It has no electricity or motive force, except for the wishes of the operator and in suitable hands it can give amazing results, but being based on the use of thought force alone, it can become an instrument of deception if used by the wrong type of person. Later models have an electronic impulse included to increase sensitivity.

De la Warr in his Oxford Laboratory has also adapted his box for use as a "camera", with which he can produce photographs of alleged diseased organs, energy patterns of crystals and other objects. The affecting of photographic emulsions by thought may be within the realm of possibility, but unfortunately when used by any orthodox scientific investigators, or even in their presence, the results are nil. The de la Warr photographs have been published but until they can be produced under strict scientific control are not likely to be accepted for general use in medicine.

The whole fallacy of the box is that no one can explain how the process works. As the instruments are both costly and complicated, it is as well for the student to practice extension of his extra-sensory-perception by using a pendulum or rod. These are inexpensive and can be proved to work with very little effort. Once you have proved to yourself that they work there is little difficulty in extending your researches into the realms of chemical analysis, colour therapy, suitability of items of diet, etc.

S. M. Pike. *Water-divining*. 1945 Research.
F. A. Archdale. *Elementary Radiesthesia*. 1950 Bournemouth.
Georges Bartarin. *Qu'est-ce que la Radiesthésie*. 1947 Paris.
Vicomte H. de France. *The Modern Dowser*. 1939 Bell.
Gabriel Lesourd. *Methode Radiesthésique*. Paris.
Gabriel Lesourd. *Cours Pratique de Radiesthésie*. 1947 Paris.
Baron de P. du Senneron. *Magnetism and Magic*. 1929 Allen & Unwin.
Langston Day. *New Worlds beyond the Atom*. 1956 Vincent Stuart.
G. Brochenin. *Traite de Radiesthésie*. Paris.

Chapter 7. Alchemy

The word Alchemy derives from the Arabic article al and the noun khemi. The noun probably refers to Egypt whose Coptic name is Khem. The Mahommedan scholars held that the alchemical art was derived from the wisdom of the Egyptians and this view was also the proud boast of Plato, Pythagoras and others, as also it was the source of their illumination. The modern interpretation of the word has more of a Greek origin and as such it implies nothing more or less than the chemical art of making and mixing infusions. The earlier meaning of chemistry was the art of extracting juices from plants and herbs.

Modern scholars are doubtful as to whether alchemical writings should be classified as mystical, magical or simply primitively chemical. It is probably reasonable to assume that at different times various authors applied one or more of these objects to their particular studies according to their abilities and interests. Some authors undoubtedly believed that gold could be transmuted from base metals—and in fact our modern scientists have proved that this is not an impossibility. Other writers, however, show quite clearly that their approach was purely a mystical or religious one.

The art is also termed Hermeticism. Hermes was the Egyptian god of Wisdom and Magic and all that is therein implied. Writers such as Robert Fludd, Henry Kunrath and Jacob Boehme aspired to and wrote about spiritual perfection; a state or mystical condition which was represented to them by the Stone of the Philosophers. Paracelsus had the primary object of curing disease and the prolongation of life. At the same time he was the discoverer of opium, zinc and hydrogen. Van Helmont was one of those rare geniuses who have increased human knowledge by his conception of gas. These two workers were chemists as well as alchemists.

Besides the genuine researchers who employed a psychological or spiritual technique and were both chemists and healers, there grew up a large body of men who utterly failed to penetrate the secret of the true doctrine on any level. These false alchemists went under the derisive name of Puffers. Their works are useless to the true seeker. Persecution by the church and propagation of the secrets of power were equally dreaded by the adepts of the art. In the immense volume of literature it is difficult to find the truth. Very few authors write without extensive concealment of their real secrets.

An unbiased examination, however, indicates quite clearly that certain sections of alchemical literature reveal the fact that the art relates to what was known to the ancients as Theurgy—the divine work. Its basic object was to afford by technical methods of meditation, reflection and magical practices and forms of prayer, a more rapid mode of spiritual development and an acceleration of intellectual evolution.

Towards the middle of last century, Mrs. M. A. Attwood published a critical examination of alchemy in a book entitled *Suggestive Enquiry*. No sooner was it published than she was struck with remorse at having exposed such a closely guarded secret. Whereupon she caused nearly all copies of the book to be withdrawn and burnt. It was not until some years after her death that the work was finally issued to the public. Mrs. Attwood and her father were probably amongst the finest classical scholars of their day and had an enormous library of alchemical works in their original languages.

Briefly, her exposures showed that the secret of alchemy was the power of the mind. It was not long previously that Mesmer had greeted the public with his theories of the magnetic fluid. Hypnotism or trance was therefore the *modus operandi* of alchemy, but this perhaps is an over-simplification of her story. In her own words "Alchemy is Philosophy; it is the philosophy of seeking out the Sophia of the mind".

Israel Regardie relates the seven metals to the seven astrological planets and these again to the constituents of man's own nature:

Saturn	lead	libido; synthetic symbol of (crude) unformulated spiritual nature.
Jupiter	tin	consciousness; memory in particular.
Venus	copper	emotion; passion and feeling.
Mars	iron	will.
Mercury	quicksilver	nervous force, prana, vital magnetism.

Luna	silver	the astral; the quick ever-changing substance which is the vehicle of consciousness, plastic to every passing thought.
Sol	gold	soul; the redeemed and regenerated ego.

When purified by art and illuminated by the process of alchemy, inner consciousness may transmute all the other metals, or principles in man. Transforming them, it enables them to perform their perfect and proper function in the psychic economy without hindrance, and without interference from any others—uniting them all into a single whole.

Mrs. Attwood provides a mystical and religious conception which far transcends the previous popular ideas of magnetism (mental). She writes "The trance state when justly and perseveringly ordered for that end affords the metaphysical condition pre-eminently perfect, for it removes the sensible obstruction and presents a clearer glass before the mind than it can ever regard in the natural state. The patient is no sooner lightly entranced than he begins to feel an internality never before known to him and which may be intensified as the intention is fixed and the calibre of the mind and circumstantial conditions are favourable. The passive personality collapses from is circumferential and phenomenal life with that central omnipresence whose circumference is not; whilst the mind, rightly disciplined and related to the Universal, becomes universalized and one with the great magnetic Will of Nature, revolving with the Infinite Medium (the pure ether) through all its spheres, perceiving all things in all and in itself, until at length becoming perfectly converted to its principle, the divinized microcosmic epitome moves with demiurgic power and grace".

Thus, Mrs. Attwood describes the technique of personal magnetism to produce a trance state leading to inner consciousness. That apparently is the object of all deeply religious exercises. We know that the magnetic method of enhancement was widely practised in Greece. Thousands of years ago the Phrygian Dactyl, the initiate priests, spoken of as magicians and exorcists of sickness, healed disease by these processes. These methods were the principal agents in theurgic mysteries as also in the Aesculapiea—the healing temples of Aesculapius, where the patients were treated during the process of "incubation", as it was termed, magnetically in sleep.

Alchemy is the science of multiplication and is based on the mental phenomena of growth. The Supreme One manifests Himself through growth, which is an urge from within outwards; a struggle for expression and manifestation. God is the spiritual seed planted in the dark earth (the material universe). By art it is possible so to grow and expand this seed so that the entire universe is tinctured thereby and becomes like the seed—pure gold. In the spiritual nature of man this is termed regeneration; in the material body of the elements it is called transmutation. As it is in the spiritual and material universes, so it is in the intellectual worlds. Wisdom cannot be imparted to an idiot because the seed of wisdom is not within him, but wisdom may be imparted to an ignorant person, because the seed of wisdom exists in him and can be developed by art and culture.

Through art (the process of learning) the whole mass of base metals (the mental body of ignorance) is transmuted into pure gold (wisdom). Thus, through faith and proximity to God the consciousness of men may be transmuted from base animal desires (the planetary metals) into a pure, golden and godly consciousness. As the way for redemption of the soul is concealed in the Mysteries, so the secrets of the metals are also concealed, that they may not fall into the hands of the profane and become perverted.

M. A. Attwood. *A Suggestive Enquiry into the Hermetic Mystery.* 1920 Belfast.
Israel Regardie. *The Philosopher's Stone.* 1938 Rider.
Anon. *The Lives of the Alchemical Philosophers.* 1955 Watkins.
C. J. S. Thompson. *The Lure and Romance of Alchemy.* 1932 Harrap.
M. M. Pattison Muir. *The Story of Alchemy.* 1902 Newnes.
A. Cockren. *Alchemy, rediscovered and restored.* Rider.
E. J. Langforth Garstin. *The Secret Fire.* 1932 Search.

Chapter 8. Mental Exercise

Interesting though the study of Alchemy is, it is a waste of time and effort to attempt these processes unless one has the true alchemical knowledge. A person who wants to be an alchemist must have within himself the "magnesia", which means the magnetic power to attract and "coagulate" the unstable astral elements. Unless a man be born again he cannot accomplish the "Great Work". If the student of alchemical formulae would remember this, it will save him much sorrow and disappointment. Cutting out the technical phraseology, mental exercises to be of use must consist of a clearly defined routine; comfortable posture; relaxing the body; regular rhythmic breathing; and with a strong persistent effort compelling the mind to work along a previously decided path. A casual indifference of attempt is doomed to failure.

In the simple exercises already suggested it should be apparent that the primary object is to still the mind in order to reduce the speed of the thought vibrations. By now it will be obvious that to do this is very difficult. In order to create correct and harmonious conditions it is necessary to prepare the body by gaining control over the breathing rhythm. Without this control developed to a high degree of efficiency mental efforts will not be effective owing to the lack of oxygen in the blood. The calculated slow rhythm induced by correct breathing exercises can form a gateway to controlled psychic excursions which without this basis might lead to danger.

Before starting any breathing exercises it is essential to attain complete muscular relaxation as far as possible. Be seated or lie down comfortably. Start relaxing the muscles of the feet and legs, then relax those of the arms starting with the fingers, next the abdomen, chest, neck and head. When a degree of calm has been achieved start breathing deeply. Let your lungs expand naturally at first and gradually breath deeper and deeper so that the lungs are filled almost to bursting point. It will eventually surprise you how little the average person uses the full capacity of the lungs. Proceed carefully at this point as dizziness may be produced in bodies which are unaccustomed to deep breathing. If this occurs pause for a while and continue when refreshed.

Make sure that the breath is entering by both nostrils. If only one is working place the fore-finger on that side of the nose and get the other one into action. Most people on awakening in the morning have only the left side working, corresponding to the lunar side of the body. It will be noticed, as consciousness of the breath develops, that when in a receptive state the left nostril is in action, and when in an active positive mood the right one works. Thus it can be understood that to produce a balanced breathing it is necessary to ensure that both nostrils are functioning equally.

It is well to remember at this point the play of the five elements in the constitution and functioning of the various bodily organs and in the manifestations and focusing of the pranic and other life forces of the body. The physical constituents represent the element earth; the bodily fluids, the element water; the animal heat, the element fire; the gaseous parts, the element air; and the more subtle psychic vitality, the element ether or spirit. In performing exercises the student should eventually become vividly conscious of the circulation of the blood and prana, of the functioning of all the bodily organs and of the arising and disappearing of each thought. At this point in our studies our first object is to develop a technique of full and efficient breathing.

Yoga has many complicated breathing styles. For our present purpose it is advisable to start on the simplest and most efficient rhythm. Now having become proficient at deep breathing, begin by finding a balanced position which is comfortable and relaxed as instructed. The Four-Fold breath as taught by the Golden Dawn is probably the most suitable technique to commence with :

1. Empty the lungs and hold while counting four.
2. Inhale while counting four so that you feel filled with air up to the throat.
3. Hold this breath while counting four.
4. Exhale counting four until the lungs are empty.

This exercise will eventually produce comfort and peace of mind. It should be done at first counting not too slowly. As practice makes it easier the counting can become slower, and eventually it can be extended for a minute at least. Having attained this rhythm prolong the exercise for two or three minutes, until you feel quiet and then you are in a fit condition to repeat the point and colour meditations.

Consider a point as defined in mathematics. Afterwards note carefully with pen and paper the ideas to which this gives rise. Concentrating all your faculties on this, try to realize the oneness and immanence of the Divine throughout all nature and in all its aspects.

At this stage the student may well ask—Why bother? The answer to that depends on what the student wants to do. The secret of all magical processes depends upon concentration and correct orientation of thought processes. The object of the exercise, therefore, is to develop control of thoughts and emotions, basing that control on a foundation of peaceful vibrations so that an impartial and unbiased analysis can be obtained. Having set the scene correctly the power of thought can thus be utilized in the desired direction. If this direction is in conformity with the cosmic design this power can have immense force. This promise is the ultimate reward for the preliminary and tedious exercises which must be regularly performed in order to attain the desired goal.

There are only two basic factors to be observed at this stage— begin and continue. Formulate the intention in your mind and then proceed without allowing stray invasive thoughts to disturb. If other worldly matters are hovering on the margin of the mind deal with them rapidly and ruthlessly, definitely lay them aside as one would chain up a fractious puppy until it was time to take it for a walk. In the same manner deal with each desire that threatens the mind's serenity. As the whole object of concentration is to learn to focus the attention on a single idea and to hold it there at will, it follows that the more simple the object chosen the more intense will be the concentration upon it. Experience has shown that until one's mental power is considerably developed, the field of truly concentrated attention is very limited, and such an expansive object as a pure abstraction is beyond the range of the beginner. Having experienced the difficulty of concentrating on a point, next try to concentrate on a line. This forms the basis of the third exercise.

There are nine basic rules in meditation which applied with common sense will eliminate most of the dangers associated with these practices; the first three are most important.

41

1. Seek wisdom and not power.
2. Avoid stunts and excesses.
3. Never be negative.
4. Do not begin unless you intend to continue.
5. Beware of self-congratulation.
6. Beware of "Guru" hunting.
7. Ignore psychic experiences, or the appearance of psychic powers.
8. Learn to want to meditate.
9. Do not neglect existing duties.

"Know Thyself" said the Delphic Oracle. The way of meditation is the way to knowing and the aim of all such knowing is to find and identify oneself with the Self within. It is therefore of extreme importance to possess some knowledge of the nature of Self and its vehicles in order that the purpose and technique of meditation may be understood. The simplest analysis is that of Body, Soul and the Spirit; the first including the complex personality; the second all that is thought of as the Higher Self; and Spirit being a useful term as any for the "Unborn, Unoriginated, Uncreated and Unformed". The aim of meditation is to differentiate and become knowledgeable about these different parts of your own life.

As meditation proceeds you may notice an ever increasing strain on the body which must be compensated by deliberate relaxation of both body and mind. In the early stages of concentration this strain is chiefly muscular, but as the effort of prolonged meditation develops there will appear evidence of strain of the nerves. You may notice yourself subject to irritability and hyper-sensitivity. This is a common experience and must be carefully controlled by paying attention to deep and rhythmic breathing, and purification of the body in every possible way. This is necessary so that the progressive refinement of the bodily instrument may keep pace with the development of the mind. Thus alone can the Spiritual Wisdom of the Universal Mind become mirrored in the heart.

Israel Regardie. *The Middle Pillar*. 1955 O.U.P.
Buddhist Lodge. *Concentration and Meditation*. 1935 London.
Geoffrey Hodson. *The Secret of Seership*. Occult Book Society.

Chapter 9. Astrology

Long years ago Astrology was included in the basic studies of the wise men. The Egyptian records are reputed to go back many thousand years before our present era; one of the earliest historians of Egypt (Herodutus *II*. 142) estimates a time of 11,340 years, during which the sun had four times risen out of his usual quarter and had twice risen where he now sets. The building of the Great Pyramid and orientation of the temples previously mentioned help to confirm that an extensive knowledge of the stars was possessed by the Ancient Egyptians.

The Zodiacs of Dendrah and Esneh represent star maps which are considered to be nearly 5,000 years old. There is a giant star map built in relief around the Tor at Glastonbury. Mrs. Maltwood has described it and indicated its limits on ordnance maps. Another of her books shows these enormous figures outlined in aerial photographs. The star map is about 10 miles in diameter. A number of the local place-names take their origin from the part of the figure in which they are found. It has been suggested that the legend of the King Arthur and the Holy Grail is the story of the initiation ceremonies enacted on this site.

A few years ago Marie Reich discovered a similar gigantic star map in the mountains of Peru, near a town called Nazca. The figures here are in some cases of a different character and of Aztec design.

Fundamentally astronomy and astrology are the same—the study of the stars. The difference being one of approach. Astronomy deals with the subject from the scientific or mathematical angle, its interest being primarily quantitative. Astrology on the other hand is more concerned with the inner qualities of the starry bodies and the effect of their varying positions on life.

It is not proposed to teach Astrology here. This information can be obtained very easily elsewhere. Our approach is one of quality, especially the inner meanings of the subject. Let us start by considering what Ptolemy says about the matter:

"It is clearly evident, that a certain power passeth from the

43

Ambient to the Earth. The two Elements beneath the moon, namely Fire and Air, are the first to feel the effects of the Ambient by which they are surrounded and these in return encompass the earth and water and effect them in a similar manner, together with the plants and animals they contain.

"The Sun, in conjunction with the Ambient, operates on all earthly substances, not only by the changes of seasons bringing the seed of animals and plants to perfection, causing the tides to flow, and substances to change; but also in its diurnal progress producing heat and moisture, cool, and dryness, according to its position with respect to the Mid-heaven. The Moon also, only by her proximity to the Earth, operates very powerfully upon it, affecting the changing of everything animate or inanimate, increasing or diminishing rivers according to her light, varying the tides as she rises and sets, causing plants and animals to increase and decrease with her. The Stars also, whether fixed or movable, are in their courses the causes of many vibrations, by means of heat, wind and storms; whereby all sub-lunary things are subject to their influence, and undergo various changes according to their several mysteries and configurations. But of all those powers, that of the sun is more prevalent and universal, the others only operating in a subordinate degree, by increasing or diminishing his influence; this is more particularly manifested in the moon at her quarters and syzigies. The effect of the other stars are more slow and obscure, as they appear, or disappear or decline. Not only are all perfect substances subject to astral influence, but even the germs from whence such bodies are produced, are moulded according to the state of the Ambient; hence the experienced husbandman, judging from the winds at the time when the seed is sown, or animals copulate can foretell what what accidents will happen to the produce; and even the most ignorant persons can judge the power of the Sun' abstractedly, when in connection with that of the Moon and Stars. Many brutes can distinguish the change of seasons; and even of the winds; their effects are chiefly caused by the Sun alone; but there are others of a more complicated nature, which may be known by observation, as miners foretell storms and hurricanes, produced by the moon and fixed stars in their courses, although they are often deceived through want of experience, and not being acquainted with the times, places or courses of the planets; whereas if they were greatly known, it would enable them to predict with certainly; what, therefore, should prevent those who are familiar with the motion of the Sun, Moon and Stars, their times, places and aspects, and the qualities belonging to them as that the Sun is hot, the Moon moist, etc., what I say, should prevent them from knowing their joint effects in all seasons, or that the atmosphere will be more warm or more moist according to the aspects of the Moon and Stars with the Sun? And if they can thus foretell the Seasons, why not also predict respecting man?

"Astrology is a science as infallible as astronomy itself, with the condition, however, that its interpreters must be equally infallible; and it is this condition, *sine qua non*, so very difficult of realisation that has always proved a stumbling block to both. Astrology is to exact Astronomy what psychology is to exact physiology. In astrology and physiology one has to step beyond the visible world of matter, and enter into the domain of transcendent spirit.

"By the radiant light of universal magnetic ocean, whose electric waves bind the cosmos together, and in their ceaseless motion penetrate every atom and molecule of the boundless creation, the disciples of mesmerism—how be it insufficient their various experiments—intuitionally perceive the alpha and omega of the great mystery. Alone the study of the agent, which is the divine breath, can unlock the secrets of psychology, of cosmical and spiritual phenomena.

"There are various nature spirits known to various teachings by many names. These beings are known by the adepts to be attracted towards certain quarters of the heavens by something of the same mysterious property which makes the magnetic needle turn towards the north, and certain plants to obey the same attraction. The various elementals are also believed to have a special sympathy with certain human temperaments, and to more readily exert power over some than others. A bilious, lymphatic, nervous or sanguine person would be affected favourably or otherwise by conditions of the astral light, resulting from the different aspects of the planetary bodies. Having reached this general principle, after recorded observations extending over an indefinite series of years, or ages, the adept astrologer would require only to know what the planetary aspects were at a given anterior date, and to apply his knowledge of the succeeding changes in the heavenly bodies to be able to trace, with approximate accuracy the varying fortunes of the person whose horoscope was required, and even to predict the future. The accuracy of the horoscope would depend, of course, no less upon the astrologer's knowledge of the occult forces and races of nature than upon his astronomical erudition."

We can assume that the Zodiac belt of the Fixed Stars on the Ecliptic forms the matrix indicating the conditions into which a soul is born. The position of the native on the left hand meridian or ascendant gives a clue to his material environment as indicated by the signs on the various houses of the horoscope. The spiritual factors playing on this mould shown by the planetary positions indicate the directing forces he is likely to meet. This is fundamentally the basis of Mundane Astrology which can be applied to all problems met in life, and can help in giving a full analysis of factors involved at any particular time.

We can thoroughly recommend our students to a study of Astrology. Start with simple works like Heindel's *Simplified Scientific Astrology* and his *Message of the Stars*, or Mayo's *Teach Yourself Astrology*. Then you can proceed to the more advanced works by Leo and others. Owing to the number of variables and uncertainties we must warn against too much easy acceptance of forecasts. The qualities taught are most helpful and useful as a guide to a system of correspondences.

Ptolemy. *Tetrabiblos* (trans. James Wilson). 1820 Hughes.

Max Heindel. *Simplified Scientific Astrology*. 1916 California.

Max Heindel. *Message of the Stars*. 1927 California.

W. Drummond. *Memoir on the Antiquity of the Zodiacs of Esneh and Dendrah*. 1821. London.

K. E. Maltwood. *Temple of the Stars*. 1935 Watkins.

K. E. Maltwood. *Temple of the Air View Supplement*. 1937 Watkins.

Maria Reich. *Mystery on the Desert*. 1948 Lima.

D. MacNaughton. *A Scheme of Egyptian Chronology*. 1932 Luzac.

Chapter 10. Egyptian Beliefs

The study of Magic, which has now fallen into disrepute was, among the Egyptians, regarded with a veneration hardly accorded to the highest Philosophy in modern times.

To the Ancient Egyptians the most eminent man was he who had by hard training gained supremacy over the Elements, from, which his own body and the manifested world were alike formed; one whose will had risen Phoenix-like from the ashes of his desires; one whose Intuition, cleansed from the stains of material illusion, was a clear mirror in which he could perceive the Past, the Present and the Future.

The Kings and Priests of Egypt were the select of those who had studied with success in the "School of Wisdom", a Philosophical Aristocracy; they were chosen because they were not only wise, but could use their wisdom. They could give strength to the Armies of the nation and they had the means of transmitting their power, for the Staff of the "King-Initiate" held so strong a magical potency, that, with it at his hand, the leader of armies became as mighty as Pharaoh himself.

The King-Priests gave forth an exoteric religion to the people, by which to guide their footsteps until they had reached that stage of development (it may have been only after repeated failures, incarnation after incarnation), when they might also join the ranks of the initiated yet it appears extremely possible that the whole Egyptian race was allowed a certain participation in the Mysteries; for the tests of a candidate were of such a nature that none but human beings developed to a considerable degree of perfection could hope to stand them.

There is every reason to suppose that only those who had received some grade of initiation were mummified; for it is certain that, in the eyes of the Egyptians, mummification effectually prevented reincarnation. Reincarnation was necessary to imperfect souls, to those who had failed to pass the test of initiation; but for, those who had the Will and the capacity to enter that secret Adytum, there was seldom necessity for that liberation of the soul which is said to be effected by the destruction of the body.

The body of the Initiate was therefore preserved after death as a species of Talisman or material basis for the manifestation of the Soul upon earth.

The first principle of Egyptian magic was based on an elaborate system of correspondences depending on the formula that, the evolution of what is material follows the type and symbol of the emmanation of the spiritual; that spirit and matter are opposite faces of the selfsame mystery. The Egyptian Adepts regarded the conception of the mind, the aspiration of the soul, the words of the mouth and the functions of the body, as possessing analogies from which a complete system of rules of life and death could be constructed. Moreover they looked upon each body, or manifested being, as the material basis of a long vista of immaterial entities functioning as Spirit, Soul and Mind in the Formative, Creative, and Archetypal worlds.

The Initiated Egyptians regarded themselves as being far from simply soul and body. They gave names to several human faculties, and postulated for each the possibility of a separate existence. The Kat, Khat or Body, was only a vehicle or material basis for the operations of the Ego upon this plane of human earth-life.

The fundamentals of the Egyptian Philosophy of Life are described partially on the obelisk of Queen Hatshepsu. A human hammemit or Primal Entity circled round the Sun for a period of One Hundred and Twenty years before incarnation. During that period certain cosmic and elemental forces would be more powerful than others; these environing the Primal Entity would give it a certain characteristic bias and guide it in the choice of the means and moment of incarnation. In the meantime the reflections of the higher elemental forces affecting the Primal Entity would be at work in the material world. These reflections would bias the human parents in like manner. When the natal epoch arrived the Great Mother-Force, symbolized by the Vulture holding the Seal, imprinted upon the Primal Entity the symbols dominant at the selected moment; and this is the rationale of the Astrological Horoscope.

The human mother had in the meantime become the centre of elemental forces that formulated an illusive attraction around her. This is the formulation of the Sahu, or the Astral body of the future human being, under the magic of the natural elemental forces. For, the plainest woman, for a time, becomes beautiful in the eyes of the lover. No sooner, however, is the co-operation of the parent forces accomplished than the Sahu hastily attaches itself to the vitalized germ and remains until it is an invisible pattern towards which solid matter gravitating forms the material body. This operation of the Sahu accounts for the vision which some clairvoyants have perceived in regard to the Vegetable Kingdom, of an Astral plant form attached to seeds or ponds before they are sown in the ground. It may also account for some of the "photographs" obtained by the de La Warr camera—mentioned in Lesson 6.

The Elemental body then having concentrated round the vitalized ovum, leaves the human mother in her natural state, stripped of the illusive beauty it had imparted to her; and she does not, or should not, regain her specially attractive power until she has done her part by the human being she is about to foster.

The unborn child is prepared for its emergence into life by the parents who contribute the principle called by the Egyptians the Hati or "whole heart". That is, the Seat of the Inherited Instincts, racial and individual; including such functions as digestion, hearing, smelling and so on. In one word the Hati is the heredity. It is clothed by a body formulated by the Elemental forces, the Sahu. The Sahu, or astral body, both before and after conception, possessed that power of radiation which formed the sphere of attraction round the human mother, which was sealed by the great Vulture—Mother—Force—at the time of conception and was withdrawn instantly to form the sphere or aura of the future human being—this is called the Khaiet, or radiating aura.

At the moment of birth the "Ego" joins the body, and there are extant many pictures which show the birth of great princes; in these the double forms of the Celestially and Terrestially generated bodies are recognizable. This is to say that the circling Hammemit now throws off an emmanation which is called the Ka or double of the newly-formed child, and thus forms its link with the earthly body by means of another principle, the Ab. The Hati is spoken of in Egyptian texts as associated with the Ab or Heart. Just as we, in our conversation, often confuse and combine our instinct and will. Will is a quality latent in every animal; it can in man be developed and cultivated until it becomes Free Will. In the same way the Ab (Will), a Red Vessel

49

of the Heart, is represented in the *Book of the Dead* as containing an egg, and a concave germ; when this concave germ is developed by cultivation the real life and full development of the Ego could begin; that is to say the Ka could progress in its celestial evolution just as the body could progress in its terrestial evolution.

In thousands of cases the celestial body was restricted; the fatal moment of conception loaded the terrestial being (composed of the Sahu, Hati and Ab within the Kab or material body) with chains of destiny too strong for him to break through. The Ka or Ego had to return to the Hammemit in the Place of Spirits and await the time when it might again have a chance of regenerating matter Astral and Material and be one of the the number of the Shining Ones, who are like jewels in the diadem of the Lord of Spirit and Life, made One.

In this we have at once the explanation of the dogma regarding the sacrifice of self to self. For the Ka or Ego can only grow and become potent through ardent and patient perserverance and struggle. The man who cannot "be Himself" must be melted down in the casting ladle of Phtha. The artist craftsman of the gods will disperse the elemental material which in its present combination cannot and will not be regenerated; he bides his time for a happier moment of operation. This doctrine is depicted in the parable of the Talents, St. Luke XIX 26 "but to everyone which hath shall be given; and from him that hath not, even that which he hath shall be taken away from him".

W. Marsham Adams. *The Book of the Master of the Hidden Places.* 1933 Search.
E. A. Wallis Budge. *The Book of the Dead.* 1910 Kegan Paul.
Thomas Taylor. *Iamblicus on the Mysteries.* 1895 Reeves & Turner.
S. S. D. D. (Florence Emery). *Egyptian Magic.* 1896 T.P.S.
Various Authors. *Records of the Past,* 18 vols. 1873–92 Bagster.

Chapter 11. Egyptian Beliefs – *continued*

From the dark side of the Egyptian Faith which dooms the impotent soul to extinction let us proceed to discuss the career opened before those who, taking the reins of the chariot of life in their own hands, guide the elemental forces which are linked to that vehicle, safe to the desirable goal.

The seeds placed with the Heart or Ab may now be considered as symbolizing the powers of Thought and Will; these once set in action by Theurgic practices or self devotion to the highest aspiration of the conscious being produce a curious result. Remembering that in the representations of the Ab the principles are reversed as though reflected in a vessel of blood—the concave germ being uppermost. We can then see that the two ends of the concave mass stretch round and form a receptacle for the eggs; this symbolizes a more quintessential influx from the primal entity or Hammemit descending upon the upstretched arms or Ka in the form of Hawk or Baie. The Cultivation of Thought and Will is again shown by the uplifted hands in the hieroglyph which represents the Ka; and the altitude of aspiration enables it to formulate a resting place for the piercing, penetrating spirit, the Baie. This latter principle is represented in four ways; by a hawk crowned, or the Horus Baie; by a human headed hawk; by a Bennu bird or by a ram. The Baie (spirit) can operate through the egg-like principle contained in the Ab and the Ka (human Ego) through the concave principle.

The four hieroglyphs used for the word Baie showed distinct orders or genera of souls; for instance, the hawk soul is only represented as resting on the Ka of the King or Queen. It is called the Royal Soul. The human headed hawk hovers over the mummies of great initiates and doubtless represents the soul after incarnation had ceased, its human head is the symbol of the quintessence of the human individuality which the bird bears to the Abode of Blessed Souls.

The Baie represented by the ram would be the progressive, penetrating power which breaks down the barriors and enables

51

the energized human soul to pass into regions, the guardians of which could hold their own against meeker enquiry.

The Bennu bird is also remarkable for transfixing and piercing its prey. There is considerable difficulty about this hieroglyph; if it represents the phoenix as it has been commonly supposed to do, it would be easy to understand that it was the symbol of a soul belonging to a more complex range of being, only to be evolved through a long series of labours on the part of its human counterpart; but if it is simply a form of common hernshaw it might imply a milder and less fiery nature of the soul.

The ram-head is often on the stone scarabaeus (symbol of self creation) which replaces the heart in the body of the mummy; representing what the medieval mystics meant when they talked of the "Stone of the Wise". That is, the Will which had become self-created and was united eternally to its celestial, progressive, penetrating faculty. The consecrated Will and purified Thought of the true Magus.

The Soul called by the Egyptians the Yekh or Khou had magical power. In nearly all the magical tales it was through the initiative of the Khou that these acts were performed. The degraded Khou became a demon and the torturer of mankind. The fate of such was to sacrifice the negatively evil, those who had neglected their opportunities; but the evil Khous could not themselves be annihilated. An evil immortality awaited the great evil-doer or destroy amongst mankind; just as a beautiful immortality awaited the Shining Ones who had added to the beauty of life in their mortal days. Between these extremes of beauty and destruction lay the impotent and ignorant where blindness doomed them to annihilation.

In the *Book of the Dead* there are elaborate formulae for the assistance of the Khou of the deceased. The justified Khou was obliged to pass many tests; it had to cultivate the gardens of heaven, destroy monsters, take on certain obligatory forms, escort the gods in their heaven-traversing ships, take part in the ceaseless struggle between the two contending forces, cross burning and desolate zones, suffer in the regions of hunger, thirst and terror, submit to proofs, reply to questions and pass the armed and hideous Deity who guarded the Portals of Wisdom.

If an Egyptian failed in standing such tests as these in the ceremony of his initiation, he was regarded as a man liable to become an evil Khou, if his power was developed; and in their wisdom the priests rejected him, and left him in that ignorance which led to oblivion and the annihilation of the incarnating Ego. Not only this, but if he, by underhand means, found out magical formulae and was able to use them effectively, the punishment was death.

It is easy to see that a great part of Egyptian magic lay in a species of hypnotism, called by later Magicians, enchantment, fascination, and so forth. Anybody with intelligence and charm can hypnotize an innocent person that interests him, but such a practice is derogatory both to the fascinator and fascinated, even when it takes place in matters of ordinary passional life. How much more so when it leads to debauchery of the soul. In this way we perceive the possibility of an uninitiate successfully performing the spells he had discovered.

Rituals or Ceremonies are frequently regarded as a waste of time by those who have to assist at their celebration; but they have a potent effect when the symbolism of each action is fully recognized, and when the imagination was extended and ultra-sensitive and the Will concentrated firmly and repeatedly on the object to be accomplished. The Ka of the Ritualist was thus at high tension acting upon its counterpart the concave germ in the Ab (heart), or vessel of conscious desire; this reacts on the Hati (Instinctive habit or unconscious executant). The whole human Ego thus being in a state of theurgic excitation the Baie (spirit) descended and the whole being became a luminous Khou, or Shining Body of super-human potency, the Augoeides of the Great Mysteries.

This glittering being established in the midst of the Sahu (Elemental Body) then by its radiation can awake corresponding potencies in nature. For this purpose the Khaibt was used as a link between the Ego and the non-Ego, and the spiritual body or Sahu was established.

When this condition was brought about, a man became in the Eyes of the Egyptians, Osirified. That is to say, a microprosopus, a perfect copy of the macroprosopus. But he who ignorant and unpurified performed these rites, became the habitation of an illusive and fatal force, ever dragging him down to the deep abysses of blind potency.

To sum up therefore the Egyptian Theologian distinguished in the economy of man the following separate but interconnected parts :

1. The Khat or material, corruptible body.
2. The Ka, Ego, or Double.
3. The Khabit, Aura or Shadow.
4. The Baie, Ba, or Heart Soul.
5. The Hati, Ab or Heart.
6. The Sekhem or vital Power.
7. The Yekh, Khou, Khu, Aakhu or Spirit Soul.
8. The Ren or name.
9. The Sahu, Sah, spiritual, astral or elemental body.
10. The Hammemit or primal entity.

The seat of instinct is the heart, which was weighed in the balance against a feather or image of truth or power of perception (*Book of the Dead*). To the Egyptians of old the cultivation of discernment was the aim of life, the want of it was a deadly sin in their eyes, and included the annihilation of the individuality. To gain perception of Truth, and so guide these fatal instincts, was the object of initiation. From the first step even, the Aspirant was taught to work upon himself as the centre of a universe of instinctive force, made on the pattern of the vast universe of which he formed a microscopic portion. Over him brooded the ways of the invisible. Daily the initiate studied the names, and meditated on the inward significance of the sounds and forms symbolizing the habitations of the Aeons and the Absolute within.

H. M. Tirard. *Book of the Dead*. 1910 S.P.C.K.
E. A. W. Budge. *The Mummy*. 1925 C.U.P.
F. Chabas. *Le Papyrus Magique Harris*. 1860 France.
William Oxley. *Egypt and the Wonderland of the Pharaohs*. 1884 Trubner.
Gerald Massey. *Ten Lectures*. Glasgow.
Larouse. *Encyclopaedia of Mythology*. 1964 Hamlyn.

Chapter 12. The Stars

To introduce some of the theories on the origin of the religions of antiquity we quote Arthur Dymot Thomson at length:

"The World, says Pliny, and what we call the heavens, which in their immense expanse embrace all other beings, must be regarded as a God, who is eternal, vast, unbegotten, and indestructable. To seek for other beings external to it, is not only useless to man, but is also beyond his mental powers; it is a sacred, vast, eternal being which encloses all in itself; it is at once the work of nature, and nature herself. It is mere folly to wish to go beyond it to seek for anything else. And Ocellus, who was a pupil of Pythagoras, says, the Universe, considered as a whole, displays nothing to us which betrays a commencement or which foretells destruction, no one has seen it created, or increased, or improved, deteriorated, or descreased; it is ever the same, existing in the same way, always equal and similar to itself. Hence the worship of nature formed the basis of all religions of antiquity; and the worship of the sun, moon and stars was common to the most learned and the less civilized nations of the ancient world. The Egyptians and Phoenicians knew in reality no other gods than the heavenly bodies and the sky in which they move, and in their hymns and theogonies sang the praises of Nature alone. The Syrians worshipped the stars of the constellation Pisces and had the sacred images of them in their temples. The worship of Adonis was established at Byblos and in the neighbourhood of Mount Libanus, and all ancient authors are agreed that Adonis was the Sun. There was a magnificent temple to the Sun at Palmyra, which was plundered by Aurelian soldiers and which the emperor ordered to be restored and dedicated anew. The Pleiades, under the name of Succoth-Benoth, were publicly worshipped by the Babylonian colonies established in the country of the Samaritans (2 Kings XVII, 29, 30). Saturn, or the planet which bears that name, is called Rempham by the Copts, and the Acts (Chap. VII. 43) reproach the Jews with having adopted the worship of the Star Rempham. Jupiter was called Baal, Mars,

55

Moloch; Venus, Astroth and Astarte; Mercury, Nebo; and all these names are also of the Syrian, Assyrian, Phoenician and Cananite deities.

"Eusebius says that the Phoenicians and Egyptians have the same religious opinions respecting the origin of all things, and respecting the divinity of the sun and stars, the only rulers of the world, he relies upon Diodorus Siculus, who informs us that the most ancient inhabitants of Egypt acknowledge two great deities, the first in rank the eternal, viz. the sun and moon . . . that they held that these two deities governed the world and that everything that receives nourishment or increase received it from them; that the whole work of generation and the perfection of all the works which are produced in nature, depended upon them". Porphry tells us that Cheremon (one of the most learned of the Egyptian priests) and a number of other learned Egyptians are convinced that we ought not to admit anything external to the universe or to the visible creation and they fortify themselves by the opinions of the ancient Egyptians. We also learn from Lucian, that all the Egyptian worship, even that of animals, related to the stars, and was founded entirely on astrology. Clemens Alexandrinus says that the book of astrology was one of the sacred books which were carried by the priests at the head of processions, and the palm, which was considered to be the symbol of astrology, was also carried in them. He also says that the four sacred animals, which were lead in the processions, were considered as emblems of the four signs or cardinal points which determine the seasons at the equinoxes and tropics and which divide the annual progress of the sun, their great deity, into four parts.

"From this also is derived the expression, the Year of God, which designates the great solar period, of which the celestial Dog, one of these four animals, fixed the commencement. The Curds of Mount Lebanon who were at times masters of Egypt followed the worship of the Dog-star from them. The dogmas of their religion were contained in a book called Souph-Sheit, or Book of Seth, to whom they attributed it. Seth is one of the names of Canis Major or rather of Sirius, the principal star of this constellation; which is the most beautiful star in the Heavens and the one which the Persians said had been appointed by Ormuzd to be the chief and superintendent of the whole heavens. This naturally made Seth or Sirius to be the inventor of astrology, and gave rise to the story of the astrological books written by

Seth and to that of the columns on which the astronomical knowledge of the antediluvians were said to be engraved.

"Bryant says, 'The worship of Ham, or the sun, as it was the
most ancient, so it was the most universal of any in the world.
It was at first the prevailing religion of Greece and was promul-
gated over all the seacoast of Europe, from whence it extended
itself into the inland provinces. It was established in Gaul and
Britain and was the original religion of this Island, which the
Druids in after times adopted.'

"The names of the gods allotted to each day of the week are
as follows; Sunday to the Sun, Monday to the Moon, Tuesday to
Mars, Wednesday to Mercury, Thursday to Jupiter, Friday to
Venus and Saturday to Saturn. This system was invented by the
Egyptians according to Dio Cassius and Herodotus and spread
to all the civilized nations of the world. They were called the
days of the gods, because the planets to which they belonged
were called gods."

In the religion of Judaism we are told how God promised that
Abraham's seed should be as numerous as the sands on the sea-
shore. His grandson, Jacob, had twelve sons and one daughter
by four wives.

This is an astronomical allegory dealing with the migration
of the heavenly bodies. A careful perusal of the 49th chapter of
Genesis and the 33rd chapter of Deuteronomy shows how they
are identified with the signs of the Zodiac, as indicated by the
blessings of Jacob : Simeon and Levi sharing the sign Gemini,
the Twins, and the feminine sign Virgo being allotted to Jacob's
only daughter, Dinah. God represents the sign Aries; Issachar,
Taurus; Benjamin, Cancer; Judah, Leo; Asher, Libra; Dan,
Scorpio; Joseph, Sagittarius; Nepthali, Capricorn; Reuben,
Aquarius; and Zebulun, Pisces. The four wives are the four
phases of the moon and Jacob is the sun. Josephus tells us that
the Jews carried the twelve signs of the Zodiac on their banners
and camped around the tabernacles which held the seven-
branched candlestick representing the sun and the heavenly
bodies which move inside the circle formed by the twelve signs
of the Zodiac. The banners used in the Royal Arch Chapter
maintain the tradition.

Now to revert to the meditation exercises. How have you been
progressing? You alone are your own and only true examiner,
so be critical. You cannot achieve any mental control without

persistent effort; you cannot become a magician without powerful thought concentration, so it is up to you. If you have neglected the first meditations start again and continue for at least a week before continuing:

The Earth meditation: First quieten the mind with the fourfold breathing, then consider a line; then outline a square; next mentally formulate a cube. Meditate upon minerals and crystals especially salt. Enter into it and actually feel yourself as a crystalline formation.

Looking out from this point of view identify yourself with the Earth Spirits in love and sympathy. Meditate upon the Earth Triplicity, realizing the Bull, Virgin and Goat which represent them as Kerubic or Fixed, Mutable and Cardinal Earth. Make a note of ideas and pictures which these meditations awake in your mind.

F. Rolleston. *Mazzaroth.* 1862–5 Rivington.
A. D. Thomson. *On Mankind; their destiny and origin.* 1872 Longmans, Green.
Max Heindel. *Western Wisdom Bible Teachings.* California.

Chapter 13.   The Chakras

There are many methods of psychic developments, some of which commence with the development of one centre and some with another, but in the scheme advocated in Ancient Egypt and continued in Freemasonry, the centre is indicated by the sign of the degree being worked. So when a Freemason makes that movement he not only indicates the opening up of that centre for special work from the occult point of view of this degree, but he also commands the aid of the powers in nature connected with and controlled through that centre in whatever work he is about to undertake. The gestures and words taught in Freemasonry are not chosen at random; each has a definite meaning and a definite signification on the physical plane. Masons generally however know nothing of all this.

The seven centres exist as points of connection at which energy flows from one vehicle or body of a man to another. Anyone who possesses a slight degree of clairvoyance may easily see them in the etheric double, where they show themselves as saucer-like depressions and vortices in its surface. When quite undeveloped they appear as small circles about two inches in diameter, glowing dully in the ordinary man; but when awakened and vivified they appear as blazing corruscating saucers much increased in size. They are sometimes spoken of as roughly corresponding to certain physical organs; in reality they show themselves at the surface of the Etheric double (the aura) which projects slightly beyond the outline of the physical body. If we imagine ourselves looking down into the bell of a flower of the convolvulous type, we shall get some idea of the general appearance of a chakra. The stalk of a flower in each case springs from a point in the spine, so another view might show the spine as a central stem, from which flowers shoot forth at intervals, showing the opening of their bells at the surface of the etheric body. It was in order to avoid the arousing of the lower centres that so much importance was attached in Egypt to the apron and the etheric web which stretched across it.

In India the spine is called the Brahmadanda or stick of Brahma. It is formed etherically of two-five-coiled serpents around a rod surmounted by a spherical knot and two wings. This is the original of the caduceus of Mercury. The two snakes symbolise the Kundalini or serpent fire which is presently to be set in motion along those channels, while the wings typify the power of conscious flight through the higher planes which the development of that fire confers. Initiation in the first degree of Freemasonry could stimulate the current, starting on the left hand side near the base of the spine which is crimson in colour and known as Ida. The second degree assists the right hand side and is yellow in colour and known as Pingala. In the third degree the triad is completed by the activation of the deep blue stream of the Sushumna, or Middle Pillar.

It is part of the hidden secret of Freemasonry to stimulate into activity these forces in the human body, so that the evolution of the individual may be accelerated. This stimulation is applied at the moment when the Right Worshipful Master creates, receives and constitutes. In the Initiation it affects the Ida or feminine aspect of this force, thus making it easier for the candidate to control passion and emotion. In the passing it is the Pingala or masculine aspect which is strengthened, in order to control the mind and in the raising it is the central energy itself, the Sushumna, which is aroused, thereby opening the way for the influence of the pure spirit on high.

It is by passing up through this channel of the Sushumna that a yogi leaves his physical body at will in such a manner that he can retain full consciousness on higher planes and bring back into his physical brain a clear memory of his experiences.

In a man the Ida starts from the base of the spine to the left, the Pingala being on the right, that is, the left and right of the man, not the spectator. In a woman their positions are reversed.

The Chakras, then, are positioned in the areas described below, each vortex or flower being attached by a cord to the spine.

Chakra	Sanskrit Name	Colour	Approx. Portion of Root	Sympathetic Plexus
1. Root	Mûlâdharâ	Orange-red	4th Sacral	Coccygeal
2. Spleen	Svârdhisthâna	Rose	18th Lumbar	Spleen
3. Navel	Manipûra	Green	8th Thorasic	Coeliac
4. Heart	Anâhata	Yellow	8th Cervical	Cardiac

5. Throat	Vishuddha	Blue	3rd Cervical	Pharyngeal
6. Brow	Âjnâ	Dark Blue	1st Cervical	Carotid
7. Crown	Sahasrâra	Violet		

The Spleen Chakra is not given in the Indian books, its place being taken by a centre called the Svâdhisthâna situated in the neighbourhood of the generative organs to which the same six petals are assigned.

The divine energy which pours into each centre from without, sets up at right angles to itself (in the surface of the etheric double) secondary forces in undulatory circular motion, as a bar-magnet thrust into an induction coil creates a current at a right angle to the axis of the magnet. The number of spokes differs in the various centres and determines the number of waves or petals which each of them exhibits. Because of this they are often spoken of in oriental books as resembling flowers.

The first chakra or Root has four spokes, dividing it into quadrants alternately red and orange in colour. This makes it appear to be marked with the sign of the cross which is frequently used to symbolize this centre. This is the seat of the serpent fire which stirs into activity consciousness and awakens the astral life of the man.

The Splenic Chakra is divided into six compartments and is devoted to absorption into the system of the sun's vitality. The awakening of this centre which is rose in colour enables the person to travel astrally but with only a vague recollection of his journey.

The Third or Umbilical has ten undulations and is a blend of red and green with the latter predominating. It is closely associated with feelings and emotions. It awakens in the astral body the power of feeling and sensitivity to all sorts of influences, but without the definite comprehension that comes from seeing or hearing.

The Fourth or Heart Chakra has twelve divisions and is mainly yellow in colour. When awakened it enables the person to comprehend and sympathize with the vibrations of the other astral entities.

The Fifth or Throat Chakra has sixteen divisions generally silvery and gleaming blue; almost a suggestion of moonlight on rippling water. Awakening this gives the power of hearing on the astral planes.

The Sixth or Brow Chakra between the eyebrows is dark blue with ninety-six divisions. The awakening produces astral sight with the power to perceive definitely the shape and nature of objects.

The Seventh or Crown is at the top of the head and has 96 divisions which are predominantly violet in colour. The awakening completes the development of the candidate.

This Chakra is frequently depicted in Indian works of art in the form of a jewelled crown or head cap.

The Yoga Tattwa Upanishad gives meditations related to the areas of the body. These are assigned to the five elements in the following manner: they are given for information, but can be used for concentration exercise if the student wishes.

The region of earth is from the feet to the knees. It is four-sided in shape, yellow in colour and has the letter La. Carrying the breath with this letter along this region one should contemplate Brahmâ with four faces and a golden colour.

The region of water extends from the knees to the thighs. It is semi-lunar in shape and white in colour with the letter Va. Carrying the breath along this region meditation is upon the god Nardyana, having four arms and a Crowned head, the colour of crystal and dressed in orange clothes.

The region of fire is from the pelvis to the heart, triangular in shape and red in colour with the letter Ra. Raising the breath made resplendent by the letter Ra along this region, he should meditate on Rudra who has three eyes and grants all wishes. The colour is of the midday sun and is smeared all over with holy ashes and has a pleasant countenance.

From the head to the middle of the eyebrows is the region of air, hexangular in shape (i.e. two interlaced triangles). The colour is black and shines with the letter Ya. Carrying the breath along this region, meditation is upon Ishvara, the Omniscient with faces on all sides.

From the centre of the eyebrows to the top of the head is the region of ether or spirit. It is circular in shape, smokey in colour and shines with the letter Ha. Raising the breath along this region, meditation is upon Sadâshiva as producing happiness. The shape is as a drop (spherical) shining like pure crystal, as the Great Deva wearing the crescent crown on his head, having five faces, ten heads and three eyes. He has a pleasing countenance and armed with all weapons, adorned with all ornaments, has the goddess Umâ in one half of his body, as the cause of all causes and ready to grant favours.

C. W. Leadbeater. *The Chakras.* 1938 T. P. S.
V. G. Rele. *The Mysterious Kundalini.* 1927 Bombay.

Chapter 14. Initiation

How many Masons realize the inner meaning of true initiation? They have gone through their several degrees with beating hearts and shaking knees. After that they sit back and watch with complacent satisfaction the discomfort of others taking the same steps. How often does the real meaning of that ceremony impress its truth on their minds?

It is difficult to describe in words matters which cannot be illustrated by symbol or diagram. Veiled in allegory the expression of thought may be understood by those prepared to see the light. As the words of the Volume of the Sacred Lore expresses it "He that hath an ear to hear, let him hear".

All candidates for Masonry enter by the help of God, being free and of good report. Phrased in somewhat different language we might say that candidates must be assisted by the forces of Nature, independent and capable of reasoned action. Expanded, that means that candidates must be assisted by the help of the secret and everlasting forces of Nature, have full and complete self possession to isolate him from blind or hampering tendencies, and lastly he must be possessed of reason illuminated by science. Thus equipped he can advance through darkness and see the light of truth. Nature's power is for all, but we must learn to use it before we can acquire it. Liberty is for all who know how to be free, and reason we all have—but many do not know how to use it.

Let us see what light may be shed on this dark subject by the ancient mysteries. "The candidate abandoned his life and liberty entirely to the masters of the Temples of Thebes at Memphis; he advanced resolutely through unnumbered terrors, which might have lead him to imagine that there was a premeditated outrage intended against him. He ascended funeral pyres; swam torrents of black and raging water; hung by unknown see-saws over unfathomed precipices. . . ." (Levi, 1923). This was blind obedience in the strict meaning of the term. Nevertheless the most absolute exercise of liberty is surely to abjure liberty for a time so that we may attain emancipation.

In the Elysian Mysteries of Ancient Greece, we are told (Spence) that at the moment of complete revelation an ear of corn was presented to the candidate, who was then told that herein was the heart and depth of the mysteries and that it symbolizes in itself all and everything that they had undergone so much to understand. The ear of corn tucked away on many ancient monuments rightly symbolizes life. Being sown, it grows and multiplies to replenish the earth, then at Autumn there are still grains of corn just like the first, apparently dead, but ready under favourable circumstances to burst forth into life once more. This symbol of rebirth is probably more clearly understood if one compares the earlier ideas on reincarnation. Christianity teaches of death and resurrection in another and better life. The pre-Christian idea was a series of progressive rebirths. *The Tibetan Book of the Dead* describes in great detail the peculiar phenomena met in the Spirit World during the forty-nine (or seven times sèven days) that the soul spent in the other world between each death and rebirth. This series of incarnations was dependent upon the spiritual development of the man. If he progresses he became more proficient in spiritual matters with each birth till at last he attained to Buddhahood or at one ness with the Gods. The Christian word atonement bears a suggestive resemblance to this idea. To the Tibetan initiation was death, to the Mason initiation is birth into a fellowship and an inner life which is sheltered from the storm of worldly turmoil. Briefly, the ear of corn symbolizes the mystery of the trinity of Past, Present and Future, or if you prefer it, of the Whence, Why and Whither. As true liberty can only be realized by sacrificing it to a purpose, so initiation should teach us that we have a purpose by helping each other to make a daily advance in the knowledge of ourselves.

Sacrifice in various forms is the basis of most religious teachings and frequently is symbolized by a lamb or lambskin. The Entered Apprentice's apron is more ancient than the Golden Fleece, more noble than any Order in existence, being the badge of innocence and the bond of friendship. When placed on the apprentice with its flap upturned it denotes a five-sided figure similar to that which was drawn on the floor of ancient lodges and erased by the E.A. after the ceremony, with mop and pail. This five-sided figure represented the combination of the square and triangle, and so the rough ashlar fresh from the quarries is shaped by the forces of education into the perfect stone suitable for the builders to use as a solid foundation upon which to stand the knowledge of the trinity or triangle—the number three numerically and geometrically being symbolical of the deity or nature. The candidate by his initiation is enabled, if he so desire to take his first step in the knowledge of himself. But ceremony itself is not enough. The symbol and allegory alone are no use, the hidden or esoteric meaning can only be obtained by reading the wisdom of the ancients. To impress this upon your mind consider the words of Spence: "The countless centuries of experience hoarded and preserved by an ancient world which knew little of the hectic haste and unrest of ours, its extraordinary earnestness regarding things divine, make it manifest that the lessons it inculcated should be profoundly considered by that English-speaking race which have long ago inherited and comprehended the wisdom of Egypt. Many of us do not realize that for lack of consideration, for the pitiful sake of immediate emolument, we are throwing away the greatest and richest treasure the world has to give us".

Initiation therefore is the development of the inner light, the gentle fanning of the flame of consciousness of the internal being. It requires peace of mind and the exercise of awareness of one's subconscious activities. In modern phraseology—it is personal psychology. When one reaches these inner recesses of one's own personality one can then communicate with the universal power. This power can be brought into the physical world and used for the improvement of mankind.

Initiation is the first step in the world of magic. Ceremonies by themselves are but signposts and vehicles. The true initiation is the inner light which urges the candidate to pursue the path to knowledge with a persistence which cannot be diverted. These lectures are of themselves dead marks on rotting vegetation. They are like the ear of corn, capable in their symbolism of coming to life and multiplying. Therefore, read and re-read, consider what they mean and encourage your inner self to follow those signposts and persist in daily exercises to control your unruly thoughts.

The story of the "Fall" is understood to have been occasioned by man's impulsive and ignorant use of the sex forces at times when the interplanetary rays were inimical to conception of the purest and best vehicles. Thus man became gradually imprisoned in a dense body crystallized by sinful passion and consequently an imperfect vehicle, subject to pain and death.

Then commenced the pilgrimage through matter and for millenia we have been living in this hard and flinty shell of body, which obscures the light of heaven from the spirit within. The spirit is like a diamond in its rough coat, and the celestial lapidaries, the Recording Angels, are constantly endeavouring to remove the coating so that the spirit may shine through the vehicle which it ensouls.

When the lapidary holds the diamond to the grindstone, the diamond emits a screech like a cry of pain as the opaque covering is removed; but gradually by many successive applications to the grindstone the rough diamond may become a gem of transcendent beauty and purity. Similarly, the celestial beings in charge of our evolution hold us closely to the grindstone of experience. Pain and suffering result, which awaken the spirit sleeping within and the man, hitherto content with material pursuits, indulgent of sense and sex, becomes infused with a divine discontent which impels him to seek the higher life.

Initiation is a word frequently surrounded by clouds of mysterious ignorance. The dictionary simply interprets as meaning beginning or rites relating thereto. This then can relate to any stage of the development of consciousness, consequently when one starts a new phase of life or thought process, it is initiation. Life being a continuous development any fresh excursion into strange fields of study is an initiation. It is not the beginning that matters, rather is it the persistent progress which carries the seeker to his chosen goal. For that reason the name—The Initiate—is frequently used to designate a being of a much higher order.

Eliphas Levi. *Transcendental Magic*. 1923 Rider.
W. Y. Evans-Wentz. *The Tibetan Book of the Dead*. 1927 O.U.P.
Israel Regardie. *The Golden Dawn* (4 vols.). 1948 U.S.A.
W. E. Butler. *Magic and the Quabalah*. 1964 Aquarian.

Chapter 15. The Tattwas

In nature we find seven forces, or seven Centres of Force, and many things seem to respond to that number, as for instance, the septenary scale in music or sounds and the septenary spectrum in colour.

There are reasons, however, why only five Tattwas are given in the Hindu systems. Owing to our having reached only the fifth race and being (so far as science is able to ascertain) endowed with only five senses, the two remaining senses that are still latent in man can have their existence proven only on phenomenal evidence which to the materialist is no evidence at all. The five physical senses are made to correspond with the five lower Tattwas; the two as yet undeveloped senses in man and the two forces, or Tattwas, forgotten by the Brahmas and still unrecognized by science, being so subjective and the highest of them so sacred, they can only be recognized by and known through the Highest Occult Sciences. It is easy to see that these two Tattwas and the two senses (the sixth and the seventh) correspond to the two highest principles—Buddhi and the Auric Envelope, impregnated with the light of Atma. Unless we open in ourselves by occult training the sixth and seventh senses, we can never comprehend correctly their corresponding types. Thus the statement sometimes made that in the Tattwas scale the highest of all is the Akasha (followed by four, each of which becomes grosser than its predecessor), if made from the esoteric stand point, is erroneous. For once Akasha, on almost homogeneous and certainly universal principles, is translated ether, then Akasha is dwarfed and limited to our visible universe, for assuredly it is not the Ether of Space. Ether, whatever modern science makes of it, is differentiated substance; Akasha having no attributes save one—Sound, of which it is the substance—is no substance even exoterically and in the minds of some orientalists, but rather chaos, or the Great Spatial Void. Esoterically, Akasha alone is Divine Space, and becomes Ether only on the lowest and last plane, or our visible universe and earth. In this case the blind is in the word "attribute", which is said to be Sound. But Sound is not an attribute of Akasha, but its primary co-relation, its primordial manifestation, the Logos, or Divine Ideation made word, and that "Word" made "Flesh". Sound may be considered an "attribute" of Akasha only on the condition of anthropomorphizing the latter. It is not a characteristic of it though it is certainly as innate in it as the idea "I am I" is innate in our thoughts.

While Sanskrit and Hindu philosophy generally speak of five Tattwas only, occultists name seven; this making them correspond with every septenary in nature. The Tattwas stand in the same order as the seven Macro and micro-cosmic Forces; and as taught in esotericism are as follows :

1. Adi Tattwa, the primordial universal Force, issuing at the beginning of manifestation, or of the "creative" period, from the eternal inimitable Sat, the substratum of all. It corresponds with the Auric Envelope, or Brahma's Egg, which surrounds every globe, as well as every man, animal and thing. It is the vehicle containing potentially everything—Spirit, Substance, Force and Matter. Adi Tattwa in esoteric Cosmogony, is the Force we refer to as proceeding from the First or Unmanifested Logos.

2. Anapadaka Tattwa, the first differentiation on the plane of being, or that which is born by transformation from something higher than itself. With the occultists this Force proceeds from the Second Logos.

3. Akasha Tattwa is the point from which all exoteric philosophies and religions start. Akasha Tattwa is explained in them as Etheric, Force, Ether. Hence Jupiter, the "Highest" God was named after Pater Aether; Indra once the highest god in India is the etheric or heavenly expanse. The Christian biblical god is spoken of as the Holy Ghost, pneuma, rarified wind or air. This the occultists call the Force of the third Logos, the Creative Force in the already Manifested Universe.

4. Vayu Tattwa, the aerial plane where substance is gaseous.

5. Tejas Tattwa, the plane of our atmosphere, from Tejas luminous.

6. Apas Tattwa, watery or liquid substance or force.

7. Prithivi Tattwa, solid earthy substance, the terrestial spirit or force, the lowest of all.

All these correspond to our principles and to the seven senses and forces in man. According to the Tattwa Force generated or induced in us, so will our bodies act.

In exoteric Yoga Philosophy and the Hatha Yoga practice, Akasha Tattwa is placed in the head (or physical brain of man); Tejas Tattwa in the shoulders; Vayu Tattwa in the navel (the seat of all the phallic gods, creators of the universe and man); Apas Tattwa in the knees, and Prithivi Tattwa in the feet.

Certain symbols and colours are traditionally associated with the Tattwas:

Tattwa	Quality	Symbol
Akasa	Ether or Spirit	Black or indigo egg
Vayu	Air	Sky blue disc or circle
Tejas	Fire	Red equilateral triangle
Apas	Water	Silver crescent
Prithivi	Earth	Yellow square

It would be well to remember that in discussing things of the higher realms words are somewhat inadequate. Therefore at all times try to find and contact the hidden quality by the development of inner knowledge and remember the maxim "as above, so below".

Let us now take a look at these five planes in other world systems. The following are given by Gaskell:

Christian	Kabbalah	Egypt	Rome
Father God	Ain Soph	Ra	Jupiter
Son of God	The Crown	Osiris	Bacchus
Holy Ghost	World of Emmanation	Isis	Juno
Mental faculties	World of Creation	Thoth	Mercury
Lower Emotions	World of Formation	Set	Pluto
Sensations	World of Action	Nephthys	Vesta

Greece	Greek (philosophy)	Mediaeval	Boehm
Zeus	Father Aether	Ineffable	Verbum Fiat
Apollo	Good Mind	Light	Light Breath
Hera	Fire	Fire	Fire Breath
Hermes	Air	Mental	Air Breath
Hades	Water	Astral	Water
Hestia	Earth	Physical	Earth

69

Sweedenborgh	Indian	Ottoman Sufi	Chaldea
The Infinite	Paran-atma	The Unity	Ea
Celestial	Atma	Absolutely Invisible	Marduk
Spiritual	Buddhi	Relatively Invisible	Istar
Rational	Manas	World of Man	Nebo
Proprium	Kama	World of Similitudes	Enlil
Physical	Strula	Visible World	??

Iran	Japan	China	New Zealand
Zerana Akerana	Ameno	Heaven	Rangi
Ormazd	Ninigi	Water	Tangaroa
Armaiti	Ama-terasu	Fire	Rongo-matane
Tistyra	Shmatsu-hiko	Metal	Tuma-tauenga
Ahriman	Susu-no-wo	Wood	Tane-Maluta
??	Haigi-no-Kami	Earth	Haumea-tiki-tiki

In all these there are correspondences, although at first sight there may appear to be discrepancies. Look at all times for the hidden quality and make allowances for the special interpretation of the followers in each system. The four worlds of the Quabala are probably the simplest basis from which to start.

In order to put these Tattwa symbols to practical use it is advisable to draw them on a piece of card (about 5″ x 4″) each symbol being about 2″ high. They can then be coloured as directed in this lesson. Alternatively, pieces of coloured paper can be cut to the appropriate shape and stuck on the white card. The technique for practical use is simple : the chosen symbol is held in front and the student gazes at it for about twenty seconds or more. Do not forget to produce a state of calm and quiet before attempting any excursions. The gaze is then transferred to any white surface, such as the ceiling, when the symbol should be seen in the complementary colour.

When this has been done several times the student should be able to visualize this figure easily. It is then made to expand to the size of a door. The next step is to imagine that one is actually passing through as if it were an open door. Do not go beyond the threshold until you become more experienced. As an exercise in visualization it can be recommended, but unless you are proficient in the Banishing Ritual (lesson 36) it is unwise to enter.

H. P. Blavatsky. *The Secret Doctrine.* T. P. S.
G. A. Gaskell. *A Dictionary of the Sacred Languages.* 1923 London.

Chapter 16. The Quabala

The clearest definition of the Quabala is given by Crowley:

"(*a*) A language fitted to describe certain classes of phenomena, and to express certain classes of ideas which escape regular phraseology. You might as well object to the technical terminology of chemistry.

"(*b*) A unisectarian and elastic terminology by means of which it is possible to equate the mental processes of people apparently diverse owing to the constraint imposed upon them by the peculiarities of their literary expression. You might as well object to a lexicon, or a treatise on comparative religion.

"(*c*) A symbolism which enables thinkers to formulate their ideas with complete precision, and to find simple expression for complex thoughts, especially such as include previously disconnected orders of conception. You might as well object to algebraic symbols.

"(*d*) An instrument for interpreting symbols whose meaning has become obscure, forgotten or misunderstood by establishing a necessary connection between the essence of forms, sounds, simple ideas (such as numbers) and their spiritual, moral, or intellectual equivalents. You might as well object to interpreting ancient art by consideration of beauty as determined by physiological facts.

"(*e*) A system of classification of omniform ideas so as to enable the mind to increase its vocabulary of thoughts and facts through organizing and co-relating them. You might as well object to the mnemonic value of arabic modification of roots.

"(*f*) An instrument for proceeding from the known to the unknown on similar principles to those of mathematics. You might as well object to the use of square root of minus one, x to the 4th power, etc.

"(*g*) A system of criteria by which the truth of correspondences may be tested with a view to criticizing new discoveries in the light of their coherence with the whole body of truth. You might as well object to judging character and status by educational and social convention."

The matter contained in the Quabala deals with the nature of God, the Sephiroth or divine emanations, of angels, and of man. God, known as Ain Soph, fills and contains the universe. As he is boundless, mind cannot conceive him. In a certain mystical sense he is non-existent. The doctrine of the Sephiroth is undoubtedly the most important to be met with in the pages of the Quabala. To justify his existence the Deity had to become active and creative and this he achieved through the medium of the ten Sephiroth or intelligences, which emanated from him like rays from a luminary. The first Sephiroth or emanation was the wish to become manifest, and this contained nine other intelligences or Sephiroth, which again emanate one from the other—the second from the first, the third from the second, and so forth.

The ten Sephiroth are :

No.	Name	Meaning	Represents	Position
1.	KETHER	The Crown	Premium Mobile	IM
2.	CHOKMAH	Wisdom	The Zodiac	2R
3.	BINAH	Understanding	Saturn	2L
4.	CHESED or GEDULAH	Mercy	Jupiter	3R
5.	GEBURAH or PAHAD	Strength	Mars	3L
6.	TIPHARETH	Beauty	Sun	4M
7.	NETZACH	Victory	Venus	5R
8.	HOD	Splendour	Mercury	5L
9.	YESOD	Foundation	Moon	6M
10.	MALKUTH	Kingdom	Elements	7M

These Sephiroth are connected together by "Paths", twenty-two in number and designated by the 22 letters of the Hebrew alphabet, each of which also has a number. The 22 trumps of the pack of Tarot cards are also related to these paths (although the numbers do not correspond). The 22 Paths, added to the ten Sephiroth form the "Thirty-two Ways" by which Wisdom descends by successive stages upon man and may enable him to mount to the Source of Wisdom, by passing successively upwards through these 32 Paths. This process of Mental Abstraction was the Rabbinical form of what the Hindu knows as Yoga, or the Union of the human with the Divine, by contemplation and absorption of the mind in a mystical reverie.

Path No.	Hebrew letter	Correspondence	Connecting	Trump No.
11	Aleph	Air	1 – 2	0
12	Bes	Mercury	1 – 3	I
13	Gimel	Luna	1 – 6	II
14	Daleth	Venus	2 – 3	III
15	Heh	Aries	2 – 6	IV
16	Vau	Taurus	2 – 4	V
17	Zayin	Gemini	3 – 6	VI
18	Cheth	Cancer	3 – 5	VII
19	Teth	Leo	4 – 5	VIII
20	Yod	Virgo	4 – 6	IX
21	Kaph	Jupiter	4 – 7	X
22	Lamed	Libra	5 – 6	XI
23	Mem	Water	5 – 8	XII
24	Nun	Scorpio	6 – 7	XIII
25	Samekh	Sagittarius	6 – 9	XIV
26	Ayin	Capricorn	6 – 8	XV
27	Pe	Mars	7 – 8	XVI
28	Tsaddi	Aquarius	7 – 9	XVII
29	Qoph	Pisces	7 – 10	XVIII
30	Resh	Sol	8 – 9	XIX
31	Shin	Fire	8 – 10	XX
32	Taw	Saturn	9 – 10	XXI
32 Bis		Earth		
31 Bis		Spirit		

The Quabala envisages four worlds :

1. World of ATZILUTH—Archetypal or emanation.
2. World of BRIAH—Creation.
3. World of YETZIRAH—Formation.
4. World of ASSIAH—Action.

These four worlds can be referred to respectively as Sephiroth 1; 2 and 3; 4, 5, 6, 7, 8 and 9; and 10. Alternatively they can be referred to four complete sets of 10 Sephiroth.

The Dogmatic or Theoretical Quabala indicates philosophical conceptions respecting the Deity, Angels and beings more spiritual than pre-existence and reincarnation and the several worlds or planes of existence.

The Practical Quabala attempts a mystical and allegorical interpretation of the Old Testament, studying each phrase, word and letter; it teaches the connection between letters and numbers and the modes of their inter-relation; the Principles of Gematria, Notaricon and Temura; the formation and uses of the divine and angelic names as Amulets; the formation of magic squares; and a vast fund of allied curious lore, which subsequently formed the basis of Medieval Magic.

Now to change the exercise. Practice the *Moon Breath* which is exactly the same as the four-fold breath except that it is done through the left nostril only. At the same time say mentally the word AUM. Then meditate upon the waxing and waning crescents while visualizing a silver crescent on an indigo background. Now call to mind the signs of the Airy Triplicity; Gemini, Libra and Aquarius. Enclosed in these, meditate on the number five and the form of the Pentagram. Now rise in imagination above the mineral world into the realm of trees and flowers and identify yourself with the Powers of the Air beyond these.

This meditation may appear at first to be complicated. However take it in stages and after a few trials you can complete it. It is important to keep notes of your efforts and any results you may notice. Beware of allowing your mind to become empty— always keep it directed firmly on a positive action and watch inwardly. Beware of voices—if you hear any, dismiss them.

These exercises should help you to realize the mental world where the mind rules over matter and make you ponder over the ideas of appearance and reality.

Should you have lost continuity in your exercises start again from the beginning. Without persistence you will never reach that perfection of mental control which will enable you to operate the forces developed in ceremonial magic.

Aleister Crowley. 777. 1955 Neptune Press.
Lewis Spence. *An Encyclopaedia of Occultism.* 1920 Routledge.
J. F. G. Fuller. *The Secret Wisdom of the Quabalah.* Rider.
W. W. Westcott. *An Introduction to the Kabalah.* 1910 Watkins.
C. D. Ginsburg. *The Kabbalah.* 1925 Routledge.

Chapter 17. The Tree of Life

In order to assist visualization it will now be necessary to delineate for yourself the Quabala Diagram or, as it is usually called, the "Tree of Life". For this you will need some white foolscap-size paper, a compass for pencil and pen, a ruler and a drawing board. Cartridge paper is more suitable than ordinary thin paper. It can be bought in sheets and cut to the correct size (13″ x 9″) with scissors or a sharp knife.

First draw a fine pencil line vertically down the paper at one inch to the right of the centre of the paper. This allows an inch margin on the left for filing. Setting the compass at $2\frac{1}{2}″$, two points up and two down from the centre of the vertical line are marked. This gives five points equally spaced on the vertical line. Using the top four marks as centres draw in pencil four "generating" circles. Next in ink and using the six points of intersection of the "generating" circles, draw six circles $1\frac{1}{4}″$ diameter (set compasses at $\frac{5}{8}″$). Four more $1\frac{1}{4}″$ circles are now drawn using the points marked on the centre line as centrea (omit the second mark from the top). You should now have four circles on the centre line, with three others on each side at regular spacing.

You now have a diagram of the ten Sephiroth correctly proportioned and large enough to insert whatever names or signs you wish. To repeat or copy the diagram all you have to do is to prick through onto another sheet of paper at the centre points of the ten circles. This will transfer the points to a fresh sheet and makes it a simple matter to duplicate the diagram as often as required.

These circles should now be numbered as indicated in the table on page 72. Columns 1 and 5 e.g. 1 M(iddle) is No. 1; 2 R(ight) is No. 2; 2 L(eft) is No. 3 and so on. All directions are to be taken as you look at the paper. No. 2 being on your right as you look at it. The importance of this will be pointed out at a later stage.

The next step is to draw in the paths. Draw a fine pencil line from the centre of each Sephiroth to the next as indicated in column 4, of page 73. On each side of these connecting lines draw an ink line from the circumference of the circles, but not penetrating them. These lines should be just over $\frac{1}{8}''$ on each side of the pencil lines giving a band of just over $\frac{1}{4}''$. Note that the paths numbered 14, 19 and 27 should be drawn first as the paths behind these are cut at the points of crossing, that is, these three paths are shown in front. Next number these paths neatly (col. 5) and mark them with the Hebrew names as in col. 2. You have now completed the diagram of the Tree of Life. The width of the paths should be $\frac{1}{2}$ of the radius of the Sephiroth.

For those who find a difficulty in lettering neatly, there are sets of stencils available. There are quite a range of styles and sizes— one type known as 'Uno'—and together with special pens and ink can be obtained through any good stationers. Ask for the catalogue before choosing the style and size you require. The cost is quite moderate.

We are now in a position to consider the traditional qualities of the ten Sephiroth.

1. Kether, the crown, represents "I am" as being, that is, as pure existence. It is neither positive nor negative but both and though sexless has the potential of male and female. Though the primordial point of light, it is nevertheless the circumference of all things, the centre of which is nowhere, because it is in No-Thing; containing all the potency of Tetragrammaton YHVH), it is simultaneously past, present and future. In the letter Yod, which corresponds to it, is enclosed the immanence of the ten Sephiroth. It is frequently called the Ancient of the Ancients, the Ancient, or the Ancient of Days. In the Book of Daniel, VII, 9, we read: "I beheld till the thrones were cast down and the Ancient of Days did sit, whose garment was white as snow and the hair of his head like pure wool: his throne was like the fiery flame, and his wheels as burning fire".

Kether is also called the White Head, the Long Face, Macro-prosopos and Adam Qadmon or Adam Illah—the Supernal or Primordial or Heavenly Man. The remaining Sephiroth are the Short Face.

In the angelic order, Kether is represented by the Beasts of Ezekiel, the Holy Living Creatures of the Chariot-Throne, namely the four Kerubim—the Eagle, Man, Lion and Bull— which represents the four elements—Air (smell), Water (taste), Fire (sight) and Earth (touch). It includes in its mysterious nature the four letters of the Tetragrammaton, namely YOD (Lion), HE (Man), VAH (Eagle), and HE (Bull). As in itself Kether is also the Shekina (the Glory of God), in it is hidden the SHIN or fire, which symbolizes Spirit.

As the Ain Soph is represented by the closed eye, so Kether is represented by the open eye. (Compare the eye of Shiva in Hindu mythology). As long as this eye remains open, the universe is maintained in being, but when it shuts it vanishes into Non-Being, that is No-Thingness. In the threefold division of Man's nature, Kether represents Neshamah—Spirit.

2. Chokmah or Wisdom is the Son or Logos and the First Born. It represents abstract ideas, the fruit of "I am" forming in the mind, the only begotten mind. Its colour is red orange or yellow, the colour of Christ. It is positive and male.

3. Binah, the mind, generally called Understanding. It is feminine and negative—the matter (mater, mare—sea) in which Kether can later form and propagate itself. It is often called the Heavenly Mother or Holy Spirit. Her dimension is depth, whilst Kether's is length (compare the yoni and lingam of Hindu mythology); her colour is sky-blue, the colour of the Virgin Mary.

4. Chesed or Gedulah means Grace, Love, Mercy and Compassion. From Chokmah emanate six Sephiroth, which symbolize the dimensions of matter. Chesed is the right arm of the Macrocosmos; it endows the world with feeling and sentiment.

5. Geburah, also known as Pahad, carries the idea of Rigour, Punishment, Fear or Severity. This is the left arm of the Macrocosmos. It is feminine and passive, as Chesed is masculine and active. As Chesed symbolizes life, so Geburah symbolizes death.

6. Tiphareth or Beauty is the common centre or harmony of Chesed and Geburah, of life and death, the active and the passive in the moral world. Its symbol is the Sun, the heart of the universe and also the heart of Adam Qadmon—the Supernal Adam. It is the seat of the sentiment and the ethical qualities; it is inhabited by the Ruach—the reasoning Soul.

7. Netzach means Triumph, Firmness or Victory. It is the part of the three energetic principles. It represents the right leg and thigh of Macrocosmos.

8. Hod means Splendour or Glory and is the left leg and thigh of Macrocosmos. "By Triumph and Glory we comprehend extension, multiplication and force, because all the forces which

were born into the universe went out of their bosom and it is for this reason that these two Sephiroth are called: the armies of YHVH (Jehovah)"—Myer.

9. Yesod, the Foundation, is the seat of the Generative Principle and also has strong connections with the astral world. "Everything shall return to its Foundation, from which it has preceeded. All marrow, seed and energy are gathered in their place"—Myer.

10. Malkuth is the Kingdom or Dominion. As Kether is the harmony at the beginning, so Malkuth is the harmony at the end; the first the head and the last the feet of Adam Qadmon. The divine name attached to this Sephiroth is Adonai—the Tetragrammaton. It is also called the Queen, Shekinah and Havah—Eve. It is the seat of the Nepesh, the instincts, and its angel is Metraton, the Angel of the Covenant.

The Ten Sephiroth when combined with the 22 letters form what is known as the Tree of Life, which constitutes the framework of the Adam Quadmon, heavenly Adam, similar in anatomy to his human counterpart—Earthly Adam. Man is a combination of three spheres of force, the intellectual, the moral and the physical, which are related to the Neshamah, Ruach and Nepesh.

Dion Fortune. *The Mystical Quabalah*. 1941 Williams & Norgate.

Chapter 18. The Aura

Around certain electrical discharges in various gases, such as Crooke's tubes, Neon lights, etc., there is a high degree of activity. Around the human body can be seen, by clairvoyants and others whose sight has been trained, a similar zone of activity. This is the aura or as it is sometimes called—the etheric double of man. It is not in any sense a separate vehicle, but must be considered as part of the physical body. It is clearly visible to the clairvoyant as a mass of faintly luminous violet-grey mist, interpenetrating the denser part of the body and extending slightly beyond it. This etheric matter is the link between the astral and physical, which has also a very important function as the vehicle of the vital forces on the physical plane.

This vital force is poured over us from the Sun, which is the source of life in this inner sense as well as by means of its light and heat in the outer world. Complementary forces are also poured out by the moon and planets and probably also from the fixed star groups in the Zodiac. The earth's atmosphere is full of this force at all times, though it is in special activity in brilliant sunshine and it is only by absorbing it that our physical bodies are able to live and keep healthy. The force itself is naturally invisible like all other forces; but after it has been absorbed into the human body it takes on a beautiful pale rose colour and flows in a constant stream over and through the whole body along the nerves and arteries of Ida, Pingala and Sushumma (see Chapter 13).

Some authorities trace the existence of the aura in such scriptural instances as the bright light shining about Moses, which the Children of Israel were unable to look upon, when he descended from the mountain bearing the stone tablets engraved with the Ten Commandments; in the exceedingly brilliant light which shone round about St. Paul at the time of his conversion; and in the transfiguration of Jesus Christ, when his raiment shone so brightly that no fuller on earth could whiten it. Many of the medieval saints were said to be surrounded with a cloud of light. Of St. John of the Cross it is told that when at the altar or kneeling in prayer, a certain brightness darted from his face; St. Philip Neri was constantly seen enveloped in light; St. Charles Borromeo was similarly illuminated. This is said to be due to the fact that when a person is engaged in lofty thoughts and spiritual aspiration, the auric colours become for the time being, more luminous and translucent and therefore more easily discernable. In Christian art, round the heads of saints and sacred characters, is to be found portrayed the halo or nimbus which is supposed to represent the aura; sometimes the luminous cloud is shown around the whole of the body as well as the head, when it is called the aureola. It is also thought that the colours of the body and clothing in medieval paintings and stained glass are intended to represent the auric colours of the person portrayed. The crowns and distinctive head-dresses worn by the kings and priests of antiquity are said to be symbolic of the aura. In many sacred books of the East, representations of the great teachers and holy men are given with the light extended round the whole of the body. Instances of this may be found in the temple caves of India and Ceylon, in the Japanese Buddhistic books, also in Egypt, Greece, Mexico and Peru.

Paracelsus, in the 16th century, mentions the aura in the following terms: "The vital force is not enclosed in man, but radiates round him like a luminous sphere and it may be made to act at a distance. In these semi-natural rays the imagination of man may produce healthy or morbid effects. It may poison the essence of life and cause diseases, or it may purify it after it has been made impure and restore it to health". Again "our thoughts are simply magnetic emanations, which, in escaping from our brains, penetrate into kindred heads and carry thitherto, with a reflection of our life, the mirage of our secrets".

The aura is a highly complicated and entangled manifestation, consisting of many influences operating within the same area. Some of the elements composing the aura are projected from the body, others from the astral principles connected with the "Higher Self", or permanent Ego; and the various auras are not lying around the others, but are all blended together and occupy the same place. Guided by occult training, the clairvoyant faculty may make a complete analysis of the various elements in the aura and can estimate the delicate tints of which it is composed—though all blended together—as if each were seen separately.

Classified more exactly the divisions of the aura are stated to be : 1. the health aura; 2. the vital aura; 3. the Karmic aura, that of the animal soul in man; 4. the aura of character; 5. the aura of the spiritual nature.

1. The health aura is almost colourless but becomes perceptible by reason of a curious system of radial striations. 2. The vital aura is under a certain extent of control of the will, when it circulates within the astral body, of a delicate rosy tint, which it looses, becoming bluish as it radiates outward. 3. The Karmic aura is the field of manifestation, or the mirror in which every feeling, every desire is reflected. Its colours constantly change to the clairvoyant vision. 4. The character aura is permanent and is said to contain the record of the past earth lives of the personality. 5. The spiritual aura is not often seen even by clairvoyants, but it is described by those who have seen it, only in the cases where spiritual nature is the most powerful factor, as "outshining all the rest of the auras with startling brilliancy".

The auric colours cannot be adequately described in terms of the ordinary colours discernible to the physical vision, being very much brighter and of varied hues and shades : the symbolic meaning of these is roughly of the following order : rose, pure affection; brilliant red, anger and force; dirty red, passion and sensuality; yellow, of the purest lemon colour, the highest type of intellectual activity; orange, intellect used for selfish ends, pride and ambition; brown, avarice; green, is a colour of varied significance, its root meaning is the placing of one's self in the position of another, while in its lower aspects it represents deceit and jealousy. Higher up it signifies adaptability and at its very highest, when it takes on the colour of bright foliage, the very essence of thinking for other people. Green merging into yellow stands for the lower intellectual and critical faculties; blue indicates religious feeling and devotion, its various shades corresponding to the various degrees, rising from fetishism to the loftiest religious idealism; purple represents the psychic faculty, spirituality, regality, spiritual power arising from knowledge and occult pre-eminence.

Most people can see the aura given suitable conditions. Having placed a dull black cloth about a yard in front of you, sit comfortably with the light from a candle coming over your shoulder. Now relax and use the four-fold breath with your eyes closed for a few minutes. Then hold your arms out with your hands placed with your palms facing you. Place the tips of the fingers about an inch or two apart and move your hands slowly. As your sight becomes sensitive you should see a faint flame between the fingers which appears to bend as the fingers move apart.

There is another way to see the aura and that is the use of Kilner Screens. These are a special hollow pair of spectacles in which is placed a solution of di-cyanin blue. This is an expensive chemical and difficult to handle in solution. A very good substitute is to have a pair of ordinary motor-cycle goggles fitted with Bristol blue glass. This can very easily be obtained from a glass factory and should be a rich dark brilliant blue similar to that used in cathedral windows. Staring at a bright light for a few minutes with these on will sensitize the eyes and make the aura easier to see.

When you get accustomed to the use of these glasses another curious phenomenon may be observed. Go into the garden in bright sunlight and look at the vegetation. Dead or dying foliage will appear quite white and opaque, whilst young lush growth looks pink and transparent. The living processes can be seen to be at work. Further, the use of these glasses can develop clair-voyance. Try looking at a magnet and notice, if you can, the red aura at one end and the blue at the other.

C. W. Leadbeater. *Man Visible and Invisible.* 1902 T.P.S.

H. P. Blavatsky. *The Key to Theosophy.* 1893 T.P.S.

Karl, Baron von Reichenback. *Physico-Physiological Researches.* 1850 London.

Ralph Shirley. *The Mystery of the Human Double.* Rider.

Chapter 19. Magic

The Goetia or First Part of the Lemegeton, or Lesser Key of King Solomon states that "Magic is the Highest, most Absolute and most Divine Knowledge of Natural Philosophy, advanced in its work and wonderful operations by a right understanding of the inward and occult virtue of things; so that true adepts being applied to proper patients, strange and admirable effects will thereby be produced. Whence magicians are profound and dilligent searchers into Nature, they, because of their skill, the which to the vulgar, shall seem to be a miracle".

Crowley in his *Magic* puts the matter more comprehensively : "Definition : Magic is the Science and Art of causing Change to occur in conformity with Will.

"Postulate : Any required Change may be effected by the application of the proper kind of degree of Force in the proper manner through the proper medium to the proper object.

"Theorems :

   1. Every intentional act is a Magical Act.

   2. Every successful act has conformed to the postulate.

   3. Every failure proves that one or more requirements of the postulate have not been fulfilled.

   4. The first requisite for causing any change is thorough qualitative and quantative understanding of the conditions.

   5. The second requisite of causing any change is the practical ability to set in right motion the necessary forces.

   6. Every man and every woman is a star.

   7. Every man and every woman has a course, depending partly on self, and partly on the environment which is natural and necessary for each. Anyone who is forced from his own course, either through not understanding himself, or through external opposition, comes into conflict with the order of the Universe, and suffers accordingly.

   8. A man whose Conscious Will is at odds with his True Will

is wasting his strength. He cannot hope to influence his environment efficiently.

9. A man who is doing his True Will has the inertia of the Universe to assist him.

10. Nature is a continuous phenomenon, though we do not know in all cases how things are connected.

11. Science enables us to take advantage of the continuity of Nature by the empirical application of certain principles whose interplay involves different orders of ideas connected with each other in a way beyond our present comprehension.

12. Man is ignorant of the nature of his own being and powers. Even his idea of his limitations is based on experience of the past, and every step in his progress extends his empire. There is, therefore, no reason to assign theoretical limits to what he may be, or to what he may do.

13. Every man is more or less aware that his individuality comprises several orders of existence, even when he maintains that his subtler principles are merely symptomatic of the changes in his gross vehicle. A similar order may be assumed to extend throughout nature.

14. Man is capable of being, and using, anything which he perceives, for everything that he perceives is in a certain sense a part of his own being. He may thus subjugate the whole Universe of which he is conscious to his individual Will.

15. Every force in the Universe is capable of being transformed into any other kind of force by using suitable means. There is thus an inexhaustible supply of any particular kind of force that we may need.

16. The application of any given force affects all the orders of being which exist in the object to which it is applied, whichever of these orders is directly affected.

17. A man may learn to use any force so as to serve any purpose, by taking advantage of the above theorems.

18. He may attract to himself any force in the Universe by making himself a fit receptacle for it, establishing a connection with it, and arranging conditions so that its nature compels it to flow towards him.

19. Man's sense of himself as separate from, and opposed to, the Universe is a bar to his conducting currents. It insulates him.

20. Man can only attract and employ the forces for which he is fitted.

21. There is no limit to the extent of the relations of any man with the Universe in essence; for as soon as man makes himself one with any idea the means of measurement cease to exist. But his power to utilize that force is limited by his mental power and capacity, and by the circumstances of his human environment.

22. Every individual is essentially sufficient to himself. But he is unsatisfactory to himself until he has established himself in his right relation with the Universe.

23. Magick is the Science of understanding oneself and one's condition. It is the Art of applying that understanding in action.

24. Every man has an indefensible right to be what he is.

25. Every man must do Magick each time that he acts or even thinks. Since a thought is an internal act whose influence ultimately affects action, though it may not do so at the time.

26. Every man has a right, the right of self-preservation, to fulfil himself to the utmost.

27. Every man should make Magick the Keynote of his life. He should learn its laws and live by them.

28. Every man has a right to fulfil his own will without being afraid that it may interfere with that of others; for if he is in his proper place, it is the fault of others if they interfere with him".

Such then are the fundamental points as outlined by the greatest self-styled magician of all times. Whatever went wrong with his application of magic to his personal ends, there is no doubt that by digging amongst his leg-pulling and pornography can be found many pearls of wisdom. The two books by John Symonds are worthy of deep study. Whether his achievements are an illustration of the following warning from the Golden Dawn manuscripts, we leave the student to determine for himself.

"Obsession always entereth through a cutting off of a Higher from the Lower Will, and it is ordinarily first induced by a Thought-Ray of the Spiritual Consciousness (whence one danger of evil thoughts ill-governed, penetrating the sphere of Sensation and admitting another potency, either human embodied, or human disembodied, elemental or demonic). The first action of such a force is to flatter the lower will, until he shall have established firmly an entrance into the Sphere of Sensation and thus shall cause a strain on the Nepesch which shall render the

Ruach less concentrated. As soon as the Ruach is sufficiently dispersed to repair the strain on the physical body, the lower will is weakened and is soon seized upon and bound by the intruder. Whence arise the sensations of chill and drowsiness which are the usual forerunners of obsessions. Now to yield the force necessary to overpower the lower from any chance of communication with the higher, the obsessing idea proceeds by seizing upon the Daath, and this consequently is the great point of attack, especially the part in the physical body which is at the back of the head about the junction of the spine. Now unless the lower will shall reluctantly endeavour to restore the connection, it is impossible for the Higher Will to intervene, seeing that the Lower Will is King of the Physical Body. Remember that no obsessing force can overpower the lower will, if it shall bravely and in spite of all opposition aspire unto the Higher Will.

"Death superveneth in the natural man, when the mental action of the Ruach and the Nepesch is definitely and thoroughly interrupted in the physical body. In the adept, death can only supervene when the Higher Will consenteth thereto, and herein is implied the whole mystery of the Elixir of Life."

Take note moreover of what Madame Blavatsky says: "To become a Neophyte, one must be ready to devote himself heart and soul to the study of mystical sciences. Magic—the most imperative of mistresses—brooks no rival. Unlike other sciences, a theoretical knowledge of formulae without mental capacities or soul powers, is utterly useless in magic. The spirit must hold in complete subjection the combativeness of what is loosely termed educated reason, until facts have vanquished cold human sophistry."

John Symonds. *The Great Beast*. 1957 Rider.
John Symonds. *The Magic of Aleister Crowley*. 1958 Rider.
Franz Hartman. *Magic, White and Black*. 1914 Kegan Paul.
Eliphas Levi. *The Magical Ritual*. 1896 Redway.

Chapter 20. The Tarot

Tarot is a French name for a species of playing cards: sometimes they are called Thora Rota. The Italian name Tarocchi—used for the game—is so called from the Tarotees, that is, having plain or dotted lines on the back. The German Taroch-karte were chequered on the back and it is also suggested that the Hungarian Gipsy name for the cards was Tar, and the Hindustani—Taru.

Whatever there is in a name, it seems likely that these ancient mystery cards may have been brought back to Southern Europe by the warriors and possibly the Knights Templars, from the Saracens, or one of the mystic sects flourishing in Syria. Tradition goes further and suggests that they originally came from Egypt. When the Gipsies arrived in England is very uncertain, but they are first noticed in our laws by several statutes against them in the reign of Henry VIII, in which they are described as outlandish people, who do not profess any trade or craft, but call themselves Egyptian. The legend relates that after the destruction of the Serapeum in Alexandria the larger body of attendant priests banded themselves together to preserve the secrets of the rites of Serapis. Their descendants, the Gipsies, carried with them the most precious of the volumes saved from the burning library—the Books of Enoch or Thoth (the Tarot) and became wanderers upon the face of the earth, remaining a people apart with an ancient language and a birthright of magic. Thus the ancient lore was veiled in allegory and illustrated by symbols to be preserved in a common plaything till time or circumstance should reveal its true meaning.

Count de Gebelin believed that the word Tarot was derived from two Egyptian words; Tar, meaning road and Ro, meaning Royal. Thus together indicating the Royal Road to Wisdom. Christian, the mouthpiece of a French secret society, gives an account of these cards, which when enlarged were the basis of the initiation in the Egyptian Mysteries, each card being explored in turn. Schure hints at the same sort of thing in the Hermetic Mysteries.

This tradition, in a modified form, is the basis of modern Hermetic rituals, such as the Golden Dawn and similar orders.

There are several modern packs available and there are many ways of interpreting them. In these pages we follow the general correspondences of the Golden Dawn workings. This will tend to avoid confusion and, when you gain more experience, you can compare the others and accept only what appears reasonable to you. In Chapter 16 we give these in table form.

The Tarot pack in use today contains seventy-eight cards of which 22 are more properly known as the Tarots and are considered the keys. These correspond to the twenty-two letters of the Hebrew alphabet. The suits are four: Wands, Sceptres or Clubs, which are usually shown in leaf, indicating life and animation and representing fire; Cups, Chalices, Goblets or Hearts, which naturally refer to the water which appears in all the court cards of this suit; Swords, corresponding to Spades or air and generally suggesting strife; Pentacles, Money or Circles, corresponding to Diamonds or earthly possessions.

Each suit consists of fourteen cards, the Ace and nine others, together with four court cards, the King, Queen, Knight and Knave. The Knave was known anciently as the Princess and is basically a female figure. There are several packs available from the many bookshops specializing in occult literature.

First: the Waite Pack which has recently been reprinted and has a descriptive book entitled *The Pictorial Key to the Tarot*. This pack was originally published by Rider, who commissioned A. E. Waite. The designs were executed by Pamela Coleman Smith under his instruction. This can be recommended as the best of the modern packs.

The Marseilles pack by B. P. Grimaud (dated 1748-1930) is also available. This is a good copy of an ancient pack and is very colourful and has a descriptive book *Le Tarot de Marseille*, in French.

An Egyptian (?) set of cards is published by the Brotherhood of Light. This pack is in black and white to be coloured by the owner. They are very crude and the numbering and symbols are not in conformity with the G.D. They are described in a book *The Sacred Tarot* by C. C. Zain and are similar to those depicted in a book by Henry Frichet published in Paris in 1924 *Le Tarot Divinatoire et le Livre de Thot*. This book, which is very rare, also depicts an Italian Tarot pack.

Gareth Knight has produced a set in collaboration with the Dutch artist and astrologer, Sander Littel. These are claimed to be esoterically correct. The drawings are very colourful but somewhat crude. There is a book accompanying these cards called *The Tarot* and some of the cards have been used as cover illustrations to the early issues of the occult magazine, *New Dimensions*.

Unfortunately the most perfect and correct rendering has never been published complete as a pack. The full designs are in the hands of a private collector. This is the pack designed by Crowley and drawn by Lady Freda Harris under his instructions. These are described in his *Book of Thoth*, published in 1944, with a few plates in colour and the rest in black and white. It incorporates the traditional symbols and correspondences as taught secretly by the Hermetic Order of the Golden Dawn. It gave a modern style to the ancient forms by the use of mathematical, scientific and geometrical designs. The colours illustrate the meanings, so that each card is not only a work of art but a talisman of the force that it represents. Where the force is adverse, as in 9 and 10 of Swords which represent cruelty and ruin respectively, the balance has been restored by the inclusion of the protective angel concerned. The Rosicrucian tradition is restored by the placing of "The Fool" in the front of the pack and numbering it 0 instead of XXI or XXII. Several trumps have been renamed to correspond with their true meanings :

No. 1. The Juggler becomes the Magus suggesting the wisdom of Thoth, rather than the juggling of Mercury.

No. VIII. Justice becomes Adjustment because nature is exact rather than just. Justice has a human and consequently relative sense.

No. XI. Strength is renamed Lust implying not only strength, but the joy of strength determined. It is the very vigour and rapture of vigour.

No. XIV. Temperance has become Art to signify the conscious meeting of opposites to produce a balance.

No. XX. The Last Judgement or the Angel has become the Aeon to depict the new era of the twentieth century, instead of the end of the world. Thus departing from the old tradition in order to renew that tradition.

Finally, the court cards are now called by their hitherto secret names—King, Queen, Prince or Emperor, and Princess or

Empress, instead of King, Queen, Knight and Knave or Page. The new names are in accordance with the Formula I.H.V.H. Thus each card becomes the talisman of the forces which it represents by tradition.

Let your meditations now include the symbols of the Rhomboid and Vesica. Seek out their meanings and correspondences. Contemplate the symbol of Mercury and the number 8. Identify yourself with the Powers of the Water Triplicity in all its aspects, with its attributes and correspondences.

Learn to control your emotions and on no account give way to anger, hatred or jealousy, but turn the force previously expended in these directions towards the attainment of perfection, so that the malarial marsh of your nature may become a limpid and clear lake, reflecting the Divine Nature truly and without distortion.

A. E. Waite. *Pictorial Key to the Tarot*. Rider.
P. Marteau. *Le Tarot de Marseille*. 1930 Paris.
C. C. Zain. *The Sacred Tarot*. California.
Gareth Knight. *The Tarot*. 1963 U.S.A.
Henry Frichet. *Le Tarot Divinatoire*. 1924 Paris.
H. Curtis. *The Key to the Universe*. 1917 Washington.
H. Curtis. *The Key of Destiny*. 1923 San Francisco.
Papus. *The Tarot of the Bohemians*. 1910 Rider.

Chapter 21. Constellations

Manilius, author of the Poeticon Astronomicon, flourished under Augustus and Tiberius in the first century B.C. He was the first Latin author to write at length on astronomy and astrology; he adhered closely to Aratos' (225 B.C.) description of the heavenly bodies. We give an extract from Book I of the translation by Thomas Creech, dated 1696 and published in London four years later.

"Now Constellations, Muse, and Signs rehearse, *Signs of the*
In order, let them sparkle in thy verse. *Zodiac and star*
Those which obliquely bound the burning Zone, *groups*
And bear the Summer and the Winter Sun,
Those first : then those which roll a different way
From West : nor Heaven's Diurnal whirl obey :
Which Nights serene disclose, and which create
The steady Rules, and fix the Laws of Fate.

"First Aries, glorious in his Golden Wool, *Aries*
Looks back, and wonders at the mighty Bull, *Taurus*
Whose back-parts first appear : He bending lies
With Threat'ning Head, and calls the Twins to *Gemini*
rise,
They clasp for fear, and mutually embrace;
And next the Twins with an unsteady pace
Bright Cancer rolls : then Leo shakes his Mane : *Cancer, Leo*
And following Virgo calms his Rage again : *Virgo*
Then Day and Night weigh'd in Libra's Scales, *Libra*
Equal a while, at last the Night prevails,
And longer grown the heavier Scale inclines
And draws bright Scorpio from the Winter signs : *Scorpio*
Him Centaur follows with an aiming Eye *Sagittarius*
His Bow full drawn and ready to let fly :
Next narrow Horns the twisted Caper shows, *Capricorn*
And from Aquarius' Urn a flood o'erflows. *Aquarius*
Near their loved Waves cold Pisces take their *Pisces*
Seat,
With Aries joyn and make the Round compleat. *Aries*

"Now view the point where turn the shining   *Bears*
    Bears,
And from their height look down on other Stars.
Which never set but only change their Sites
To the same point; and whirl the meaner Lights;
Thither the Axis runs, whose adverse Poles   *Poles*
Bears the poiz'd World, and Heaven about it rolls;
No solid substance that the weight might bear
But an imagin'd Line stretcht through the Air;
Begun from either Pole the Line extends
Earth's Center through and in the other ends.
For since the frame turns round, that fancy'd
    Line
Which cuts the middle, too minutely thin
By turning round itself to measure space,
But still confin'd to one imagin'd place,
Is called the Axis; cause unapt to move   *Axis*
It sees Stars whirl, the shining Planets rove,
And swiftly measure the vast space above.
   "Fixt near the Pole appear those friendly Stars
Well known to wretched greedy Mariners;
Which guide their Sails, and which direct their
    Oars,
When mad for gain they fly to foreign Shores.
(Whilst Heaven itself befriends their Avarice,
What Pleas may wretched Mortals make for
    Vice?)
Seven equal Stars adorn the greater Bear,   *Great Bear*
Which measure larger Circles of the Sphere,
And teach the Grecian Sailors how to steer.
The smaller Bear, though less in size and light   *Little Bear*
In narrower Circles she commands the Night,
Yet Tyre prefers, for though the Ocean tost
They sail by her and find the foreign Coast;
These stand not front to front, but each doth
    view
The others Tayl, pursu'd as they pursue.
   "Betwixt and round these two the Serpent   *Serpent*
    twines,
At once divides, and to their place confines;
Secure from meeting they're distinctly roll'd,
Nor leave their Seats, and pass the dreadful fold:
These keep the Vertex, but betwixt the Bear
And shining Zodiack where the Planets err,

A thousand Figur'd Constellations roll,
Some near the Zodiack, some plac'd near the
    Pole :
Whose differing Powers by tempering Skies
    combin'd
Make Seasons fruitful, and refresh Mankind.
    "First near the North, as conscious of his   *Hercules*
    Shame
A Constellation kneels without a Name;
And next Bootes comes, whose order'd Beams   *Bootes*
Present a Figure driving of his Teams.
Below his Girdle, near his Knees, He bears
The Bright Arcturus, fairest of the Stars.   *Arcturus*
Behind his Back the radiant Crown is view'd,   *The Crown*
And shines with Stars of different magnitude;
One plac'd i'th' front above the rest displays
A vigorous light, and darts surprising rays.
This shone since Theseus first his faith betray'd,
The Monument of the forsaken Maid.
    "Nor far from these distended Lyra lies,   *Lyra*
Well strung, the sounding glory of the Skies.
This Orpheus struck when with his wondrous
    Song
He charmed the Woods, and drew the Rocks
    along;
When Hell obeyed, when Death resign'd her
    Chain,
And loos'd his dear Eurydice again;
This gained it Heaven, and still its force appears,
As then the Rocks it now draws on the Stars.
The Planets dance, and to the tuneful Sound
The Heaven consents, and moves the fatal Round.
    "Next Ophiuchus strides the mighty Snake,   *Ophiuchus*
Untwists his winding Folds, and smooths his Back,
Extends its Bulk, and o'er the slippery Scale
His wide stretched Hands on either side prevail :
The Snake turns back his Head, and seems to
    rage,
That War must last where equal Powers engage.
    "Next view the Swan, whom Jove advanc'd   *Swan*
    above,
That Form's reward by which He caught his Love.
When shrouded in the fair deceitful shape,
He cheated trusting Leda to a Rape :

Now graced with Stars his Wings stretched o'er
    the Skies.
   "And next the Swan the shining Arrow flies :   *Arrow*
The Tow'ring Eagle next doth boldly soar,   *Eagle*
As if the Thunder in his Claws he bore :
He's worthy Jove, since He, a Bird, supplies
The Heaven with sacred Bolts, and arms the
    Skies.
Next raised from Seas the Dolphin's Tail appears,   *Dolphin*
The Glory of the Flood and of the Stars.
Whom while the Horse (one radiant Star doth   *Horse*
    grace
His generous Breast) pursues with eager pace,
His Legs before, as running, He extends,
But closed in fair Andromeda he ends.   *Andromeda*
   "Five splendid Stars in its unequal Frame   *The Triangle*
Deltoton bears, and from the shape a Name;
But those that grace the sides dim Light display
And yield unto the Basis brighter Ray.
   "Next with her Cepheus Cassiopeia shines,   *Cepheus*
Her posture sad, and mourns amongst the Signs;   *Cassiopeia*
She sees her Daughter chained, the rolling Tide
The Monster spouts, and curses her old Pride :
She fears that Perseus will inconstant prove,   *Perseus*
And now in Heaven forget his former Love;
But He attends, and bears the Gorgon's head,   *Gorgon's Head*
His Spoil, and witness of a coming aid.
Near the bent Bull a feat the Driver claims,   *Heniochius*
Whose skill conferred his Honour and his Names,
His Art great Jove admired, when first he drove
His rattling Car, and fixt the Youth above."

M. Manilius. *Ancient Astronomy and Astrology* (trans. Creech). 1700
   London.

Chapter 22. Colours

In the Equinox Vol. 1. No. 3 is given a list of colour correspondences as follows:

Elements

Air	Yellow of Tiphareth
Water	Blue of Chesed
Fire	Red of Geburah
Earth	Colours as in Malkuth

The Planets

Saturn	Indigo
Jupiter	Violet
Mars	Scarlet
Sol	Orange
Venus	Green
Mercury	Yellow
Luna	Blue

The Houses of the Zodiac

Aries	Scarlet	Cerise or magenta
Taurus	Red-orange	Cerise
Gemini	Orange	Orange
Cancer	Amber	Orange-yellow
Leo	Greenish-yellow	Yellow
Virgo	Yellow-green	Yellow-green
Libra	Emerald	Green
Scorpio	Greenish-blue	Blue-green
Sagittarius	Deep Blue	Blue
Capricornus	Indigo	Blue-violet
Aquarius	Violet	Violet
Pisces	Crimson	Cerise-violet

In the third column the colours given above are from Carey Penny.

A list of complimentary colours follows from Israel Regardie:

Violet	Citrine
Reddish-orange	Blue-green
Deep Amber	Indigo
Lemon-yellow	Red Violet
Yellow-green	Crimson
White	Black or grey
Red	Green
Blue	Orange
Yellow	Violet
Olive	Red-orange
Blue-green	Russet

If you stare at a mass of one of these colours for a short time and then close your eyes, you should see the complimentary colour. Eyes vary in their colour interpretation so you should learn to play with colours and form your own impressions of these values—which are vibrations. As such, and bearing in mind the rule "as above, so below", it will add another range to your lists of correspondences.

As a result of Chapter 17 you should have a neat and clear diagram of the Tree of Life. If not, make a fair copy as directed without numbers and names on a sheet of cartridge paper. Using bright glossy oil colours is obviously best, but they are somewhat difficult for the beginner. It is suggested that you get, if possible, a shade card of Winsor and Newton's 'Brilliant' Water Colours and a complete range of these paints (28 in all). These colours are extremely brilliant and transparent water colours, which have been manufactured for the commercial artist and designer and for teaching advanced colour harmony. With the exception of the turquoise, they are claimed to be fast to light for colours of this nature. They are supplied in 2 inch tubes and the shade card gives a range of tones which may be obtained upon dilution with water. (American, and other students abroad, may be unable to obtain this make of paints, but they are advised to enquire at their local artists' suppliers, who no doubt will be able to supply an equivalent range of colours.)

Having then experimented to get what you consider to be the correct density of colour, paint in the colours of the Sephiroth as follows:

The last column gives the number of the colour in the series mentioned:

1. White brilliance	White	
2. Cloud like grey	Grey	
3. Thick darkness	Black	
4. Pure and primitive blue	Blue	2
5. Flame red	Red	1
6. Gleaming golden yellow	Yellow	2
7. Emerald green	Sea green	3
8. Orange tawny	Orange	3
9. Deep violet purple	Purple	3
10. Greenish citrine	Leaf green	1
Red Russet brown	Brown	
Dark olive green	Sea green	3 and Black
Black	Black	

No. 10 is divided into four compartments by two lines at 45° to the vertical. The top compartment is greenish citrine, the right hand (Chesed) side is dark greenish olive, the left hand (Geburah) side is red russet brown and the bottom quadrant is black.

When the above are dry, proceed to paint the paths with the following colours:

11		Bright pale yellow	Yellow	1
	12	Yellow	Yellow	2
	13	Blue	Blue	2
	14	Emerald green	Sea green	3
	15	Scarlet	Red	1
	16	Red orange	Orange	3
	17	Orange	Orange	2
	18	Amber	Brown	
	19	Yellow greenish	Leaf green	3
	20	Green yellowish	Leaf green	2
	21	Violet	Purple	3
	22	Emerald green	Sea green	3
23		Deep blue	Blue	1
	24	Green blue	Turquoise	3
	25	Blue	Blue	2
	26	Indigo	Blue	1
27		Scarlet	Red	1
	28	Violet	Purple	3
	29	Crimson (ultra violet)	Red	3
30		Orange	Orange	2
31		Glowing orange scarlet	Orange	3
	32	Indigo	Blue	1

This, when completed, is the Diagram of the Minutum Mundum—the Small Universe or Foundation of Colour. Treasure it in your heart, and mark it well, seeing that herein is the key of Nature. It is, as you see, the diagram of the Sephiroth and the Paths with the colours approximately attributed thereto. See that you reveal it not to the profane, for many and great are its mysteries.

In the Pythagorean Tetractys—the supreme symbol of universal forces and processes—are set forth the Greek theories concerning music and colour. The first three dots represent the threefold White Light, which is the

Godhead containing potentially all sound and colour. The remaining seven dots are the colours of the spectrum and the notes of the musical scale. The colours and tones are the active creative powers, which, emanating from the First Cause, establish the Universe. The seven are divided into two groups—three become the spiritual nature of the Universe, and the four represent the inferior world.

There are numerous arbitrary arrangements setting forth the mutual relationships of the planets, colours, and the musical notes. The most satisfactory system is that based on the laws of the octave. The sense of hearing has a much wider scope than that of sight, as the eye is restricted to the cognition of seven fundamental colours, or one short of the octave, whereas the ear can generally register about ten octaves of sound. Red, when regarded as the lowest colour tone in the chromatic scale thus relates to do; orange corresponds to re; yellow to me; green to fa; blue to so; indigo to la, and violet to te. The eighth colour tone to complete the octave would be the higher octave of red—the first colour tone. This arrangement is attested by two striking facts: 1 the three fundamental notes of the musical scale—the first, third and fifth—correspond with the three primary colours— red, yellow and blue; 2 the seventh and least perfect note of the musical scale corresponds with purple—the least perfect tone of the colour scale.

Carey-Perry. *The Zodiac and the Salts of Salvation.* 1932 Los Angeles.
A. Crowley. *Equinox*, Vol. 1, No. 3. 1910 London.

Chapter 23. Allegory

The origin and the destiny of man are subjects which though inseparably connected with each other are usually treated as distinct, because, while the one is now generally admitted to be the legitimate subject of scientific enquiry, the other is held to be removed from that mode of investigation by the existence of books which contain the revelation of the destiny of the human race.

In ancient times this was not so. Theology was based upon such science as existed at that time, and Science and Theology were consequently in harmony with each other. This harmony has long since ceased to exist in consequence of the rapid progress which Science has made, while Theology has remained unchanged. One great cause of this has been that adherence to the literal interpretation of the scriptures which has prevailed for more than a thousand years to the exclusion of every other, although St. Jerome has said: "The most difficult and obscure of the holy books contain as many secrets as they do words: that is to say, too little: they conceal many things under each word". Several learned works have been written to explain the secret, that is, the real meaning, of these books. Some of these have been translated and commented upon and form the written basis for the occult tradition of the western wisdom.

The better instructed among the ancients, whether Jews or Pagans, never believed in the literal meaning of their sacred books and mythological traditions. Maimonides, the most learned of the Rabbis, says of the Book of Genesis: "We ought not to take literally that which is written in the Book of Creation, nor entertain the same ideas of it as are common with the vulgar. If it were otherwise, our learned ancient sages would not have taken so much pains to conceal the meaning and to keep before the eyes of the vulgar the veil of allegory which conceals the truths which it contains. Taken literally, that work contains the most extravagant and absurd ideas of the Deity. Whoever can guess at the true meaning should take care not to divulge it. This

99

is a maxim inculcated by our wise men, especially in connection with the work of the six days. It is possible that by our own intelligence, or by the aid of others, some may guess the true meaning, in which they should be silent respecting it; or, if they do speak of it, they should do so obscurely, as I myself do, leaving the rest to be guessed by those who have sufficient ability to understand". He also says that this enigmatic method is not peculiar to Moses and the Jewish doctors, but is common to them and to all the sages of antiquity.

Origen says: "What man of good sense will ever persuade himself that there has been a first, a second, or a third day, and that these days have each of them had their morning and their evening, when there was as yet neither sun, nor moon, nor stars? What man is there so simple as to believe that God, personifying a gardener, planted a garden in the East? That the tree of life was a real tree, which could be touched, and the fruit of which had the power of preserving life?

"It is not reasonable", he says, "to deny to Moses the possession of truth, under the veil of allegory, which was then the practice of all Eastern nations". In the same work Origen distinctly admits that there are Arcana Imperii in the Christian religion which are not fit to be entrusted to the vulgar.

"St. Augustine admits that many persons looked upon the story of Eve and the serpent, as well as the Garden of Eden, as being a fiction and an allegory, which was commonly given but which was worthless. He says it would be possible to find a better one and that he had no objection to such being found, provided one sees in it a true history also. It is impossible, however, for a story to be both allegorical and true at the same time."

Mosheim says that all the Fathers of the second century attributed a double sense to the words of Scripture: the one obvious and literal, which they treated with the utmost neglect; the other hidden and mysterious. This includes, among others, Papias, Justin Martyr, Irenaeus and Clemens Alexandrinus, to whom may be added Gregory of Nazianzen, Gregory of Nyssa and Ambrose, who all held that the Mosiac account was an allegory.

Dr. Geddes says of Genesis III, 15, "and I will put enmity between thee and woman, and between thy seed and her seed: it shall bruise thy head and thou shall bruise his heel": "Whosoever thou be-est that understandest the first elements of the

Hebrew dialect and the first elements of logic—say if thou findest in it any vestige of a seducing devil or a redeeming Saviour; then mayest thou turn to Calmet's commentary, or any commentary of the same brand and keep thyself from laughing if thou canst". Dr. Geddes also says: "The fall is an excellent mythologue, or an Egyptian allegory judiciously selected by Moses, in order to enable him to account for the introduction of evil, and of man's antipathy to the reptile race". This learned Hebraist concludes his commentary on the third chapter of Genesis as follows: "We have now got to the end of the Mythos of Moses, or whoever else was the author of this wonderful production. I trust I have done something like justice to its beauties; and that it will appear, on the whole, to be a well devised, well delineated, well executed piece—nay, that it has not its equal in all the mythology of antiquity; I mean, if it be considered not as a real history, nor as a mere mystical allegory, but as a most charming political fiction, dressed up for excellent purposes in the garb of history and adapted to the gross conceptions of a rude, sensual, unlearned and credulous people".

As Burnet observed, we receive these stories without examination because they are believed to have been written by Moses. If we found them in a Greek philosopher, or in the writings of a Mahomedan, doubts and objections would arise. It is only because Moses is supposed to be inspired that we accept them, but when we see that these books are full of repetitions and contradictions, it becomes impossible to suppose that any one person, and certainly not an inspired one, can have written them. The following are a few of the principal repetitions and contradictions in the Pantateuch, omitting for the present those in the first chapter of Genesis, which prove that it cannot have been written by a single writer: the hesitation of Moses when he received the order to deliver the Israelites from the yoke of the Egyptians is mentioned in different terms. Compare Exod. IV, 10 et seq. with VI, 28 et seq.

The miracle of the cloud resting on the tabernacle is related twice with different particulars. Compare Exod. XL, 38 with Numb. IX, 15–23. The same is the case with the tables of the Decalogue, written first by God himself—compare Exod. XXIV, 12; XXXII, 16, and XXXIV, 1, and secondly by Moses after the dictation by God, Exod. XXXIV, 27.

For the establishment of the Council of the Seventy Elders,

101

compare Exod. XXIV with Numb. XII; and with the situation of the tabernacle, which is at one time pitched outside the camp, Exod. XXXIII, 7, and at another time in the midst of it, Numb. II, 2, and 17.

Some of the laws are mentioned twice and each time they are different. In Exod. XXI, 2 and Deut. XV, 12, it is enacted that the Hebrew slave shall be free after having served seven years, as Jeremiah at a later date also states, XXXIV, 14. In Lev. XXV, 50 et seq. on the contrary the slave is to obtain his freedom only in the year of jubilee, or after the lapse of fifty years. The enactments respecting lepers in Lev. XIII are quite different from those in the next chapter. The same is the case with respect to the un-leavened bread of the Passover—in Exod. XII, 17–20 it is spoken of as a commemoration of the deliverance from Egypt, yet at verse 39 of the same chapter it is stated that "they baked unleavened cakes . . . because they were thrust out of Egypt and could not tarry, neither had they prepared for themselves any victual".

According to Exod. XX, 9–11, the Sabbath day is to be kept holy because "in six days the Lord made heaven and earth . . . and rested on the seventh day". In Chap XXIII, 12 however, this enactment is made a question of humanity and agricultural economy. "Six days thou shalt do thy work and on the seventh day thou shalt rest, that thine ox and thine ass may rest and the son of thine handmaid and the stranger may be refreshed;" and each time we are told that God Himself spake the words. In Deut. V, 15, God is represented as giving a third reason : "and remember that thou wast a servant in the land of Egypt and that the Lord brought thee out from thence . . . therefore the Lord thy God commanded thee to keep the seventh day". In verse 21 of this chapter the order of the tenth commandment is altered and an addition is made to it "thou shalt not covet thy neighbour's field".

In Origen's book against Celsus he says : "In Egypt the philosophers have a sublime and secret knowledge respecting the nature of God, which they only disclose to people under the cover of fables and allegories. All the Eastern Nations—the Persians, the Indians, the Syrians—conceal secret mysteries under religious fables; the wise of all nations fathom the meaning of them, while the common people see the symbols and the outside of them."

Chapter 24. Elementals

In Chapter 2 we took a brief look at the Elements of the Ancient Philosophers. It is now time to investigate them further, together with their inhabitants and attributes.

There are four orders of Elementals, who are Essential Spiritual beings. The Kerubim are the Living Powers of the Tetragrammaton on the Material Plane and the Presidents of the Four Elements. They operate through the Fixed or Kerubic signs of the Zodiac. Tetragrammaton means Four-Lettered name and refers to the Unpronouncable Name of God, symbolized by JEHOVAH.

The Altar of Burnt Offering for the sacrifice of animals symbolizes the Qlippoth of the plane contiguous to and below the Material Universe. It points out that our passions should be sacrificed. The Qlippoth are the Evil Demons of Matter and the Shells of the Dead.

The ritualistic attributions of the Elementals and Kerubic correspondences are as follows:

East	Air	Sylphs	Man	Aquarius
South	Fire	Salamanders	Lion	Leo
West	Water	Undines	Eagle	Scorpio
North	Earth	Gnomes	Bull	Taurus

The Eagle is the more favourable aspect of the House of Scorpio. It indicates aspiration rather than treachery and was used more often in earlier astrological applications. The Four Kerubs; Man. Lion, Eagle and Bull, if you can obtain these as small figures or plaster casts, when placed at the appropriate compass points about your room, will help to concentrate these forces and produce a balance at the centre.

For a description of these creatures we can do no better than to quote at length from W. Y. Evans-Wentz whose studies of the fairies won him degrees at Rennes (Britanny) and Oxford Universities.

"These medieval metaphysicians, inheritors of pre-Platonic,

Platonic and neo-Platonic teachings, purposely obscured their doctrines under a cover of alchemical terms, so as to safeguard themselves against persecution, open discussion of occultism not being safe during the Middle Ages, as it was amongst the ancients, and happily is now again in our generation. But they were quite scientific in their methods, for they divided all the invisible beings into four distinct classes: The Angels, who in character and function are parallel to the Gods of the Ancients and equal to the Tuatha De Danann of the Irish, are the highest; below them are the Devils or Demons, who correspond to the fallen Angels of Christianity; the third class includes all Elementals, sub-human Nature—Spirits, who are generally regarded as having pygmy stature, like the Greek daemons; and the fourth division comprises the Souls of the Dead, and the shades or ghosts of the dead.

"For us the third class, which includes spirits or pygmy-like forms, is the most important in this present discussion. All its members are of four kinds, according as they inhabit one of the four elements of Nature. Those inhabiting the Earth are called gnomes. They are definitely of pygmy stature, and friendly to man, and in fairy-lore ordinarily correspond to the mine-haunting fairies or goblins, to pixies, corrigans, leprechauns, and to such elves as live in rocks, caverns or Earth—an important consideration entirely overlooked by champions of the Pygmy Theory. Those inhabiting the air are called Sylphs. These Sylphs, commonly described as little spirits like pygmies in form, correspond to most of the fairies who are not of the Tuatha De Danann or 'Gentry' type, and who as a race are beautiful and graceful. They are quite like the fairies in Shakespeare's *Midsummer Nights Dream*; and especially like Ariel in *The Tempest*, which, according to Mr. Moreton Luce, a commentator on the drama, seems to have been shaped by Shakespeare from his knowledge of Rosicrucian occultism, in which spirits hold an important place. Those inhabiting the water are called Undines, and correspond exactly to the fairies who live in sacred fountains, lakes or rivers. And the fourth kind, those inhabiting the fire, are called Salamanders and seldom appear in the Celtic Fairy-Faith; they are supreme in the elementary Hierarchies. All these elementals, who procreate after the manner of men, are said to have bodies of an elastic half-material essence, which is sufficiently ethereal not to be visible to the physical sight, and probably comparable to matter in the form of invisible gasses. W. B. Yeats has given this explanation: 'Many poets, and all mystic and occult writers, in all ages and countries, have declared that behind the visible are chains of conscious beings, who are not of heaven but of earth, who have no inherent form, but change according to their whim, or the mind that sees them. You cannot lift your hand without influencing or being influenced by hordes. The visible world is merely their skin. In dreams do we go amongst them, and contact them. They are, perhaps, human souls in the crucible—these creatures of whim! And bringing this into relation with ordinary fairies he says: 'Do not think the fairies are always little. Everything is capricious about them, even their size. They seem to take what size or shape pleases them. Fairies in Ireland are sometimes as big as we are, sometimes bigger, and sometimes, as I have been told, about three feet high'.

"To the unbiassed student it would appear that all the fetes, rites or observances of Christianity have a relation more or less direct to paganism, and thus to the ancient Celtic cults and sacrifice offered to the dead, to spirits or fairies. The same set of ideas which operated among the Celts to create their Fairy Mythology—ideas arising out of a belief in a knowledge of the one universal Realm of Spirit and its various orders of invisible inhabitants—gave the Egyptians, the Greeks, the Romans, the Teutons, the Mexicans, the Peruvians, and all the nations their respective mythologies and religions; and we moderns are literally the heirs of all the ages".

The doctrine of spiritual beings, or the concept that a great part, if not the whole, of inanimate nature, as well as of animate beings, are endowed with reason and volition identical with that of man is termed animism and may explain the belief in elementals. It is difficult to distinguish this conception from that of personalization, but the difference exists. The savage hears the wind whistle past him, and thinks that in it he can distinguish voices. He sees movement in streams, trees and other objects, which he believes to be inhabited by spirits. Movement, therefore argued life. The cult of fetishism well instances the belief in animism, for in posits an entrance into an inanimate body of a separate spiritual entity deliberately come to inhabit it. This is probably the root of all magical belief and practice.

The evidence for the historical and ancient belief in fairies in Celtic countries appears to suggest that it is essentially animistic. Folk-imagination, social anthropomorphism generally, explains by far the greater mass of the evidence recorded, but the animistic background of these beliefs present problems which the strictly anthropological sciences are unable to solve. These problems therefore must be presented to physiology and psychology for solution. Science tends to disregard in no uncertain manner any thing that cannot be put into a test-tube, mathematically tested, weighed, dissected or otherwise analyzed in laboratories.

To say that we know reality through sensual perception is an error, as all schools of scientists should nowadays admit. Nature is for ever eluding the senses; she masquerades in disguise until science tears away her mask. We must always adjust the senses to the world itself; where there are only vibrations in ether, man sees light and he hears sounds. We only know things through the way in which our senses react upon them. We sum up the world-problem by saying "consciousness does not exhaust its object, the world". Perceptibility and reality thus not being coincident, man and the universe remain an unsolved problem, despite the noisy shouting of the materialist in his hermetically sealed and light-excluding case, called sensual perceptions. To consider a materialistic hypotheses as adequate to account for the Fairy-Faith would not even be reasonable.

The Fourth meditation will complete your adventures in the elemental spheres. After the usual preliminaries meditate on the symbol of fire and identify yourself with it; contemplate the symbol of Venus, and realize the Power of Universal Love. Consider the Fire Triplicity with its attributes and correspondences. Having achieved some control of the four elemental qualities you will then be in a position to benefit from your future exercises which will test and prove your abilities as a magician.

Eliphas Levi. *Dogme et Ritual de la Haute Magie.* 1894 Paris.
A. E. Waite. *The Occult Sciences.* 1891 London.
W. B. Yeats. *Irish Fairy and Folk Tales.* 1891 London.
W. B. Yeats. *The Celtic Twilight.* 1902 London.
W. Y. Evans-Wentz. *Fairy Faith in Celtic Countries.* 1911 O.U.P.

Chapter 25. The Four Worlds

In Chapter 16 we mentioned the four worlds : before these there are the three states or negative existence namely :

> Ain—the negative—meaning No-thing—Is not
> Ain Soph—Limitless.
> Ain Soph Aur—The Limitless Light.

There are the veils which are described in the Secret Doctrine as the Eternal Parent, wrapped in the Ever-Invisible robes before the action of "I Am" created material life. Their correspondences are :

1. Atziluth	Formation	Yod	Fire	Wands	King Scale	Abba
2. Briah	Creation	Heh	Water	Cups	Queen Scale	Aima
3. Yetzira	Archetypal	Vau	Air	Swords	Emperor Scale	Zauir Anpin
4. Assiah	Material	Heh (final)	Earth	Pentacles	Empress Scale	Malkah

Arik Anpin—Macroprosopus or the Vast Countenance—is the Title of Kether. It is also called Aatik Yomin or the Ancient of Days. Kether emanates first as Abba, the Supernal Father, and Aima the Supernal Mother. Abba is referred to as Yod of Tetragrammaton and Aima to Heh. Elohim is the name given to these two persons United. In this union they become the parents of the Son, Zauir Anpin also called the Microprosopus or the Lesser Countenance.

Abba is also referred to the Sephiroth, Chokmah; Aima to Binah. Zauir Anpin is referred to the six Sephiroth—Chesed, Geburah, Tiphareth, Netzach, Hod and Yesod, and especially to Tiphareth.

An alternative arrangement uses ten Sephiroth in each Sephiroth—making 400 Sephiroth in all—the number of the letter Tau, The Cross, The Universe, the Completion of all things.

At this stage you should make four copies of the Tree of Life as described in Lesson 17, so that you will have them ready for colouring, which will be described in a later chapter. These should be left clean, complete with the paths, unnamed and un-numbered.

The correspondences of the Tarot suits are given on page 73. The Ace is placed on the Throne of Kether—the remaining small cards of the suit go respectively—2 on Chokmah, 3 on Binah, etc. The 22 Trumps are then arranged on the Paths between them according to the numbers given. You should note here that the first column of the table given is divided into three subsidiary columns. That on the left relates to the elements. The centre one to the planets and the right hand column to the Zodiac signs.

The King and Queen of the suit are placed beside Chokmah and Binah respectively; the Knight beside Tiphareth and the Knave by Malkuth. The Tarot Trumps thus receive the equilibrium of the Sephiroth they connect and give a Key to the hidden meanings of the qualities of the various paths. See page 123.

From this you will see how the Tree lends itself to becoming a basis of a universal philosophical alphabet. It is in fact a universal filing cabinet—and can be used as a common denominator for the analysis of qualitative information on all the philosophical systems and correspondences which otherwise would be a mass of unrelated detail. You will find that correspondences given by different authors vary considerably. By the use of the Tree and the Paths, you will be enabled to verify and check this information and classify it into your own sections.

The first world or Atziluth is the world of Formation of Emanation and is the most exalted of all the Conditions and is generally considered as containing only the Holy Upper Ten Sephiroth; the Highest round of the ladder of Intermediaries, which are nevertheless only a Unit, and are between the Ain Soph, the Primal Cause of all, and the inferior emanations which develop the existences. As a totality in this Upper Condition, the Ten Sephiroth represent the operative qualities of the Divine Will, considered as the most abstract and spiritual of all the emanations of the Ain Soph. This Upper World is the abode solely of the Image, Upper Adam, or Adam Illajah, the Archetypal Man; the Protogonos, the first born. This condition is also known as the World of the Sephiroth. It is considered from its nearness to and as the direct emanation of Ain Soph, as perfect, an emanation in which Ain Soph is more immediately immanent yet transcendental. It is not ever looked upon as in any way perfectly equal to the External Boundless, which is concealed and hidden in its essence from the comprehension of man.

Atziluth is the Great Sacred Seal, by means of which all the Worlds are copied which have impressed on themselves the image of the Seal; and as this Great Seal comprehends three stages, which are three zures (prototypes) of Nepesh (the Vital Spirit or Soul), Rauch (the Etherical and Reasoning Spirit) and the Neshamah (the Highest Soul of man), so the Sealed have also received three zures, namely Briah, Yetzirah and Assiah, and these three zures are only One in the Seal.

From the Atziluth World, through the conjunction of the King and Queen, proceeds the World of Briah or Creation, sometimes known as the Throne. In this condition, creation as we understand the word began. It is considered as the abode of only pure spirits. It also contains a continuation of the emanating rays of the Ten Sephiroth of Atziluth, as a matter of course still further removed from Ain Soph, and the first Ten, but a continuation and not in any way separate and distinct from them, but nevertheless of a more limited and circumscribed potency. The purely spiritual substances which it contains have not any admixture of matter, as we understand matter; but they are inferior to the First World and superior to the following : that of the Powers or Intelligences, or Angels, of the planets and celestial spheres. As the image or archetypal man, the Prototype, occupies the First World, so the great Presence, Angel of the Covenant, Metatron, occupies the Second World. He alone constituting the entire World of Spirits or Angels. He is "the garment" or visible manifestation of the Ain Soph, and his name is equal to Shaddai (Almighty). He governs the visible world, preserves unity, harmony and the revolutions of the spheres, planets and all the heavenly bodies; and is the Commander under the Will of the Deity, of all the myriads of the Angelic hosts, of the next or Yetzirah World. These are divided into ten ranks answering to the number of the Ten Sephiroth.

Following and also proceeding from Briah by emanation is the World of Archetypes, or Yetzirah. It is the Abode of the Angels, the Intelligences of the celestial planets and stars and is also called of the Angels. It has also Ten Sephiroth, which proceed from and are only continuations of the Ten of the Atziluth World, through the Ten of Briah, being only extensions of the first manifestations of Ain Soph through the preceding Ten Sephiroth of this Condition or World, are still contemplated as without taint of earthly matter or matter as man understands the word. In this world reside those intelligent and corporeal beings, each wrapped in a luminous vestment, which are sexless and capable by the Divine permission of assuming a form sensible to mankind when they appear to him. They are also ministering spirits, energies of forces, which do the Will of the Deity.

The fourth and last Condition is termed, the World of Material or Action or Assiah, also called the World of Shells, or Rinds, the Demons. It contains the actual matter of the planets or spheres (gill-gooleem) and what man terms matter. It is the residence of Samäel, the Prince of Darkness and his legions. In it is our sublunary world which is subject to matter, rebirth and the dissolution of the matter forms, but not the destruction of the essential atoms. It has the operative qualities of all the preceding Ten Sephiroth, but much diminished because further removed from the original source, and is merely an extension of their rays or energies to their last degree or point of cessation.

The substances of this Condition or World, are considered to be of matter, limited by the dimensions and perceptible to the senses by means of the multiplicity of forms. It is subject to change, birth, death, corruption and rebirth, yet not anything in it is considered as ever totally annihilated or destroyed in essence or atom. It is the abode of the Evil Spirit and his demoniac forces. These demons and evil angels are the Qlippoth or energies or forces which are injurious and destructive to man.

Read again the notes on obsession given and realize the dangers of uncontrolled expeditions into the region of the shells. Realize the dangers of negative or passive trance, therefore always keep a positive, aggressive end in view and never falter. You will by now have found that our progressive exercises are designed to enable you to explore the elemental regions. We have tried to offer you a route through the zones of earth, air, water and fire so that you will be enabled to practice magic with the power of knowledge and without the fear of ignorance.

Isaac Myer. *Qabbalah*. 1888 U.S.A.

Israel Regardie. *Garden of Pomegranates*. 1932 Rider.

A. Ben Joseph. *Book of Formation*. (trans. by Knut Stenring). 1923 Rider.

Chapter 26. Colour Scales

In Chapter 16 was given a list of the Paths. In Chapter 25 was described how these emanated from one to another sephiroth. In an attempt to demonstrate the relative qualities of these descending or ascending qualitative vibrations we now describe the colours attributed to the four scales mentioned in Chapter 25.

In Chapter 22 was described the colour attributions of the Minutum Mundum. This depicts the Sephiroth of the feminine or Queen's Scale and the Paths in the masculine or King's Scale. The reason for this peculiar arrangement is that the Golden Dawn ceremonies are worked in the active atmosphere of the Paths, with the object of the candidates reception into the passive qualities of the Sephiroth. We must now widen our horizon and consider the four scales as a succession of continuous emanations. The colours of the paths in the four scales are given below to enable you to colour your four Trees. When finished and coloured as in this table you will have a vibrating expression of the essential ideas indicating the varying degrees of change in the Ain Soph as it becomes denser and more material in its descent towards matter.

Starting with the King Scale study the following notes and choose your colours carefully and particularly the depth of shade suitable, working from the shade card already described. In addition to the range of colours you already have two more will be required: two small tins of lacquer—silver and gold.

The King Scale represent the root of colour in the Atzituth or Formative World. This scale should be as transparent as possible a quality which water paint will not produce.

1. Brilliance represents the colourless luminosity of Kether.
2. The blue is that of the bright sky.
3. Crimson represents blood.
4. The deep violet is episcopal and combines the starry existence with the principle of blood in animal life.
5. The orange suggests the energy of the Sun.

111

6. The rose is of dawn identifying the Sun and Horus and the birth of new life.
7. Amber suggests the electric voluptuousness of Aphrodite, and the skin of women dedicated to Venus.
8. Violet purple. Crowley suggests that this might well be lavender.
9. The indigo is that of the Akasa (ether), the sky blue and mysterious darkness which surrounds generation.
10. The yellow is the sense of solar radiance, and the energy of the universe.

The Elementary Colours are orange scarlet (31) representing the activity of fire; deep blue (23) the passivity of water; and bright pale yellow (11) is the balance between them. Note that the complimentary colours of each pair of the active elements is the third. Red and blue make violet; the complimentary colour is yellow. Green is the middle colour of the spectrum and therefore the balanced receptacle of all vibrations.

The Planetary Colours follow the spiritual aspect and subtlety of the spectrum. The yellow of Mercury (12) suggests the balanced articulate movement of the Mind. The blue of Luna (13) represents purity, aspiration and unselfish love. The emerald green of Venus (14) portrays the vibration of vegetable growth intermediate between the spiritual, emotional and intellectual types of vibration. Green is the central colour absorbing all and combining all the Sephiroth in one Symbol, the spirit of Nature. The violet of Jupiter (21) which is religious and creative in contrast to the scarlet of Mars (27) which is physical, violent and gross. The orange of Sol (30) is the intense but gross physical vibration of animal life. The Indigo of Saturn (32), the eldest of the gods represents sobriety, and deep-sea calmness of meditation.

The Zodiac colours form a circle of transparent brilliance. Aries (15) being the home of Mars and the sign of the spring Equinox is scarlet to suggest the fiery outburst of the new year. Taurus (16) is red orange indicating the red earth of which man is made, combining the Solar influence with the energy of Geburah. Gemini (17) is orange since ATU VI (Tarot Trump) shows the solar twins Vau Heh. Cancer (18) is amber being connected with Netzach; Venus in her less spiritual form is the chariot through which the influence of the Supernal Mother is conveyed to man, love and electricity being implicit in this sign.

Leo (19) is pure yellow with a tinge of green suggestive of gold, the principle of the vegetable growth inherent in the Solar ray. Virgo (20) is the yellowish green of young grass. Libra (22) is emerald green the house of Venus. Scorpio (24) is greenish blue (Prussian blue) the psychological effect on the sensitive mind suggests a poisonous or putrifactive vibration. It contains the idea of life and death, continuous morbid pleasure; meditate on the blue green sea in its many moods. Sagittarius (25) is the blue of the sky and religious aspiration. Capricorn (26) is indigo carrying some of the sexuual symbolism of the goat. Aquarius (28) is violet and is both spiritual and erotic, it has the most powerful vibrations on the planes of Nephesh and Neschama. Pisces (29) is crimson and has relationship with Binah through ATU XVIII.

No.	King	Queen	Emperor	Empress
1.	Brilliance	White Brilliance	White Brilliance	White, flecked gold
2.	Pale soft blue	Grey	Blue pearl grey like mother pearl	White flecked red blue and yellow
3.	Crimson	Black	Dark Brown	Grey flecked pink
4.	Deep violet	Blue	Deep purple	Deep azure flecked yellow
5.	Orange	Scarlet Red	Bright scarlet	Red flecked black
6.	Clear pink rose	Yellow (gold)	Rich salmon	Gold amber
7.	Amber	Emerald	Bright yellow green	Olive flecked gold
8.	Violet purple	Orange	Red-russet	Yellowish brown flecked white
9.	Indigo	Violet	Very dark purple	Citrine flecked azure
10.	Yellow	Citrine, olive russet, black	As Queen scale flecked gold	Black rayed yellow
11.	Bright pale yellow	Sky blue	Blue emerald green	Emerald flecked gold
12.	Yellow	Purple	Grey	Indigo rayed violet
13.	Blue	Silver	Cold pale blue	Silver rayed sky blue
14.	Emerald green	Sky blue	Early spring green	Bright rose rayed pale
15.	Scarlet	Red	Brilliant flame	Glowing red
16.	Red orange	Deep indigo	Deep warm olive	Rich Brown
17.	Orange	Pale mauve	New yellow leather	Reddish grey inclined to mauve
18.	Amber	Maroon	Rich bright russet	Dark greenish brown
19.	Yellow greenish	Deep purple	Grey	Reddish amber
20.	Green Yellowish	Slate grey	Green grey	Plum colour
21.	Violet	Blue	Rich purple	Bright blue rayed yellow

113

No.	King	Queen	Emperor	Empress
22.	Emerald green	Blue	Deep olive-green	Pale Green
23.	Deep blue	Sea Green	Deep olive-green	White flecked purple like mother of pearl
24.	Green blue	Dull brown	Very dark brown	Livid indigo brown Black beetle
25.	Blue	Yellow	Green	Dark vivid blue
26.	Indigo	Black	Blue black	Cold dark grey nearing black
27.	Scarlet	Red	Venetian red	Bright red, rayed azure or emerald
28.	Violet	Sky blue	Bluish mauve	White tinged purple
29.	Crimson (ultra-violet)	Buff flecked Silver white	Light translucent pinkish brown	Stone colour
30.	Orange	Gold yellow	Rich amber	Amber rayed red
31.	Glowing orange scarlet	Vermilion	Scarlet flecked gold	Vermilion flecked crimson and emerald
32.	Indigo	Black	Blue black	Black rayed blue
32bis.	Citrine, olive, russet, black	Amber	Dark brown	Black flecked yellow
31bis.	White merging into grey	Deep purple nearly black	The 7 prismatic colours violet outside	White, red, yellow blue and black outside
Daath.	Lavender	Grey white	Pure violet	Grey flecked gold

The above colours are taken from the Golden Dawn documents and Crowley's works, which we consider to be better reasoned and more accurate than many other sources. As any filing system is a personal matter and very individualistic it is up to the reader to consider carefully these suggestions and to create his own scales. So our advice is that you first try the system given and later as your knowledge grows to modify where deemed advisable. 31 and 32 Bis are given by Crowley as alternative renderings to these paths, but can be ignored in your colourings of the Trees. Daath (Knowledge) is not properly a sephiroth, but is shown on some trees midway between 1 and 6 of which it is rather a conjunction.

Chapter 27. Colour Scales – *continued*

Having completed the King Scale compare it with the Minutum Mundum. Test for the feel of vibrations with your pendulum. Try it in various positions aligned in turn to the four points of the compass. In which position do you find it most active?

The Queen Scale of the Briahtic or Creative World is reflected, and represents the colours as found in nature. Kether (1) being unconditioned brilliance is non-articulate as white. The grey of Chokmah (2) refers to the cloudy appearance of semen indicating the transition from white to black. Binah (3) is black having the property of absorbing all the colours. In these three supernals we find the three possible modifications of light, above the Abyss there is no differentiation into colour.

The next three sephiroth are the three primary colours of reflected light as opposed to the violet, green and red of transparent light in the King Scale. Chesed (4) has now the blue of water. Geburah (5) is the scarlet red of fire and the Tiphareth (6) is the yellow of air.

The colours of the third Triad are derived from those of the second by a simple mixture. Netzach (7) is the blue and yellow producing the colour of Venus—Emerald. Hod (8) is the mixture of red and yellow giving orange. Yesod (9) is blue and red mingled giving violet.

Malkuth combines the colours of the second Triad by pairs more completely than the third Triad. Citrine is blue-red with a predominance of yellow; olive has a predominance of blue; russet has a predominance of red; representing respectively the airy, watery and fiery elements. The black is the link between the lowest conception, the climax of degeneration of the prime colours in the complete absorbtion of colour as black.

The Planetary colours have been suggested by clairvoyant observation, astrological and alchemical qualities. Mercury (12) combining the irridescence of quicksilver and the blue of the mercury vapour is purple. Luna (13) is metallic silver, the colour of the planet in the sky. Venus (14) has the sky blue colour of copper sulphate, an important salt in alchemy. The blue of Jupiter (21) is the bright deep blue of the sky indicative of religious aspiration. The red of Mars (27) is that of rust. The yellow of Sol (30) is that of pure gold. Saturn (32) is the blackness of night and oblivion.

The Zodiac colours are but a degeneration or dulling of the King Scale colours. In choosing these colours meditation on the Tarot cards will help.

The Emperor or Prince Scale of the Yetziratic or Archetypal World, is for the most part derived as a mixture of the two previous scales by a simple admixture of colours on a palette.

The Empress or Princess Scale of the Assiahtic or material World is a degeneration from the Emperor Scale with, in many cases an added brightness, the source of which should be discovered by meditation.

1. The Brilliance of Kether flecked with gold is indicative of the Mystery of the Holy Guardian Angel when invoked by Tiphareth.

2. The red blue and yellow flecks are the result of the creative energy of Chokmah.

3. The black of Binah is perfected to the grey of Chokmah, flecked with the pink of Tiphareth.

4. Azure of Jupiter and Water flecked with yellow of religious meditation which are the first marks of extasy.

5. Red is the most passive of Scarlet of the two previous scales, flecks of black show the perfection it receives from Binah.

6. Gold amber is the mellowness of harvest which is the perfection of the rose pink of dawn.

7. The olive flecked gold shows that Netzach has received the influence of Tiphareth.

8. Yellowish brown flecked white contains the mystery of mercury and the result of the Initiation.

9. The Citrine represents the final modification of Yesod, with the airy nature, the azure flecks are from chesed.

10. Malkuth is set on the Throne of Binah flooded with the gold of Tiphareth.

The Elements. Air (11) has been made fertile emerald by the golden flecks of the sun. Air is barren by nature, the emerald is of Harpocrates seated on the Lotus. Alchemically water (23) is indicated by its sea green iridescence. Fire (31) being pure has its original vermilion but has become the home of the crimson and emerald of Binah and her sphere of joy, Venus the abode of Love. Earth (32-bis) is the same as Malkuth but the rays are not flecked. Spirit (31-bis) is perfection complete in the Pentagram as shown by the fire colours of the Uraeus Wand.

The Planets. Mercury's perfection (12) is still and concentrated thought reaching indigo through which shines the violet of spiritual ecstasy. The defect of Mercury is cold-bloodedness. The original chastity of the Luna (13) is tinged with Love. Venus (14) is the emerald green of vegetable life and growth. Its defect is the tendency to rose or cerise romance. The religious devotion of Jupiter (21) is rewarded with the yellow rays of the Holy Guardian Angel. The energy of Mars (27) has become a proper vehicle for the blue and green rays of vegetable and spiritual growth. The Sol (30) in its perfection is fixed in the Amber of Cancer by elevation at the Summer Solstice, in this it is endowed with the vibrations of pure physical energy. The fire of Red being purer than average, being the incorruptible quality. Saturn (32) attains perfection in identification with Binah. It is adorned with the blue rays of the King Scale of Chokmah.

The Zodiac. Aries (15) is the red fire, under control as in a furnace. In Taurus (16) brown represents the rich fertile earth. Gemini (17) is completed by active thought, directed and influenced by spiritual intention. Cancer (18) is the blood which has dried to brown, still retaining the vegetable and immortal life principles. Leo's (19) red of fire is toned to amber correcting his tendency to impulse. Virgo (20) with a rich plum colour suggests that the perfection of virginity is fruitfulness. Libra (22) is a pale green which is the attribute of its ruler purified of grossness. The blue of watery putrefaction in Scorpio (24) assumes the hue of the beetle Kephra. The dark vivid blue of Sagittarius (25) is connected with the Great Sea of Binah and Chesed, the image of the sea below the Abyss. The cold dark blue of Capricorn (26) combines Chokmah and Binah. The great attainment is symbolized by marriage. The white of Aquarius (28) is tinged with purple vibrations of aspirations showing his ability to attain spiritual elevation. Pisces (29) is the symbol of the Astral plane brought to equilibrium on the mental plane showing its adaptability to receive and transmit varying vibration. Its defect is glamour and illusion.

You may wonder why we have set you such a tiresome task in drawing and colouring these diagrams. In the experience gained in creating these diagrams you have taken a firm series of steps in creating your own visualization of the Tree in its various aspects.

There are two main techniques of magical achievement. The first is the negative one of watching thoughts and forms arise in the imagination. The second is under active and positive will to create certain forms yourself. The former can to the inexperienced be dangerous and may easily develop into a type of mediumship. That, until you become fully graduated must be avoided, owing to the risk of possession or obsession. In drawing these diagrams in colour you are creating forms which have been used by powerful minds and you are linking your own mind with forces which will help you to progress in a gradual manner, and always under complete control of your own will. Learn therefore to know these Trees, especially the Minutum Mundum. This scale is balanced and therefore can be used as a fix or control at any time when thought forms try to intrude which seem to you to be disturbing. Look at it often and know it so well that you can visualize, or imagine it as a strong glowing thought form. It can then be a powerful weapon in times of psyhic danger.

The thought form of the Minutum Mundum should be created as large as yourself, with Kether above your head. Then mentally place yourself before the diagram, visualizing yourself as part of it. You are in a position to attune yourself with the total energies of nature and should be able to utilize the strength acquired to combat all evil that may assail you. For therein are represented all the Occult Forces of the Universe and the Magician can have no more powerful source of inspiration and energy.

Chapter 28. The Secret Fire

Marcus Aurelius says: "Represent incessantly the universe to thyself as a single living being composed of one sort of matter, and of one soul. This is how all that passes in it is referred to one principle of feeling. This is how one single impulse makes the whole move, and this is why all its products are an effect of a number of causes. O Universe! O Nature! Thou are the source of all, the ultimate terms of all. The same species of soul has been assigned to all animals, and the same intellectual soul to all reasoning beings, just as all terrestial bodies are made of the same terrestial matter, are as all that sees and breathes, sees but one and the same light, and breathes but one and the same air.

"The light of the sun is one, though we see it dispersed on walls, on mountains, and on a thousand different objects. This is but one sort of matter, though it be divided into thousands of separate bodies. There is but one intelligent Soul, though it seems to divide itself. We are all united by a common participation in the same intelligence. Thou hast forgotten that the soul of each of us is a god who has emanated from the Supreme Being. Just as bodies after a brief sojourn on earth become changed, and at last dissolved, so that they give place to others, so do souls after their sojourn in the air become changed, as they return to the fertile bosom of Universal Reason. All souls form a portion of the same spiritual element, just as all seas belong to the element of water. One and the same Reason gives light to them all, as the sun gives light to the earth and ocean."

The Essenes attributed the same origin to our souls, which they looked upon as an emanation from the ethereal fire. Sallust after describing the harmonious representation of the Universe or of the Spheres, defines God and the Spiritus, or the Universal Soul, as being above it. The Nous or Wisdom, is the cause of the admirable order which prevails throughout it, and the Soul or Spiritus spreads through it the life and motion which agitate it. The Manichaens believed that the substance in which thought and feeling dwelt was spread throughout it. Tatian says that

119

spirit is everywhere, not only in the stars and in the angels, but also in plants, in the waters, and in animals, and that though it is everywhere the same spirit, there are nevertheless differences, according to the subjects. Christians hold exactly the same ideas respecting the Wisdom and Spirit. The Wisdom of God is the principle of order which is visible in the Universe and the Spirit is the Principle of life which circulates in every part of it.

Most of us are unconscious of this vital principle which is the Fundamental source of the Quabala, which describes its descent into matter via the Sephiroth and Paths in the four worlds. The paths on the diagrams of Kircher are called channels, Myer calls them canals. These terms denote a freer passage of the forces than the more modern title "paths".

So now consider the Sacred Fire in all its aspects: Solar, Spiritual, Elemental, Purificatory, Sacrificial, Holy Ghost, Baptismal, Creative. Remember too the symbolical and Alchemical Lion, the Eastern Prana and Kundalini. This Fire working actively through the Tree forms the one and only power in the universe, however varied may be its manifestations.

Study its manifestations as described in the Bible. During the wandering in the Wilderness "the Lord went before them by day in a pillar of cloud, to lead them the way; and by night in a pillar of fire, to give them light; to go by day and by night." Exod. XIII 21. When God showed himself to Isaiah VI 1–4 "the whole earth is full of his glory and the house was filled with smoke". His appearance to Ezekiel I 4–6 was in "a whirlwind that came out of the north, a great cloud, and a fire unfolding itself, and a brightness was about it". John states that "His eyes were as a flame of fire" Revel. I.14. The second coming of the Messiah is promised II Thes. I.8 as a "flaming fire taking vengeance on them that know not God". Daniel VIII 9–10 describes how the "Ancient of Days did sit, whose garment was white as snow, and the hair of his head like pure wool: his throne was like the fiery flame, and his wheels as burning fire. A fiery stream issued and came forth from before him". Jeremiah XXIII 29 says "Is not my world like as fire?"

What is fire? The scientists will state that it is heat, combustion, light and motion, a combination of chemical and physical forces in general. But is it just that? Although we are so familiar with this phenomena we scarcely ever give it a thought. Paracelsus, prince of alchemists and Hermetic Philosophers, believed that the elements known to the ancients (earth, air, fire and water) consisted of a subtle, vaporous principle, and a gross corporeal substance.

Fire therefore is twofold in nature, a tangible atmosphere and an intangible, volatile substratum which may be termed spiritual fire. Man, animals, plants and minerals therefore live in a world composed of the gross side of the four elements, and from various combinations of them are constructed their living organisms. Minerals are also living things to be philosophers.

Drummond describes this process as follows : "If we analyse this material at a point at which all life starts, we shall find it to consist of a clear structureless, jelly-like substance resembling the white of albumen or white of an egg. It is made of Carbon, Hydrogen, Oxygen and Nitrogen. Its name is protoplasm. And it is not only the structural unit with which all living bodies start in life, but with which they are subsequently built up. "Protoplasm", says Huxley "simple or nucleated, is the formal basis of all life, it is the clay of the potter".

Think now on fire yourself. Darken your room and light a candle in front of a mirror placed a few inches behind it. Sit about three or four feet away from it and about eye level. Relax and look at the tip of the flame. After a time you will see the central portion, the main flame and a halo around it. When you have studied this several times notice the spectrum colours on the edge of the flame. Try to distinguish the various colours and the order in which they appear, notice if one colour is more predominant. When you have become proficient in distinguishing these and other characteristics, do your four-fold breaths and relax still further. Next try to see from within the back of your forehead, that is from within your head and behind and above your eyes. This exercise will enable you eventually to bring the third eye into operation and you should be able to see the essence of the flame.

So far your exercises have been somewhat vag e, but they were designed to enable you to control and guide your thought processes along a certain path. Now you should learn to project your thoughts, to imagine or create a visible result of your mind on the material plane. If you aspire to be a Magician it is very necessary that you should be able to create material forms by an act of will.

The gospel of St. Mark X, 14 says "Whosoever shall not receive the Kingdom of God as a little child, he shall not enter therein". The difference between the child and the adult is one of education. Education teaches the child to think in words, which are symbols and as such are far removed from the simple processes of visualization which the young child had before he was taught to think away from the real mental magic of imagination. Think again as a little child and a real magical ability will be your reward. When you have practiced and become efficient with your candle exercise, the next step is to create in the dark a flame of a similar nature. Try to project it from the tip of one finger. Constant practice is necessary, but without this ability you will not be able to proceed with the next exercise, which will give you the real key to magical attainment. So keep trying.

"The Solar rays descending from the Sun carry with them the solar alchemical sulphur, the Divine Fire. These rays are crystallized by contact with the lunar rays. The solar rays are also met by the contact with the lunar rays. The solar rays are also met by the emanation rising upward from the earth's surface and are thus still further crystallized into a partly tangible substance, which is soluable in pure water. The crystallization of the solar and lunar rays in water (dew) produces the virgin earth, a pure invisible substance uncontaminated by material matter". Such, according to Manley-Hall, is the alchemical description of what you must do in this exercise. When you can really project a flame return to the candle and by an effort of will project any colour of your choice so that the candle burns with that one colour alone.

The next few chapters will deal with the details of the Tarot Cards, although these may appear somewhat complicated and difficult you should bear in mind that the explanation and meanings of these cards form the basis of a complete system of correspondences, without which a complete system of magic is impossible.

Atranasius Kircher. *Oedipus Aegypticus.* 1652 Rome.
Henry Drummond. *Natural Laws in the Spiritual World.* 1883 New York.
A. E. Waite. *Paracelsus the Great* (2 vol.) 1894 Elliot.
Franz Hartmann. *Paracelsus.* 1896 Kegan Paul.

Chapter 29. The Tarot Cards
(Aces & Court)

In Chapter 25 we gave the positioning of the numbered cards of the Tarot Pack on the Sephiroth, each suit representing one of the four worlds. As it is obviously impossible to place these cards on the trees you have drawn it will be necessary to make a much larger glyph. For this you should get a piece of $\frac{1}{4}$ inch hardboard from any "do-it-yourself" shop, cut five feet by two feet six inches. On this paste a piece of good quality white cartridge paper and allow to dry, making sure there are no air bubbles left underneath. On this draw, as previously instructed, your large tree but the dimensions should be : Generating circles —6 inches radius (12 inches diameter). Sephiroth—3 inches radius (6 inches diameter), and the paths $1\frac{1}{2}$ inches wide. This large tree suitably coloured when properly charged by a group can become a most powerful instrument for the direction of universal energy and may be used for healing or other magical purposes. See page 73.

The Four Aces represent the force of the spirit acting in, and binding together the four scales of each element in the Kether of each. Each one has an angelic hand issuing from a cloud which represents the Radical or Root-Force. They are said to be placed around the North Pole to govern its revolution and connecting the Higher with the Material Plane.

The Ace of Wands. The issuing hand holds a heavy club with three branches surrounded by leaping flames or Yods. The whole is a flaming torch. It symbolizes natural as opposed to Invoked force, vigour, energy strength and rush. It is the Root of the Powers of fire.

Ace of Cups or Chalices. The radiant hand supports a cup from which issues a fountain of pure water which falls into the calm water below in which grow Lotus and Water Lilies. The great letter Heh of the supernal Mother (sometimes M) should be traced in the spray. The symbolism is Fertility, Productiveness,

Happiness, Beauty and Pleasure. It is the Root of the Powers of Water.

Ace of Swords. The angelic hand supports a sword on which is impaled a celestial crown from which descend on the left the Palm of suffering and on the right the branch of peace. Six Vaus fall from the point.

It symbolizes invoked force as opposed to natural force, upwards representing spiritual brightness, justice and strength in a whirling force. Reversed it is the invocation of evil, wrath, punishment and affliction. It is the Root of the Powers of Air.

Ace of Pentacles. The hand should hold a rose tree branch on which rests a large Pentacle formed in five concentric circles. The centre is white with a red Greek cross (composed of 13 squares). From the centre emerge 12 radii suggestive of the Zodiac divisions of the Heavens. Resting above is a smaller circle, surmounted by a Maltese Cross with two wings at the sides.

The Symbolism is Materiality in the sense of either good or evil. It is mainly illusionary and indicates gain, labour, power and work.

The Sixteen Royal or Court Cards

The Four Kings should be seated on steeds and clothed in armour to represent the Yod forces in each suit. They represent the swift and violent unsustained force of the radix or commencement of the Material Forces containing all others. Therefore is a knowledge of the King Scale necessary to all magical working.

The Four Queens seated on Thrones represent the Heh forces in each suit. The mother or birth of material force, steady and unshaken, enduring but not rapid. They should also be clothed in armour.

The Four Princes or Knights should be seated in chariots representing the Vau forces realizing the influence of both scales of force, the King and Queen. Its power is illusionary unless set in motion by the Father and Mother.

The Four Pages, Princesses or Knaves standing firmly by themselves represent the forces of Heh final completing the other scales. The power is at once violent and permanent, mainly material, but is the throne of the Forces of the Spirit.

King of Wands, wears a golden winged crown, his chariot is drawn by a lion, he bears a torch and flames are beneath the chariot; ruler of Salamanders and Air of Fire.

He symbolizes swift, strong and hasty action, yet just and generous. If badly placed cruel, intolerent and prejudiced.

Queen of Wands has long red gold hair, seated on a throne with flames beneath, at her side is a couchant leopard and she bears a long wand with a heavy conical head.

Symbolizes a steady force, adaptability, power to command. Kind and generous if not opposed. If ill placed, domineering, revengeful and obstinate. Queen of Salamanders, Water of Fire.

Knight of Wands is a winged warrior on a black horse with a flowing tail, wearing a winged helmet, he holds a club with a flaming end. Symbolizes activity, generous sudden and impetuous action. He is the King of Salamanders and the Fire of Fire.

Page of Wands a strong and beautiful woman, wearing a plumed helmet, surmounted by a tiger's head. Her right hand rests on a brazen altar, in her left she holds a flaming wand.

Symbolizes beauty, sudden force, desire for love, power, or revenge. If ill placed superficial, unstable, domineering and cruel. She is the Empress of Salamanders and the Earth of Fire.

King of Cups is a winged figure, with a winged crown, seated on a chariot drawn by an eagle, on the wheel is the sign of the Scorpion, beneath the chariot are the calm waters of a lake. In one hand is a lotus and in the other a cup from which issues a serpent. He is the emperor of Undines and the Air of Water.

Symbolizes crafty and artistic force in a violent way. Powerful for good or evil but tending towards the former if productive of power or wisdom. If ill placed he is evil and intensely merciless. He is the Emperor of Undines and the Air of Water.

Queen of Cups sits upon her throne under which is flowing water, she is very beautiful and fair, her hand holds a lotus and beside her is an ibis. She holds a cup from which a crayfish emerges.

Symbolizes imagination of the poetic kind, good natured and dreamy. Affected by outside influences is dependent on good or bad placing more than the other court cards. She is the Queen of Undines or Water of Water.

Knight of Cups is a young warrior seated upon a white horse, on his helmet is a peacock, he holds a cup in his hand from which crawls a crab. The sea is underneath his steed.

Symbolizes indolence, sensuality but unenthusiastic. If ill placed idle and untruthful. He is the King of Undines and the Fire of Water.

Page of Cups, standing on a sea with a dolphin on her right, she has a swan on her helmet and holds a cup in one hand from which a turtle issues, in the other is a lotus.

Symbolizes sweetness, kindness and gentleness, dreamy but courageous. Ill placed she can be luxurious and selfish. She is the Empress of Undines and the Earth of Water.

King of Swords is a winged figure with a winged crown in a chariot drawn by Fairies, their wings carry pentagrams and their wands have the same symbol on top. Grey clouds are beneath the chariot. He has a sword in one hand and a sickle in the other. He rules with the sword and slays with a sickle.

Symbolizes firmness, ideas, designs, suspicions, alpha and omega, who creates as fast as he slays. Ill aspected he is malicious, obstinate and unreliable. He is the Emperor of Sylphs and the Air of Air.

Queen of Swords is graceful with waving hair, with a crest like a winged childs head or Kerub, a drawn sword in one hand and a severed bearded head of a man in the other.

Symbolizes keen observation, speed, confidence, fond of dancing and similar amusements. Ill aspected, unreliable, deceitful, cruel, sly but with a good exterior. She is the Queen of Sylphs and the Water of Air.

Knight of Swords is winged on a brown steed and wears a winged helmet. His crest is a six pointed star. He carries a drawn sword and underneath his horse are dark clouds.

Symbolizes courage, skill, fierceness and delicate activity inclined to domineer. Ill aspected deceitful, tyrannical and crafty. He is the King of Sylphs and the Fire of Air.

Chapter 30. The Tarot Cards
(Court & Keys)

The Page of Swords wears as a crest the head of Medusa with Serpent hair. She has one hand on a small silver altar with grey smoke arising but no fire, her other hand holds a sword. Beneath her feet are white Cirrus clouds.

Symbolizes wisdom, grace and dexterity combined with strength. If ill aspected she is frivolous and cunning. She is the Empress of Sylphs and the Earth of Air.

King of Pentacles is a winged figure in a chariot drawn by a bull. He has a winged bull's head as a crest, beneath is a flower-decked band. A golden orb held downwards is in one hand, in the other is a wand with an orb and cross on top.

Symbolizes increase in all things, consolidation, reliability. Ill aspected material, stupid, carnal. Slow to action in both. He is the Emperor of Gnomes and the Air of Earth.

Queen of Pentacles is a beautiful woman with dark hair, one side of her face is light the other in shadow. Her crest is a winged goat's head, and a goat is by her side. In one hand is a golden orb, in the other a wand surmounted by a cube.

Symbolizes charming impetuosity, intelligence, open hearted, truthfulness, of many moods. Ill aspected foolish, changeable and undecided. She is the Queen of Gnomes and the Water of Earth.

Knight of Pentacles is a dark winged warrior with winged helmet, he rides a light brown horse. His crest is a winged stag's head. Under the horse's feet is a field of ripe corn. In one hand he holds a pentacle in the other a wand with a hexagon on top.

Symbolizes persistence and patience in material matters, clever and dull. Ill aspected jealousy and avariciousness. He is the King of Gnomes and the Fire of Earth.

Page of Pentacles is a strong beautiful figure standing in a flowered meadow. She has brown hair and a ram's head as a crest and wears a sheepskin coat. In one hand is a Pentacle, in the other a wand surmounted by a circular disc.

Symbolizes courage benevolence, care, kindness. Ill aspected prodigal and wasteful. She is the Queen of Gnomes and the Earth of Earth.

To further illustrate the Tarot symbolism we give Israel Regardie's tabulation of the characteristics of the Court cards. Whichever pack you may possess you will find difficulties in matching the symbols which are described in this book; this is because most of the packs available today were not drawn with the true correspondences, which are only to be found in Book T, which only exists in manuscript and is generally closely guarded as secret. The descriptions we have given are simplified from this document and therefore will be found to fit into the general pattern of correspondences. Using the appropriate suit for your world on the tree :

Two is placed on Chokmah, and symbolizes the Powers of the King and Queen uniting and initiating the force. Generally, therefore, they indicate the initiating and fertilization of a matter.

Three is placed on Binah, symbolizes that action has been commenced for good or evil. Note the central figure of each card.

Four is placed on Chesed, symbolizes perfection, completion and realization fixing the settlement of the matter.

Five is placed on Geburah, symbolizes opposition, war, strife or struggle and the opposition to the matter in question. They show ultimate success or failure according to aspect.

Six placed on Tiphareth, symbolizes the definite completion of the matter.

Seven placed on Netzach, symbolizes a force transcending the material plane, therefore a power which requires one capable of wielding it, and a result which depends on the action taken.

Eight placed on Hod, symbolizes temporary success, but not leading further than the immediate project.

Nine placed on Yesod, symbolizes a powerful fundamental force, resting on a firm footing resulting in good or evil.

Ten placed on Malkuth, symbolizes a completed and fixed force of good or evil, the ultimate fulfilled.

The cards of the Lesser Arcana present to us the vibrations of Number, Colour, and Element, that is, the plane on which number and colour function. Thus in the Ten of Pentacles we have the number Ten and tertiary colours, citrine, olive and russet, working in Malkuth, the material plane. Whereas in the Ten of wands we have the number Ten and the tertiaries working in pure energy. In these cards the Sephiroth is indicated by colouring of the clouds; the plane by the colouring of the symbols.

The four honours of each suit taken in their abstract sense may be interpreted as:

Potential Power	The King
Brooding Power	The Queen
Power in Action	The Prince or Knight
Reception and Transmission	The Princess or Knave

All these cards are coloured according to their elements plus those of the Sephiroth to which they are attributed. With the Greater Arcana, The Trumps, however, are given as keys to divine manifestation, each one an individual force to be considered independently. It must never be forgotten that the Trumps are, intrinsically, glyphs.

Special Characteristics of the Four Court Cards of the Suit

Suit	Cards	Crest	Symbols	Hair	Eyes
Wands	King	Winged black horse's head	Black horse, waving flames, club. Scarlet cloak	Red-Gold	Grey or Hazel
	Queen	Winged leopard	Leopard. Steady flames Wand with heavy head	Red-Gold	Blue or Brown
	Prince or Knight	Winged lion's head	Wand and shooting flames. Fire Wand	Yellow	Blue-Grey
	Princess or Prince	Tiger's head	Tiger, leaping flames. Gold Altar, long club, larger at bottom	Red-Gold	Blue
Cups	King	Peacock with open wings	White horse, crab issuing from cup. Sea	Fair	Blue
	Queen	Ibis	Crayfish is issuing from river	Gold-Brown	Blue
	Prince	Eagle	Scorpion, Eagle-serpent issuing from lake	Brown	Grey or Brown
	Princess	Swan	Dolphin, Lotus. Sea with spray, turtle from cup	Brown	Blue or Brown
Swords	King	Winged Hexagram	Winged brown horse, driving clouds, drawn Sword	Dark Brown	Dark

E

Suit	Cards	Crest	Symbols	Hair	Eyes
	Queen	Winged Child's head	Head of Man severed. Cumulous clouds. Drawn sword	Grey	Light Brown
	Prince	Winged Angel's head	Arch-Fairies winged. Clouds. Nimbi. Drawn Sword	Dark	Dark
	Princess	Medusa's head	Silver Altar. Smoke. Cirrus clouds. Drawn swords	Light Brown	Blue
Pentacles	King	Winged Stag's head	Light brown horse. Ripe cornland. Sceptre with Hexagram	Dark	Dark
	Queen	Winged goat's head	Barren land. Face light one side only. Sceptre with orb of gold	Dark	Dark
	Prince	Winged bull's head	Flowery land. Bull. Sceptre with orb and cross, held downwards	Dark Brown	Dark
	Princess	Winged ram's head	Grass. Flowers, grove of trees. Sceptre with disc and Pentagram	Rich Brown	Dark

22 Keys of the Book of Thoth or the titles of the Tarot Trumps

0. Fool — Spirit of Ether.
1. Magician — Magus of Power.
2. Priestess — Priestess of the Silver Star.
3. Empress — Daughter of the Mighty Ones.
4. Emperor — Son of the Morning, Chief among the Mighty.
5. Hierophant — Magus of the Eternal Gods.
6. Lovers — Children of the Voice Divine. Oracles of the Mighty Gods.
7. Chariot — Child of the Power of the Waters, Lord of the Triumph of Light.
8. Strength — Daughters of the Flaming Sword, Leader of the Lion.
9. Hermit — Magus of the Voice of Light, Prophet of the Gods.
10. Wheel — Lord of the Forces of Life.
11. Justice — Daughter of the Lord of Truth, Holder of the Balances.

130

12. Hanging Man   Spirit of the Mighty Waters.
13. Death   Child of the Great Transformers, Lord of the Gates of Death.
14. Temperence   Daughter of the Reconcilers, Bringer forth of Life.
15. Devil   Lord of the Gates of Matter, Child of the Forces of Time.
16. Tower   Lord of the Hosts of the Mighty.
17. Star   Daughter of the Firmanent, Dweller between waters.
18. Moon   Ruler of Flux and Reflux, Child of the Sons of Mighty.
19. Sun   Lord of the Fire of the World.
20. Judgement   Spirit of the Primal Fire.
21. Universe   Great One of the Night of Time.

Chapter 31. The Tarot and the Zodiac

As was hinted in the last chapter, the cards can also be related to the Zodiac. The Sphere of influence of the Aces is distributed around the North Polar star which is the fixed centre of the heavens. The Pages or Princesses then rule that part of the heavens which lie around the pole and are related to the Kerubic Signs of the Zodiac and are related to the thrones of the four aces.

The twelve court cards, four each Kings, Queens and Knights, rule the Dominion of the Heavens between the Pages and The Zodiac. Thus they are a link with the signs, the other cards, these numbered from 2 to 10 inclusive can then be laid around the Zodiac in a circle, one to each of the decans or one to each 10 degrees of the 360 degree circle. This, if you refer to any good astrological manual, now gives another set of correspondences and takes our researches into yet another dimension.

To lay the cards out as described you will require a board about 4 feet square with a circle drawn about 20 inches radius. The circle should be divided by twelve radii. Comparing the lines to a clock face and starting with the space between 8 and 9 o'clock with Aries, the signs should be written in an anticlockwise direction and numbered as in lesson 3. The cards can then be placed with the court cards in the centre as directed and the other 36 cards around the outside of the circle three to each of the spaces.

There being 36 decans and only seven planets one of these must rule over one more than the others. Consequently Mars is allotted to the last decan of Pisces as well as the first decan of Aries. This is because a greater heat is required to overcome the long cold of winter in order to initiate spring. The decans start in Cor Leonis which is the Great King Star at the heart of the lion, this is the decante of Saturn in Leo. We now give a keyword meaning of the Zodiac cards in their decans.

Sign	Decan	Card	Meaning
5 Leo	Saturn	5 Wands	Strife
5 Leo	Jupiter	6 Wands	Victory

Sign	Decan	Card	Meaning
5 Leo	Mars	7 Wands	Valour
6 Virgo	Sun	8 Pentacles	Prudence
6 Virgo	Venus	9 Pentacles	(Material) gain
6 Virgo	Mercury	10 Pentacles	Wealth
7 Libra	Moon	2 Swords	Peace (restored)
7 Libra	Saturn	3 Swords	Sorrow
7 Libra	Jupiter	4 Swords	Truce (Rest from Strife)
8 Scorpio	Mars	5 Cups	Disappointment
8 Scorpio	Sun	6 Cups	Pleasure
8 Scorpio	Venus	7 Cups	Illusionary Success (C. Debauch)
9 Sagittarius	Mercury	8 Wands	Swiftness
9 Sagittarius	Moon	9 Wands	(Great) Strength
9 Sagittarius	Saturn	10 Wands	Oppression
10 Capricorn	Jupiter	2 Pentacles	(Harmonious) change
10 Capricorn	Mars	3 Pentacles	(Material) works
10 Capricorn	Sun	4 Pentacles	(Earthly) power
11 Aquarius	Venus	5 Swords	Defeat
11 Aquarius	Mercury	6 Swords	Earned Success (C. Science)
11 Aquarius	Moon	7 Swords	Unstable Effort (C. Futility)
12 Pisces	Saturn	8 Cups	Abandoned success (C. Indolence)
12 Pisces	Jupiter	9 Cups	(Material) happiness
12 Pisces	Mars	10 Cups	Perpetual Success (C. Satiety)
1 Aries	Mars	2 Wands	Dominion
1 Aries	Sun	3 Wands	Established Success (C. Virtue)
1 Aries	Venus	4 Wands	Perfected Work (C. Completion)
2 Taurus	Mercury	5 Pentacles	Material Troubles (C. Worry)
2 Taurus	Moon	6 Pentacles	Material Success
2 Taurus	Saturn	7 Pentacles	Success unfulfilled (C. Failure)
3 Gemini	Jupiter	8 Swords	Shortened force (C. Interference)
3 Gemini	Mars	9 Swords	(Despair and) cruelty
3 Gemini	Sun	10 Swords	Ruin
4 Cancer	Venus	2 Cups	Love
4 Cancer	Mercury	3 Cups	Abundance
4 Cancer	Moon	4 Cups	Blended Pleasure (C. Luxury)

In the above table C. gives Crowley's meaning of the card as taken from the pack he designed.

For easy reference and to help you to understand the cards further we give a description of the cards together with their symbolism now in order of the suits. From this it will be seen that there are at least two methods of using the "as above so below" law to investigate the real meanings of the Tarot pack.

When relating the numbered cards to the tree the various suits should be used separately according to the scale in use, or can be placed with the four numbers together if a more general Picture is required.

Two of Wands. A hand grasps two large crossed wands, the junction produces flames. Above and below are two small wands on which are the symbols of Mars and Aries, also with flames rising from them.

133

It symbolizes strength, fierceness, authority, resolution. Ill aspected it is domination, unforgiving, obstinate, Lord of Dominion, Mars in Aries 1°–10° and the Chokmah of Yod.

Three of Wands. Two crossed wands and one upright held by a hand. Flames issue from the junction. Above and below are the Sun and Aries.

Symbolizes realization, completion, success and wealth. Ill aspected, arrogance, rudeness and insolence, conceit and obstinacy. Lord of Established Strength. Sun in Aries 10°–20°, and the Binah of Yod.

Four of Wands. Two clasped hands holding four crossed wands with flames at the junction. Above and below are two small wands with the signs of Venus and Aries.

Symbolizes completion, rest after labour, reasoning from knowledge. Ill aspected unreliable, hurried action, unready and uncertain. Lord of Perfected Work. Venus in Aries 20°–30° and the Chesed of Yod.

Five of Wands. Two clasped hands hold four crossed wands together with one upright. Above is the Saturn symbol and below is Leo.

Symbolizes quarrelling and fighting, strife. Ill aspected, violence, rashness, cruelty, lust. Lord of Strife. Saturn in Leo 1°–10° and the Geburah of Yod.

Six of Wands. Two clasped hands hold six wands in two groups of three. Above and below are two wands of Jupiter and Leo. From the junction issue flames.

Symbolizes gain, victory after strife, success after industry and energy. Sociability. Ill aspected insolence, pride. The Lord of Victory, Jupiter in Leo 10°–20° and the Tiphareth of Yod.

Seven of Wands. Two clasped hands holding six wands as before, the seventh wand is held by a third hand, crossing at the junction from which issue flames. Above and below are the symbols of Mars and Leo.

Symbolizes courageous opposition, valour in small things, opposition, difficulties. Ill aspected quarrelling, ignorance, wrangling. Lord of Valour, Mars in Leo 20°–30° and the Netzach of Yod.

Eight of Wands. Four radiating hands clasp eight wands in two groups of four. Flames issue from the junctions, with the symbols of Mercury and Sagittarius above and below.

Symbolizes, swiftness, boldness, courage, great force applied suddenly, quickly expended. Love of outdoors. Ill aspected untrustworthy, violent, oppressive, theft. Lord of Swiftness, Mercury in Sagittarius 1°–10° the Hod of Yod.

Nine of Wands. Four hands holding eight wands crossed in fours with a fifth hand holding an upright wand crossing the junction from which flames issue. The symbols are Luna and Sagittarius, the former horizontally.

Symbolizes steady and tremendous force. Success, victory preceded by apprehension, good health. Ill aspected obstinate, questioning doubt. Lord of Great Strength, Moon in Sagittarius 10°–20° and the Yesod of Yod.

Ten of Wands. Four hands as before, a fifth hand holds two wands which cross at the junction, flames as before.

Sybolizes cruel force applied for material ends, self-sacrifice, sometimes failure in a project. Ill aspected speed in evil, slander, envy, motive, lying. The Lord of Oppression, Saturn in Sagittarius 20°–30° and the Malkuth of Yod.

After a close and detailed consideration, the meaning of the Tarot cards should be memorized. This is a basic need as a key to the system of correspondences, and also helps to create the understanding of the cards so that you can later apply them to divining or cartomancy.

Mrs. V. K. V. Resselaer. *Devil's Picture Books.* 1892 London.
E. S. Taylor. *History of Playing Cards.* 1855 London.

Chapter 32. The Pentagram and Lesser Arcana

By now you should have had some success in producing the flaming fire on the astral plane. Next you should try to put it to ritualistic use. The five pointed star has been a sign of power through the ages and must always be used with two angles firmly and equally at the bottom, as reversed it becomes the sign of evil. Several points have allocated to them the Kerubs, elements, and certain words of power as indicated in the diagram.

Spirit

Aquarius
Air
YHVH

Scorpio
Water
EL

Taurus
Earth
ADONAI

Leo
Fire
ELOHIM

To perform the ritual stand facing the East and trace in the air with the first finger of your right hand a large pentagram about 5 feet high. This must be perfect in shape and closed where you began. Starting at the Earth corner practice this tracing movement till you can do it perfectly. Only then can you be trusted to combine the flame exercise and in making the figure imagine the glowing line as you trace it. Practice this diligently and frequently till it becomes an automatic and unchangeable action. This is important because it is the basis of cleansing the atmosphere from evil influences, with which you must attain proficiency, before you can undertake any real magical rituals. Further and more detailed instructions will be given in chapter 36.

The Lesser Arcana (contd)

Two of Cups. On the lower part of the card is water with lotus flowers arising, one nearly to the top of the card. Crossed on the stem below are two dolphins, gold and silver. Water overflows from the lotus bloom into two cups which in turn overflow to the water below, cascading off the dolphin's backs as it falls. Above and below are the signs of Venus and Cancer.

Symbolizes harmony of union, marriage, pleasure, mutual joy. Ill aspected disharmony, dissipation, folly. The Lord of Fire, Venus in Cancer 1°–10° and the Chokmah of Heh.

Three of Cups. A hand holds a group of Lotuses. Water falls
Y   into the top cup from one bloom and overflows into the
Y Y   two cups placed below, and then to the lower part of the
card. The signs are of Mercury and Cancer.

Symbolizes abundance, plenty, pleasure and good luck. Ill aspected the same fortunes but of very temporary nature. It is the Lord of Abundance, Mercury in Cancer 10°–20° and the Binah of Heh.

Four of Cups. Two above and two below, with water and lotuses as before. Two leaves are between the cups making a cross with the stem. The signs are Luna and Cancer.

Signifies success or pleasure nearing completion, a static period in a project. Ill aspected injustice, pleasure mixed with anxiety. It is the Lord of Blended Pleasure, Moon in Cancer 20°–30° and the Chesed of Heh.

Five of Cups. Lotuses are now leaves only with flowers falling and no buds. Neither is there any water in the cups. The signs are Mars and Scorpio.

Symbolizes disappointments in love, marriage, loss of friendship, deceit. Ill aspected, all these characters are amplified. Lord of Loss in Pleasure, Mars in Scorpio 1°–10° and the Geburah of Heh.

Six of Cups. Six flowers bend over six cups, into which they pour glistening water. The symbols are Sun and Scorpio.

Symbolizes, beginning of success, increase, gain or pleasure. Ill aspected defective knowledge, vanity and thankless presumption. The Lord of Pleasure, Sun in Scorpio, 10°–20° and the Tiphareth of Heh.

Seven of Cups. Are empty and are arranged as shown.
Y Y Y The lotus arises from the lower cup and each
Y   flower overhangs a cup. The symbols are Venus and
Y Y Y Scorpio.

Symbolizes promises unfilled, error, inability to retain success. Ill aspected, lust, drunkenness, wrath, selfish dissipation, deception in love and friendship. The Lord of Illusionary Success, Venus in Scorpio 20°–30° and the Netzach of Heh.

Eight of Cups. A hand holds a stem of Lotuses. The cups are Y Y Y arranged as shown. There are but two flowers which
 Y Y are pouring water into the centre cups. The other cups
Y Y Y are empty. The signs are Saturn and Pisces.

Symbolizes Temporary Success, things thrown away as soon as acquired. Ill aspected misery, instability, indolence repining without cause. The signs above and below are Saturn and Pisces. The Lord of Abandoned Success. Saturn in Pisces 1°–10° and the Hod of Heh.

Nine of Cups are arranged in three rows, a hand issuing from a cloud holds a bunch of Lotuses one over each cup. Water pours into each cup which are full and running over. The symbols are Jupiter and Pisces.

Symbolizes Complete Success, wishes fulfilled, and happiness to perfection. Ill aspected vanity, conceit, selfish and too much self-assumption. The Lord of Material Happiness. Jupiter in Pisces 10°–20° the Yesod of Heh.

Ten of Cups is similar to the nine with one extra cup on top. The symbols are Mars and Pisces.

Symbolizes completion of good fortune, matters arranged as desired, permanent lasting success. Ill aspected dissipation, debauchery, wantonness. Lord of Perfected Success, Mars in Pisces 20°–30° and the Malkuth of Heh.

Two of Swords are held crossed by a radiating hand, at the intersection is a five petalled rose emitting rays. At the top and bottom are two small daggers with the signs of Luna and Libra on the points.

Symbolizes, balance after strife. Pleasure after pain. Strength through suffering. Justice, quarrels made up. Ill aspected, repetition or errors, talkative, injury through speech. The Lord of Peace Restored. Moon in Libra 1°–10° and the Chokmah of Vau.

Three of Swords as before but the centre sword has apart the rose and its petals fall, no rays issue from it. Above and below are the symbols Saturn and Libra.

Symbolizes unhappiness, sorrow, tears, disruption : honesty in money matters. Ill aspected selfish and dissipated, deceitful, fun in evil pleasures. The Lord of Sorrow, Saturn in Libra 10°–20° and the Binah of Vau.

Four of Swords. Two hands each hold two swords, the radiating rose is at the intersection. The symbols are Jupiter and Libra.

Symbolizes recovery from sickness, change for the better, peace after struggle, ease and plenty. Ill dignified, may be modified by its context with other cards. Lord of Rest from Strife. Jupiter in Libra 20°–30° and the Chesed of Vau.

Five of Swords. Two hands each holding three swords falling away from the centre sword which is held by a third hand as if it had separated them. The Rose petals are again torn apart and falling. The symbols are Venus and Aquarius.

Symbolism : defeat, loss, spite, malice, trouble, poverty, slander and sorrow after gain. Ill dignified these characteristics are accentuated. The Lord of Defeat, Venus in Aquarius 1°–10° and the Geburah of Vau.

Six of Swords held by two hands with the rose at the cross in the centre. The symbols are Mercury and Aquarius.

Symbolism : Success after anxiety, patience, journey by water, work. Ill dignified selfishness, conceit, The Lord of Earned Success. Mercury in Aquarius 10°–20° and the Tipareth of Vau.

Seven of Swords as before but the third hand holds a rose and a seventh sword in the centre. The points just touch.

Symbolism : Journey by land, partial success, not enough strength to complete the matter. Ill aspected fascinated by display, betrayal of confidences, vascillating, unreliable. The Lord of Unstable Effort. Moon in Aquarius 20°–30° and the Netzach of Vau.

Eight of Swords held by four hands, two in each and touching near the top of the card. The rose is again in the centre. The symbols are Jupiter and Gemini.

Symbolism : generous in money matters, too much force applied to small matters, ignoring the main issue. Wisdom applied to unworthy ends. Ill aspected impulsive, narrow, restricted, a prison. The Lord of the Shortened Forces. Jupiter in Gemini 1°–10° and the Hod of Vau.

Chapter 33. Lesser Arcana – *continued* and the Trump

Nine of Swords as before with a fifth hand holding the one sword upright in the centre dividing the others into two groups. The rose is absent.

Symbolism; oppression, hard work, lying, dishonesty, slander, cruelty. Ill aspected increases these characteristics. Lord of Despair and Cruelty, Mars in Gemini 10°–20° and the Yesod of Vau.

Ten of Swords as before but two crossed swords are dividing the others into two groups. The symbols are Sun and Gemini.

Symbolism: Ruin, disruption, death, failure of plans, ill aspected increases the power of evil. Lord of Ruin, Sun in Gemini 20°–30° and the Malkuth of Vau.

Two of Pentacles are united by a gold and green snake like the figure eight or sign of infinity. A radiant hand grasps the centre which appears to be revolving. The symbols are Jupiter and Capricorn.

Symbolism: visits to friends, pleasant change, alternating loss and gain, fortunate for journeys. Ill aspected wavering, inconsistent, wandering. The Lord of Harmonious Change. Jupiter in Capricorn 1°–10° and the Chokmah of Heh final.

Three of Pentacles are arranged in a triangle with a branch of a rose tree and two white birds surmounting the upper circle. Above and below are the symbols of Mars and Capricorn.

Symbolism: Business, employment, commercial deals. Influence, gain in deals, increase of material things, creative work, commencement of project. Ill aspected narrow, keen to gain, prejudiced, seeking the impossible. The Lord of Material Works, Mars in Capricorn 10°–20° and the Binah Heh final.

Four of Pentacles form a square, with the Sun and Capricorn above and below. A hand holds a branch of a rose tree, no flowers except one blown white bloom in centre. The signs of Sun and Capricorn in the usual positions.

Symbolism: gain in money or influence, success, power. Ill aspected prejudiced, suspicion and discontent. The Lord of Earthly Power, Sun in Capricorn 20°–30° and the Chesed of Heh final.

Five of Pentacles are similar to the ace, with a hand holding a rose tree from which all flowers and buds have fallen. The Symbols are Mercury and Taurus.

Symbolism: loss of money or job, trouble about material things, poverty. Ill aspected makes conditions worse. The Lord of Material Troubles. Mercury in Taurus 1°–10° and the Geburah of Heh final.

Six of Pentacles are arranged in a column of twos, with a hand holding a branch of white roses which touch the pentacles. The Symbols are Luna and Taurus.

Symbolism: prosperity in business, success in material matters, power, rank, influence, success. Ill dignified prodigal, indolent and purse-proud. The Lord of Material Success, Moon in Taurus 10°–20° and the Tiphareth of Heh final.

Seven of Pentacles arranged as a square with an inverted triangle above. A hand projects from a black cloud holding a rose branch to which the pentacles are attached. The Symbols are Saturn and Taurus.

Symbolism: unprofitable speculation, and difficulty in employment, much work for little gain. Promises of Unfulfilled success. Disappointment. Ill aspected the difficulties are increased. The Lord of Success Unfulfilled. Saturn in Taurus 20°–30° and the Netzach of Heh final.

Eight of Pentacles arranged in a column of twos. The hand issues from a cloud, holds a rose branch, the flowers of which touch only the lower four pentacles. The Pentacles are similar to the aces but without the wings and cross. The Symbols are Sun and Virgo.

Symbolism: skill, cunning prudence, over careful in small things at the expense of the great. Ill aspected, mean, lacking in enterprise, avaricious. The Lord of Prudence, Sun in Virgo 1°–10° and the Hod of Heh final.

Nine of Pentacles arranged as two squares, at the top and bottom of the card, with one at the centre. A hand holds rose branch with nine white flowers. The signs are Venus and Virgo.

Symbolism: increase of goods, inheritance, completion of material gain. Ill aspected theft, knavery, covetousness. The Lord of Material gain, Venus in Virgo 10°–20° and the Yesod of Heh final.

Ten of Pentacles are touched by roses on a branch held by a hand as before. The Symbols are Mercury and Virgo.

Symbolism : Riches and Wealth, completion of material gain and fortune. Ill aspected old age, slothfulness, dullness of mind. The Lord of Wealth, Mercury in Virgo 20°–30° and the Malkuth of Heh final.

This completes the description and meanings of the Lesser Arcana.

The Tarot Trumps on the Path

The picture cards of the Pack are 22 in number and are related to the paths connecting the Sephiroth from which they take part of their attributes in the various worlds (see lesson 16).

Trump No. 0, Path No. 11, Hebrew letter Aleph, The Fool connecting Kether with Chokmah is the Primum Mobile acting through the Air on the Zodiac.

I, 12, Bes, the *Juggler* connecting Kether with Binah is the Crown of Understanding, the beginning of material, the Primum Mobile acting through Mercury or Saturn.

II, 13, Gimel, the *High Priestess* connecting Kether with Tiphareth is the Crown of Beauty, the beginning of Beauty, the Primum Mobile acting on the Sun through the Moon.

III, 14, Daleth, the *Empress*, connecting Chokmah and Binah, is the Wisdom of Understanding, the union of the Powers of Origination and Production, the sphere of the Zodiac acting on Saturn through Venus.

IV, 15, Heh, the *Emperor* connecting Chokmah with Tiphareth is the Wisdom of Sovereignity and Beauty, and the orginator of them, the sphere of the Zodiac acting upon the Sun through Aries and initiating Spring.

V, 16, Vau, the *Nierophant*, connecting Chokmah with Chesed, the Wisdom and fount of Mercury, the sphere of the Zodiac acting on Jupiter through Taurus.

VI, 17, Zayin, *The Lovers*, connecting Binah and Tiphareth the Understanding and Production of Beauty and Sovereignity, Saturn acting on Sol through Gemini.

VII, 18, Cheth, *The Chariot*, connecting Binah and Geburah, is Understanding acting on Severity. Saturn acting on Mars through Cancer.

VIII, 19, Teth, *Strength or Fortitude*, connecting Chesed and Geburah. Mercy tempering Severity. The Glory of Strength. Jupiter acting on Mars through Leo.

IX, 20, Yod, *The Hermit*, connecting Chesed and Tiphareth is the Mercy of Beauty, The Magnificence of Sovereignity. Jupiter acting on Sol through Virgo.

X, 21, Kaph, *The Wheel of Fortune*, connecting Chesed and Netzach, is the Mercy and Magnificence of Victory. Jupiter acting through Jupiter acting through Jupiter direct on Venus.

XI, 22, Lamed, *Justice*, connecting Geburah and Tiphareth, is the Severity of Beauty and Sovereignty. Mars acting on Sol through Libra.

XII, 23, Mem, *The Hanged Man*, connecting Geburah and Hod is the Severity of Splendour. Execution of Judgement. Mars acting on Mercury through Water.

XIII, 24, Nun, *Death*, connecting Tiphareth and Netzach is the Sovereignity and result of Victory. Sol acting on Venus through Scorpio.

XIV, 25, Samekh, *Temperance*, connecting Tiphareth and Yesod, is the Beauty of Firm Basis, the Sovereignity of Fundamental Power. Sol acting on Luna through Sagittarius.

XV, 26, Ayin, *The Devil*, connecting Tiphareth and Hod is the Sovereignity and Beauty of Materialism and false splendour. Sol acting on Mercury through Capricorn.

XVI, 27, Pe, *The Tower*, connecting Netzach and Hod, is the Victory over Splendour, Avenging Force. Venus acting on Mercury through Mars.

XVII, 28, Tsaddi, *The Star*, connecting Netzach and Yesod, is the Victory of Fundamental Strength, Hope. Venus acting on Luna through Aquarius.

XVIII, 29, Qoph, *The Moon*, connecting Netzach and Malkuth, is the Victory of Material Venus acting on the Cosmic elements through Pisces.

XIX, 30, Resh, *The Sun*, connecting Hod and Yesod, is the Splendour of the Material World. Mercury acting on the Moon through the Sun.

XX, 31, Shin, *The Judgement*, connecting Hod and Malkuth, is the Splendour of the Material World. Mercury acting on the Cosmic Elements through Fire.

XXI, 32, Taw, *The Universe*, connecting Yesod and Malkuth, is the Foundation of the Cosmic Elements and of the Material World. Luna acting on the Elements through Saturn.

You may wonder why we have described a set of Tarot cards which is not in accordance with any of the easily obtained packs. We have detailed the pack used by the Golden Dawn and which was never published, but had to be copied by each member individually. The nearest illustrations to be obtained are in Crowley's Equinox Vol. III No. 5. *The Book of Thoth.* We believe however, that the descriptions given in these lectures are nearer to the ancient symbolisms and thus they fit well the general pattern of correspendences we are trying to demonstrate. It is to be hoped that in the not too distant future a pack including this symbolism will be available. In the meantime as all packs differ you can only try to interpret the cards of the pack you have along the lines described. Get to know your pack, they complete the tree and can be a source of inspiration, to expand your magical alphabet.

A. E. Thierens. *The General Book of the Tarot.* Rider.

W. Brodie-Innes. *The Tarot Cards* (article in *Occult Review.*) 1919 Feb. Issue.

Aleister Crowley. *Book of Thoth* (Equinox III. 5.) 1944 London.

S. L. MacGregor Mathers. *The Tarot.* New York.

Chapter 34. Sound

The priests of Israel marched with their hosts around Jericho for seven days, on the last day they all shouted and the walls fell down flat, see Joshua VI.12-20. This demonstrates the power of vibration as a destructive agent. For the same reason soldiers break step when crossing a bridge, lest the rhythm of their marching should set up a vibration and break it.

Included in the list of Yogas in Chapter 2 was given as Mantra Yoga, which is the study of sound. In this form of Yoga, by the expert use of Mantras, which consist of words or sounds of occult power, sometimes coupled with Yantra Yoga or the use of geometrical diagrams or postures of mystical significance, the yogin's object is to establish communion on the higher planes with the deities or spirits which he invites to assist him in his endeavours.

Your four-fold breathing exercise can take on a new form and increased power by adding colour and sound. First learn to count your breathing which normally is fifteen to the minute, nine hundred to the hour and 21,600 breathings for 24 hours.

Next take note of when the breathing begins and how it enters the body. Get well acquainted with the process, how it enters the nose, to the bottom of the lungs; how long it takes and how long it is retained, and exhaled, and the pauses between.

By visualizing each expiration as white in colour, while mentally or audibly vibrating the syllable AŪM or ŌM; the retention period as red in colour while vibrating ĀH; and each inspiration as blue in colour while vibrating HŪM. This technique will enable you to know your breathing and help you to energize it and thus retain the vital prana for use in your own aura.

The magical Rituals used by the Egyptian priesthood and the Masters of India and the East were based on a complete comprehension of the human mental and spiritual factors, they could therefore be adapted for use in healing by the reaction of the body to the higher forces. Their system of vibro-therapeutics, by means of chants and mantras, the use of certain vowel and con-

145

sonant sounds set up vibratory reaction which could be utilized to reduce congestion and restore broken members and depleted organs. They also used these methods, based on the laws governing vibrations, to elevate the spiritual constitution. By intoning the latent centre of consciousness could be stimulated to increase sensitivity to subjective influences.

The Book of Coming Forth by Day has preserved many of the secrets of the Egyptian Rituals for the present time, although its translation is not perfect, a great deal can be discovered by close study of its magical passages.

Oriental races have a keen understanding of the uses of sound vibration in spiritual exploration. Every word has tremendous power and by the correct arrangement of sounds a great influence can be produced on the physical plane; the sacred word by which the World was created; Masonry is still seeking for the Lost Word; the creative threefold sound of the Hindus AÜM, and the Hebrew name of the deity JHVH are examples of the power of words. But each must be vibrated in the especial manner which is known only to initiates. Isis in one of her myths is said to have conjured the Sun God Ra to tell her his secret and sacred name. This is equivalent to the lost word of Masonry. By means of this word the magician can demand obedience from the superior and invisible deities and spirits.

In Grecian times Pythagoras developed a philosophy of music which has come to be known as the "Music of the Spheres". Unfortunately not enough of this remains to be absolutely certain of his fundamentals. The Tetractys forms the basis of the theories of the Greeks about colour and music. In this pyramid of ten dots, the three at the top represent the threefold light, which is the Godhead containing the potential of all sound and colour, the active creative powers emanating from the First cause establish and maintain the Universe. The remaining seven are divided into two groups, three and four. The three become the spiritual nature of the creative Universe and the lower group of four manifest as the inferior world. Compare this with the Tree of Life which can be divided in a very similar manner.

Our musical scale is a series of notes rising in pitch from C to C octave, but pleasing to the ear only if sounded in a particular sequence. Each note is the result of a certain number of vibrations per second, therefore each can be represented by number and colour.

Note	V. per sec.	Colour	Scale	Planet
C	32	Red	do	Mars
D	36	Orange	re	Sol
E	40	Yellow	me	Mercury
F	44	Green	fa	Venus
G	48	Blue	soh	Luna
A	54	Indigo	la	Saturn
B	60	Violet	ti	Jupiter
C octave	68			

In the above table is also given the notes of the Tonic Scale and the Planetary correspondences. Most of the scales you find in literature are arbitary and present variations. So check that correspondences do correspond.

There are many curious stories about the uses of sound. Pythagorous discovered that the various modes or keys, the seven notes of the Greek system, had power to incite or depress the various emotions. One evening he met a youth who was bemused with strong drink and was trying to burn down the house of his master by piling faggots against it. He noticed that he was activated by a nearby flautist who was playing a stirring Phrygian style of tune. Having induced the musician to change the rhythm of his playing to the slow rhythmic Spondaic mode, the youth immediately became calmer and gathering up his bundles of wood returned to his own home.

One of his pupils, by name Empedocles, saved the life of his host Anchitus by changing the style of his playing. He was being threatened with death by the sword by a person whose father he had condemned to death by public execution.

Pythagoras treated many ailments of the body and soul by certain carefully composed musical compositions, and reciting chosen selections of the poets such as Hesiod and Homer. His school or University at Crotona was opened and closed each day with a song. The morning music was designed to clear the sleep from the mind and prepare it for the inspiration of the day's activities, that in the evening was designed to soothe, relax and prepare for sleep.

In the Great Pyramid of Gizeh which Marsham Adams described as the place of initiation there is a great coffin in which has never been found a body. When this great tomb carved out of a single piece of rock was struck a note was emitted which is

147

alleged to have no counterpart in any known musical scale. This tone may have been utilized in conjunction with the rituals in order to form an ideal setting for conferment of the Highest degrees of the Ancient Mysteries.

Origen recounts that the Brahamans were well known for the spectacular cures which they performed by the use of certain words. Orioli, a learned member of the French Institute, wrote that "There are also persons who upon pronouncing certain sentences, or mantras, walk bare-footed on red burning coals and on the points of sharp knives stuck in the ground; and once poised on them, on one toe, they will lift up in the air a heavy man or any other burden of considerable weight. They will tame wild horses likewise, and the most furious bulls, with a single word".

These words are to be found in the Mantras of the Sanscrit Vedas, say some adepts. It is for the philologists to decide for themselves whether such words are in the Vedas. So far as human evidence goes, it would seem that such magic words do exist, although without personal initiation by an adept it might be difficult to find them.

A clue may exist, however, in the statement of a certain eastern teacher that the real pronunciation of AŪM is a sound-less roar on the higher planes. This apparent contradiction will become clear on meditation. These sounds intepreted on the elemental planes vary; the earthly hum is like that of a bumble-bee; the watery level produces a flute like note; the Fiery nature is harp like; the airy version is like a bell. All these notes are contained in the soundless roar of a properly intoned AŪM.

Francis Barrett. *The Magus*. 1801 London.
E. L. Gardener. *Notes on H. B. B's Instruction*. 1931 T.P.S.
Clarence S. Hill. *Harmonia Harmonica*. 1920 Novello.
Stirling. *The Canon*. 1897 London.
Sepharial. *Kabala of Numbers*. 1914 London.

Chapter 35. The Great Pyramid

The only remaining one of the Seven Ancient Wonders of the World is the Great Pyramid at Gizeh. Its base stands on an area of about 15 acres, and its present height is just over 450 feet. There are about 2,300,000 stones in its structure averaging about $50 \times 50 \times 26$ inches and weighing some $2\frac{1}{2}$ tons each, with a total weight of about 6,000,000 tons. It was built in the reign of Cheops nearly 6,000 years ago and ten years were needed in its construction. Outside it was lined with polished limestone, but unfortunately most of the casing stones have been removed for use in Cairo buildings many years ago.

It is the north eastern of a group of three large pyramids about 10 miles west of Cairo, and there are several smaller ones nearby, as well as the Sphinx. It is oriented so that its faces are aligned to the four points of the compass. It can be assumed that the top thirty feet was never built thus making a truncated pyramid with a flat top, giving a platform about 30 feet square.

The Pyramid has been a source of wonder and awe for countless years and many legends are associated with it. The Guardian of the Eastern Pyramid was an idol, who had both eyes open, and was seated on a throne, having a sort of halberd near it, on which, if anyone fixed his eye, he heard a fearful noise, which struck terror in his heart, and caused the death of the hearer. There was a spirit appointed to wait on the guardian who departed not from before him. The keeping of the other two pyramids was arranged in a similar manner.

It possessed up to the Arab conquest, its facing of white marble polished and so subtly joined that it looked like a single slab from top to bottom. Its site at the apex of the Nile Delta on the 30° longitude places it in a position of some importance. Its main entrance on the eighteenth course of masonry, about forty-five feet from the ground, was so concealed by a movable flagstone working on a pivot, that its position was impossible to find except by the priests and custodians. From this a passage runs downwards, from which there are other passages leading to chambers of which the two most important are known as the Queen's and King's.

It was known in ancient times variously as the Horizon, the Khut or Lights, and the City of the White Wall. The *Book of the Dead* or Funeral Ritual is called the Book or Scroll of the Master of the Secret House. The Rubric to Chapter CLXII (Budge) ends with "this is a composition of exceedingly great mystery. Let not the eye of any man whatsoever see it, for it is an abominal thing for everyone to know it; therefore hide it. Book of the Mistress of the Hidden Temple is its name". The original papyrus of this chapter was found in the coffin of a priest named Auf Aukh and is now in the Turin Museum.

It was because a number of references to light in the various sections of the *Book of the Dead*, were accompanied by references to parts of a building that gave Marsham Adams the clue to connect the book with the pyramid. The ritual has many references to passages, opening doors, going out, and other masonic phrases. From that inspiration he assumed and proved in a well-reasoned manner that the Ritual was that of the Pyramid.

On the coffin of Amamu of Abydos was an inscription which demonstrated that the secret places of the pyramid determined the order of the Ritual. "Thou hast not gone dying, thou hast gone living to Osiris. Now that thou hast found the words of order, the Mystery of the Secret Places". Here was the link, the little 'Light' of the Great Pyramid, was not the light of day, but the Invisible Light of the unseen world, renewed forever in the splendour of Osiris. Chapter LV states "I draw air from the presence of the God of Light to the bounds of heaven, and to the bounds of Earth". Therefore the doctrine contained in those mystic writings was nothing less than an account of the Path pursued by the Just; when the bonds of flesh were loosed, he passed through stage after stage of spiritual growth to the Entrance on Light to become indissolubly united with Him whose name, says the Egyptian Ritual, is Light, the Great Creator.

"The intimate connection" writes Adams, "between the secret doctrine of Egypt's most venerated books, and the secret significance of her most venerable monument, seems impossible to dissever and each form illustrates and interpenetrates the other. As we pursue the dark utterances and recognize the mystic allusions of the Book, we seem to stand amid the profound darkness enwrapping the whole interior of the building. Dimly before our eyes, age after age, the sacred procession of the Egyptian dead moves silently along as they pass to the tribunal of Osiris. In vain do we attempt to trace their footsteps till we enter with them into the Hidden Places and penetrate the secret of the House of Light. But no sooner do we tread the chambers of the mysterious pyramid than the teaching of the Sacred Books seems lit up as with a tongue of Flame.

"With the sacred writings in hand" he says, "I went through the secret places of the Great House; and I doubt whether anyone will do the same, bearing in mind the traditions of the priests, and picturing to himself the midnight watch of the lonely neophyte amid the impenetrable darkness of those solemn chambers, without recognizing how apt was that awe-inspiring structure for the initiation into the secrets of the unseen world".

Refer back to Chapter 1 and the quotation from the *Golden Ass* and see how this theory throws more light on the brief description of the mysteries described by Apulius. There have been many theories and speculations about the pyramid but for our purpose there is none more rewarding than that of Marsham Adams which well repays investigation with an unprejudiced mind.

Leadbeater relates "The initiates of the Egyptian Mysteries were symbolically engaged in the building of the pyramid, just as in our modern masonry we are engaged in erecting the temple of King Solomon, both structures being intended to be emblematical of the building processes of nature. In the halls below the pyramid, those underground chambers which were mentioned by Herodotus as being contained in an island, fed by a channel from the Nile, certain of the ceremonies of the Mysteries were held. These and other halls in and near the Great Pyramid are still unknown to the explorer, though they may yet be opened by "the proper steps", the secret doors turning upon pivots according to an elaborate system of counterpoise, and being set in motion by treading upon certain spots in the floor in a certain order".

The Ceremonies of the Mysteries were also intended to portray the higher evolution of men, his return to the divine source whence he came, through the development of the higher part of his nature, which is not merely consequent upon practices of meditation and ceremonial, but even more upon the living out of the ethical precepts which were taught. Many people of our day imagine that we know ethical truths without being taught them, but that is not so; they seem to us quite natural now, but long ago they were discoveries or revelations somewhat analogous to the steps of advancement in material science and invention.

Each degree of the Mysteries was designed to reflect one or other of the Great Initiations of the White Lodge, so that the initiates of the lower level might prepare themselves ultimately to enter the Path of Holiness, and so strive after the fulness of union with Osiris, the Hidden Light. This teaching was graded and the initiates who were properly prepared were enabled to reach the true knowledge which they were seeking. The whole scheme of initiation provided a complete chart of man's spiritual evolution, and it was for the individual candidate to endeavour to put the teachings into practice and to make real in his own consciousness that which was symbolized in the ritual.

The Great Pyramid is the House of a Tomb; but it is not a closed tomb, but an open tomb. It is the tomb, not of a man but of a God; not of the dead but of the risen. It is the tomb of the divine Osiris, in unison with whom the holy departed, achieved the path of illumination, and passed in safety the divine tribunal. Compare 1 Cor. XV 51-54. "Behold I show you a mystery; we shall not all sleep, but we shall all be changed. In a moment, in the twinkling of an eye, at the last trump. . . . For this corruptible must put on incorruption, and this mortal put on immortality". Thus and only thus can "Death be swallowed up in victory" (Isaih XXV. 8).

William Kingsland. *The Great Pyramid*. Vol. 1. 1932 Rider.
William Kingsland. *The Great Pyramid*. Vol. 2. 1935 Rider.
D. Davidson and H. Aldersmith. *The Great Pyramid its divine message*. 1924 Williams and Norgate.
Basil Stewart. *History and Significance of the Great Pyramid*. 1935 Bale.
Paul Brunton. *A Search in Secret Egypt*. 1944 Rider.
E. A. W. Budge. *Egypt and the Egyptian Sudan*. 1925 Cooks.

Chapter 36. The Banishing Ritual

The pentagram or five pointed star is the figure of the micro-cosm, the magical formula of man. It is the one rising out of the four, the human soul rising from the bondage of animal nature. It is the true light, the Morning Star, Stella Matutina. It locates the five mysterious centres of force, the awakening of which is the supreme secret of White Magic.

This magic pentagram, or star of the microcosm, is the five pointed star of occult masonry, the star with which Agrippa drew the human figure the head in the upper point, the four limbs in the four others. The flaming star, which when turned upside down, is the hieroglyphic sign of the goat of Black Magic, whose head may then be drawn in the star, the two horns at the top, the ears to the right and left, the beard at the bottom. It is now the sign of antagonism, fatality and instability. It is the goat of lust attacking the heavens with its horns. It is a sign execrated by initiates of superior rank even at the Sabbath.

So that you may understand what is being described you should now draw and colour your own pentagram. On a sheet of cartridge paper draw two circles, with a common centre, one two inches radius and one with three inches radius. Keep your pencil lines fine so that later they can be rubbed out. Next divide the outer circle into five equal parts and join these points to the centre. Start at the top so that the uppermost mark is right at the top of the outer circle. The easiest way to divide the circle is with a protractor marked in degrees. This gives 72° to each segment the five segments making the full circle of 360°. Now mark and number the radii on the outer circle starting at the top and proceeding clockwise. Next join the intersecting points on the outer circle 1 to 3, 3 to 5, 5 to 2, 2 to 4 and 4 to 1. This will give a five pointed star in the outer circle. Next in a similar order draw another smaller star within the inner circle. Yoy now have a double pentagram which can be inked in two ways. Each full triangle can be inked so that the corners overlap in one direction;

or a continuous band can be left in the centre as a five-sided figure, with the two other sides of each triangle standing on a side of the centre pentagram. The figure can now be coloured as indicated. Try it with gold, or alternatively any appropriate colour for the work in hand. The angles can have their own colours as in the table below, and this makes the most useful form.

Element	Colour	Kerub	Wind
1. Spirit	Black or Indigo		
2. Water	Sky blue	Eagle	West
3. Fire	Red	Leo	South
4. Earth	Yellow	Taurus	North
5. Air	Silver	Aquarius	East

These are the colours of the tattwas. This symbol was used by most of the secret and occult societies, by the Rosicrucians, the Illuminati and the Freemasons. Modern Occultists interpret the meaning of the pentagram as symbolic of the human soul in its relationship with God.

The Symbol when placed properly with one point at the top, represents the great spirit. The line drawn from there to the left-hand angle at the base suggests the descent of spirit into the base matter earth. It then ascends to the right angle which suggests matter in its higher form, the grain of man, or spirit moving on the water. From here to the left upper angle indicates man's development in intellect, his airy nature. This in the progress of material civilization is the point of danger, from which all nations have fallen eventually into moral corruption as indicated by the line the right angle at the base. The soul of man being derived from God cannot remain here, and must struggle upwards as is symbolized by the line again reaching to the apex, from which it originated.

Didorus calls five "the union of the four elements with Ether". There are 5 orders of Architecture; the 5 senses of the human body now commonly known and described (but the whole are seven); Geometry was technically called the 5th Science. In Masonry the Grand Scheme is the 5 points of Fellowship, and the rule that 5 Brethren are necessary to hold a Fellowcraft Lodge. Ther are 5 regular Euclidean bodies, tetrahedron, hexahedron or cube, octohedron, dodekahedron and icosahedron.

The 5 points of Fellowship as given by Carlisle are :

1. Hand to hand—I greet you as a brother.
2. Foot to foot—I will support you in all your just and laudable undertakings.
3. Knee to knee—Being the posture of my daily supplications, shall remind me of your wants.
4. Breast to breast—shall be a safe and sacred repository for all your just and lawful secrets.
5. Hand over back—that I will support a brother's character in his absence, equally as though he were present.

The fifth Element, the Quintessence of the Alchemist was derived from four by progression. At first the Ens, then the two Contraries then the Three Principles, then the four Elements. Separate the pure from the impure, gently and with judgement, and you obtain the Quintessence, the Son of the Sun. Similarly note the progression in nature; stone, plant, animal, man, god.

The Triad Society of China, concerning which there is an article in the *Freemason's Quarterly Review 1845* p. 165, boasts of great antiquity; it resembles Freemasonry in some points; five is a chief mystical number in its concerns. Its seal is pentangular, on its angles are five characters representing TOO or Saturn, MUH or Jupiter, SHWVY or Mercury, KWY or Venus, and HO or Mars.

Now we come to a most important practice know as the Banishing Ritual of the Pentagram. In the table above the elements given corresponding to nature of the winds and not as to their natural position in the Zodiac which are as follows: Fire in the East, Earth in the South, Air in the West and Water in the North. So in performing the ritual you should stand erect with your face to the cardinal point of the element in which you wish to banish. For general use it is customary to use the pentagram of earth in order to prepare and clear the place for the performance of magical ritual or meditation, or protection against opposing forces.

Standing with your face to the East imagine before you a large pentagram in the colours as you have drawn it about 5 feet high and 6 feet in front of your body. Having completed the four fold breathing and energizing yourself as directed, stretch your hand out towards the earth angle opposite your left foot. You may use your finger, a wand or dagger to transfer the glowing energy towards the imagined figure. Next bring the finger upward to opposite your brow at the same time transfer the glowing energy to the pentacle. Then come down to a point opposite your right foot. Next come over to opposite your left shoulder straight across to opposite your right shoulder and then back to your point of commencement. Make sure that your pentagram is accurate. Finally stab the centre point thus completing the figure and you will have a vibrating glowing image of an astral pentagram. From the centre go to the south holding the hand straight out and perform the same ritual there. Continue in the west and north and finally return to the East thus completing the circle.

Thus you will have four glowing signs in each quarter so that your room should be cleansed and guarded against unwanted influences. Practice this ritual till you are so familiar with the movements that you can do so without reference to these pages.

The Key to the working of the Pentagram ritual is use of the words or Divine names given in Chapter 32. As you point to the centre of each figure vibrate the name for the element in which you are working. Vibrate the names letter by letter as much as possible with the outgoing breath, vibrating inwardly but not necessarily loudly. "The man of genius differs from the dreamer and the fool in this only, that his creations are analogous to breath, while those of the fool and the dreamer are lost reflections and betrayed images. Hence for the wise man, to imagine is to see, or, for the magician, to speak is to create. It follows that by means of the imagination demons and spirits can be held really and in truth; but the imagination of the adept is diaphanous, whilst that of the crowd is opaque; the light of truth traverses the one as ordinary light impinges upon a vitreous block, full of scoriae and foreign matter : that which most contributes to the errors of the vulgar is the reflection of the depraved imaginations one in the other. But in virtue of positive science, the seer knows that what he imagines is true, and the event invariably confirms his vision"—Levi.

Eliphas Levi. *The Key of the Mysteries*. Trans. Aleister Crowley. 1959 Rider.
Eliphas Levi. *History of Magic*. 1922 Rider.
W. Wynn Wescott. *Numbers*. 1902 T.P.S.

Chapter 37. The Tarot Trumps

The remaining cards of the Tarot Pack now to be described are known as Trumps, Atus of Thoth, or the 22 Keys. They correspond to the Paths of the Quabala (see page 73) which are numbered 11 to 22 inclusive. The cards however are numbered 0 to XXI to avoid confusion by using similar notations. You can now place these cards on your large tree, which will complete the set of symbols.

Some schools put 0 as the 22nd card which can cause complication. Placed before number 1 as in the present arrangement the correspondence with the Hebrew alphabet is reasonable and the cards demonstrate the qualities of the paths connecting the various sephiroth.

Path 11, card 0. The Fool strides along, head in the air regardless of the dog which attacks him. A naked child stands beneath a yellow rose tree (of Joy and Silence), he holds a grey wolf in leash, wisdom held in check by innocence. It is linked with the name of Kristna and Dionysus. The colours, pale yellow, blue and greenish yellow, suggesting an early spring dawn. The Hebrew letter is Aleph.

Symbolizes spirituality, ideas. Ill aspected it is too unstable to be good on the material plane, folly.

12. I. The Magician or Adept is consecrating his magical instruments. He is reflected in the Intellect which stores knowledge and transmits it to Life. The number of the path 12 suggests the Zodiac belt. It is linked with Tahuti and Hermes. The colours yellow, violet, grey and indigo indicate the mysterious astral light around the Adept. The letter is Bes.

Symbolizes skill, wisdom, adaptation particularly in occult spheres. Ill aspected craft and cunning.

13. II. The High Priestess is the great feminine principle controlling the ultimate source of life, gathering the energizing forces and keeping them solvent until their time of release. She rules the path from Kether to Tiphareth. Her colours are pale blue darkening into sky blue, silver, with touches of flame and orange. The letter is Gimel.

Symbolizes increase, change, alteration. Ill aspected decrease and change for the worse. Generally representing a religious tendency and orthodoxy; compare with XVIII.

14. *III. The Empress* is the creative side of nature as in the Egyptian triology Isis, Hathor and Nephthys and their symbols respectively the crescent, full moon and gibbous moon. The Positive feminine is the force indicated. It is the door to the inner mysteries. The colours are emerald sky blue, blue green and cerise or rose pink. The letter is Daleth.

Symbolizes success, beauty, happiness, pleasure; if ill aspected dissipation and black magic.

15. *IV. The Emperor* is the doer and indicates by various degrees of red the great energizing forces. Note that all red paths remain red although varying in shades in all planes. Aries is blood red and deep crimson red, vermillion or fiery red. He is not passionate and carries the forces of Mars in love and war. He is positive masculine force. The letter is Heh.

Symbolizes war, conquest, victory, strife. Ill aspected these powers are contrary to wishes.

16. *V. The Hierophant* or High Priest is the counterpart of 11 and reflects the mystical aspect of the masculine. He is the Thinker. Taurus is the house of Venus and the exhaltation of the moon. His colours vary considerably, red, orange, maroon, deep brown. Indicates interior power, contemplation. The letter is Vau.

Symbolizes Divine Wisdom, Teaching, the Prophet, Occult Wisdom and the guardianship of the masters. Ill aspected, the antagonistic working of these qualities.

17. *VI. The Lovers* and Perseus rescuing Andromeda from the Dragon of Fear and the Waters of Stagnation. They illustrate the impact of inspiration on intuition, giving liberation and illumination. The colours are orange, violet, purplish grey. The letter is Zayin.

Symbolizes sympathetic understanding, inspiration and power resulting therefrom. Ill aspected, these qualities are reduced or negative.

18. *VII. The Chariot* represents the spirit of man controlling his lower principles, soul and body, passing through the astral plane to the higher spheres. It shows the sublimation of the

Psyche. The colours are amber, silver grey, blue grey, and blue violet of the night sky. The letter is Cheth.

Symbolizes Victory, Success, Health, Triumph. Ill aspected unenduring or temporary success.

19. VIII. Strength represents the mastery of the lower by the higher. The Soul with her feet on earth holds in check the passions. A dark veil is around her head and body. The colours are greenish yellow, yellowish grey and reddish amber, deep rose gives a contrast. The letter is Teth.

Symbolizes Fortitude, Strength and courage, Power as a starting factor. Ill aspected obstinacy.

20. IX. The Hermit or Prophet is a man wrapped in a hood and mantle carrying a lantern to light the Path, and a staff to support his footsteps. He is the Seeker and Pilgrim Soul. His vestments are the brown of earth, the delicate yellow greens, and bluish greens of spring. The letter is Yod. Together with the Hierophant and Magician these cards are the 3 Magi.

Symbolizes Prudence, Divine Wisdom in the active sense as compared with the Lovers. Ill aspected the card carries a bad influence.

21. X. The Wheel of Life or Fortune presided over by the cynocephalus below and the Sphinx above is the Riddle which can only be solved by attaining liberation. It is the revolution of the Zodiac, experience and progress, under the influence of Light and Darkness. The basic colours are blue, violet, deep purple and blue speckled with yellow. The Zodiac spheres are in the colours of the Spectrum, the ape as those of Malkuth, the Sphinx in black and the primary colours. The letter is Kaph.

Symbolizes good fortune and happiness according to the aspects.

22. XI. Justice as opposed to love illustrated by Nephthys, the twin sister of Isis who is the third aspect of the Moon. The colours are green clothes, but a colder colour than the pure emerald of Isis, the other colours are blue, blue green and pale green. The letter is Lamed.

Symbolizes Balance and Eternal Justice, arrested force; compared with VIII. Ill aspected these properties are reduced.

23. XII. The Hanged Man is the sacrifice, the sublimation of the lower man by submergence of the higher. The descent of Spirit into Matter illustrates the incarnation of God in Man. The colours are deep blue, white and black mixed (not grey), olive, green and greenish fawn. The letter is Mem.

Symbolizes punishment, loss, involuntary sacrifice. Ill aspected suffering generally.

24. XIII. Death is the transmuting power of the Spirit from above working downwards. The skeleton survives the destruction of time, suggests the evolutionary changes which leave the Spirit relatively unchanged. The colours are blue-green, dark and light, orange and red-orange. The letter is Nun.

Symbolizes transformation, time, involuntary change. Ill aspected death and destruction.

25. XIV. Temperance sums up the equilibrium in the arrow of Sagittarius, which clears its way by the impetus given by the bow. It requires the balance of Fire and Water (Shin and Qoph) controlled by the restrictive power of Saturn, and the active energies of Mars to initiate their impelling force. These are shown by the figure standing between Earth and Water, holding two jars with streams of living water, and the volcano in the distance. The colours are bright-blue, blue grey, slate blue and lilac grey. The letter is Samekh.

Symbolizes material action; combination of forces, realization. For good or evil according to aspect.

26. XV. The Devil indicates the lower nature of man as indicated by the chains on the smaller figures and the beastial nature of their lower limbs. The lower nature of man hates the transmitting process which is necessary to preserve continuity and stabilize the life force. This card should be studied in connection with XIII as they indicate the two great controlling forces of the universe, destructive and reproductive, centrifugal and centripetal, dynamic and static. The colours are indigo, livid brown, golden brown and grey. The letter is Ayin.

Symbolizes material force, temptation, materiality. Ill aspected obsession and worldly obstacles.

Kurt Seligmann. *The History of Magic.* 1948 Pantheon.
Mouni Sadhu. *The Tarot.* U.S.A.
Eden Gray. *Tarot Revealed.* U.S.A.
Paul F. Case. *The Tarot, a Key to the Wisdom of the ages.* U.S.A.

Chapter 38. The Tarot Trumps and Divination

27. XVI. The Tower struck by lightning suggests revolution instead of transmutation and sublimation. The destructive and powerful force ejects those who try to abandon themselves to ease and tradition. The colours are red in various shades, thrown into relief with shades of green. Compare with Emperor.

Symbolizes courage, war, fighting, ambition. Ill aspected danger, ruin, destruction.

28. XVII. The Star is the seven pointed star of Venus shining over the Waters of Aquarius. It is the guarding force of love illuminating the soul in human bondage. The dove of Spirit hovers over the Fire of Knowledge, and on the other side is the Tree of Life. The colours of dawn are amethyst, pale grey, fawn, dove and white with pale yellow of the star.

Symbolizes unexpected help, faith and hope. Ill aspected dreamers and deception.

29. XVIII. The Moon is the path of blood, tears and sweat, in which weakness and fear must be overcome. The river is the troubled waters of Night, the Crayfish is similar to the Scarab beetle. From the waters' edge leads a dark path of toil, and possible failure. The threatening watchdogs intimidate the travellers, while in the distance are fortresses on the hills further guarding the way to attainment. The colours are dark crimson, reddish brown, brownish crimson and plum; these are contrasted by faint greens and yellows.

Symbolizes voluntary change (in contrast to XIII), dissatisfaction. Ill aspected, error, deception, lying.

30. XIX. The Sun with its fiery rays may melt the waxen wings of the Icarius urged by Ambition and Curiosity. But the Pilgrim protected by an encircling wall may approach the Light with humility and absorb warmth and vitality to fit him for the coming struggle. The Watery Paths of probation are balanced by the Fiery path of Temptation and Decision. The colours are clear orange, golden yellow, amber flecked with red and the blue and purple as contrast. The sombre colours of Aquarius and Pisces opposing the flaring hues of the Sun and Fire.

Symbolizes riches, glory, gain. Ill aspected, display, arrogance and vanity.

31. XX. The Last Judgement shows the cosmic concentrating on the pilgrim from all sides. Judgement is pronounced. Lazarus cannot emerge from the Sepulchre till the voice cries "Come Forth". Man himself is helpless, the impulse to ascend must come from above. It is only by this impulse that he can transcend the tomb, cast aside his desire attractions, and become one with the source of life itself.

Symbolizes Judgement, Final decision, aspects modify the nature of determination of the matter.

32. XXI. The Universe is represented and not the world. To the ancients Saturn passing through his spiral path in the Zodiac represented the confines of the Solar System. They had no knowledge of Uranus, Neptune or Pluto. The white gleam of the stars shining in the dark has the misty figure of Aimah Elohim in the midst. This card may be taken as the synthesis of the whole Tarot. If the central figure be Hathor, Athor or Ator instead of Isis the hidden anagram can be interpreted as follows; ORAT—many prays. ATOR—to the Great Mother. TARO—who turns. ROTA—the Wheel of Life and Death.

Symbolizes Synthesis, The Matter itself, World, Kingdom and this depends on its aspects more than the other cards.

The student will notice that the cards have been described in order from above downwards according to the numbers of the Paths as life descends from above. It would be well now for him to study the cards in the reverse sequence so that he may be enabled to see the various paths or qualities with which he will need to become familiar in his search for the ultimate.

The trumps VIII and XI, carrying the correspondences of Leo and Libra, were transposed in the older cards, revolving on the pivot of Pisces. Crowley also transposed IV and XVII. He did this on the authority of Verse 57 of Chapter 1 of the *Book of the Law*. This only appears once in *777* (revised) and once in his *Book of Thoth*.

Tarot Divination

Having considered the cards in detail and their correspondences on the Tree there is another use to which they can be put. The technique to be described is given by A. E. Waite as an ancient Celtic method of divination. There are many other methods but it is wise to become expert first with a simple one. The diviner selects a card to represent the person or matter about which the enquiry is to be made, using one of the following sixteen Court cards:

Wands	fair haired and complexioned, and red haired persons
Cups	fairish
Swords	dark
Pentacles	very dark
Kings	men
Queens	women
Princes (Knights)	young men
Princesses (Knaves)	young women

This card is placed upright on the table in front of the diviner who notes which way the figure looks. The pack is then given to the enquirer who shuffles the pack concentrating on the matter which should first have been written down as a definite question. The cards are then placed on the table and cut, with the top lot placed below the others, all face down. The upper cards are taken one at a time and placed as follows in accordance with the diagram.

S. *The Significator.*
1. What covers him.
2. What crosses him.
3. What crowns him.
4. What is beneath him.
5. What is behind him.
6. What is before him.
7. Himself.
8. His house.
9. His hopes or fears.
10. What will come.

Care must be taken with 5 and 6 bearing in mind the direction in which the significator is looking.

Now take a sheet of paper, from your loose-leaved notebook, put the question and date and time at the top. On the left-hand side write the figures 0, 1 to 10 in a column. Opposite these write the key words in the table above. In the third column write the

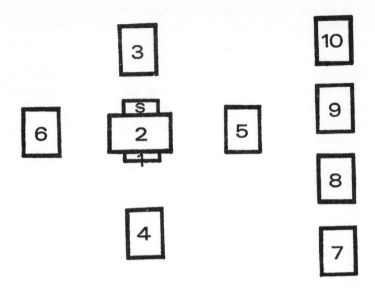

card (number and suit or individual number and name of trumps). In the next column write the Keyword as in Chapter 31. The trump card keywords you should be able to work out for yourself from Chapter 30 and others dealing with the trumps. This now gives you a complete picture and a permanent record of your divination and can be kept to verify or otherwise the truth of your prognostications. You should now, by working at the cards and their symbolism with your inner consciousness, be able to put together comprehensive reply to the original question.

It is not to be expected that you will be completely successful at the first trial, but with practice and an increasing knowledge of the cards you should easily give a reasonable forecast and sensible reply to any question asked. This technique may be regarded as fortune telling but it can help to develop your awareness of other people's problems, and does assist in developing sensitivity in a positive way. The latent faculty of insight can be stimulated and the method is free of all complications.

At first it is advised that you attempt only questions in which you have no emotional envolvement. This is because those who are psychic but do not know themselves sufficiently, may find the various methods of divination including telling the cards may be a fruitful source of self-deception. Under no circumstances must you allow yourself to advertise only your successes. Learn to assess your diagnosis accurately, record it and test in the light of later events. Only thus can you expect to develop your intuition scientifically and correctly.

It is most important to observe the correct correspondences of the symbols employed, otherwise the link between them and the inner occult forces may become strained which will yield a false answer. The Diviner must have his mind clear and unprejudiced, neither disturbed by anger, fear nor love, and with a sound knowledge of the correspondences of the symbols employed. It is unwise to repeat the divination on any one question.

To facilitate memorizing and working with the cards you should obtain 80 plain unprinted postcards. On the top of each write the name and number of the card. 22 for the Trumps, that is 0 to I to XXI in Roman numerals. 56 numbered 4 each for the different suits numbered 1–10 and the four named court cards of each suit (refer to lessons 29 and 30. Below the names write the keywords given in lessons 16, 25, 26 and others dealing with this subject). You should by now have sufficient knowledge to pick the key-words which are best suited to your requirements—be that divination or assessment of the qualities of the paths for magical purposes. These personal cards can be used instead of or in conjunction with an ordinary tarot pack.

Chapter 39. The Gnostics

Little reliable information remains to us of the early Christian and Pagan Gnostics. As they were somewhat at variance with the better organized and simpler teachings of the early church fathers, it is not surprising that most of their literature was destroyed. Their secret information and philosophical teachings were concealed from the profane and taught to small groups of especially initiated people. They existed during the early days of the Christian Church and it was claimed that their mystic teachings were based on the secret doctrines of Christianity interpreted according to pagan symbolism. The word *gnosis*, from the Greek, means wisdom or knowledge.

Simon Magus, the magician of the New Testament is reputed to be the Founder. Everything which did not correspond to the teachings of the Church was alleged to be of the Devil; consequently a great wealth of real information has been suppressed. Hippolytus is alleged to have stated "To you, therefore, I say what I say, and I write what I write. And the writing is this; of the Universal Aeons (periods, planes, or cycles of creative and created life in substance and space, celestial creatures), there are two shoots, without beginning or end, springing from one root, which is the power invisible, inapprehensible silence (Bythos). Of these shoots one is manifested from above, which is the Great Power, the Universal Mind ordering all things, male; and the other (is manifested) from below, the Great Thought, female, producing all things. Hence paring with each, they Unite in the Middle Distance, incomprehensible Air, without beginning or end. In this is the Father who sustains all things, and nourishes those things which have a beginning and end".

From this it would appear that manifestation is the result of a positive and negative principle, acting in the middle plane or point of equilibrium called the pleroma. This is a peculiar state produced by the blending of the spiritual and material. Out of which was individualized the Demiurgus, the immortal mortal from which comes our physical existence and the suffering con-

166

nected therewith. In the Gnostic System three Syzygies or pairs of opposites emanate from the Eternal One. The first two were Mind (Nous) and Thought (Epinoia). Next came Voice (Phone) and its opposite Name (Onoma). The third pair was Reason (Logismos) and Reflection (Enthumesis). From these primordial six, united with the Eternal Flame, came forth the Aeons (Angels) who formed the lower worlds under the direction of the Demiurgus.

The Gnosis, therefore, in its simplest and earliest form taught the Knowledge of God and of Men, of the being and providence of the former, and of the creation and destiny of the latter. While the ignorant and superstitious were degrading the glory of the incorruptible God into an image made with hands, and were changing the truth of God into a lie, and worshipped and served the creature rather than the creator, the ancient Gnostics held purer and truer ideas. When these corrupted and idolatrous forms of religion and worship became established and were popularly regarded as true and real in themselves, the Gnostics held and secretly taught an esoteric theology of which the popular creed of multitudes of deities, with its whole ritual of sacrifice and worship was but an exoteric form. Hence all the mysteries which, almost if not all, the heathen religions possessed. Those initiated into the mysteries, whilst they carefully maintained and encouraged the gorgeous worship, sacrifice and processions of the national religion, and even openly taught Polytheism, and the efficacy of the public rites, yet secretly held something very different, at the first, probably a purer creed, but in the course of time, like the exoteric form degenerating.

The principle works dealing with the Gnostics are the *Pistis Sophia* and the two *Books of Enoch*. Otherwise one has to study many ancient works by authors who regarded the Gnostics as heretics. The introduction to Mead's *Pistis Sophia* gives a comprehensive list of sources. King's *Gnostics and their Remains* deals with these in greater detail.

The only manuscript of the *Pistis Sophia* known to exist was bought by the British Museum from the heirs of Dr. Askew before an auction of his library which lasted twenty days in 1785. (Its number is M.S.Add.5114.) There is no evidence as to how it was originally acquired. It is written on Vellum in Greek Unical letters, and is in the Upper Egyptian dialect, called Thebaidic or Sahidic. It makes known to us the deepest secrets of the celebrated Egyptian mysteries which are identical with the Rabbinical Quabala, the only alteration being that of putting them into the mouth of Scripture personages, in order to adapt them to the prevailing change of ideas. The book, therefore, supplies an elucidation of contemporary monuments not found elsewhere, for the Christian Fathers discuss only the doctrines of their adversaries, not condescending to notice their application to everyday life. In it is a whole category of Holy names, of such talismanic virtue; the powers and titles of the actual genii, the constitution of the Soul; and its state after death. It exhibits the leading principles of the Quabala applied to demonstrate the highest truths. All this is in the form of a record of the higher teachings of the Saviour communicated to his disciples during the eleven years he is supposed to have passed with them after his crucifixion.

There are two *Books of Enoch*, the first or Ethiopic, known as *The Book of Enoch the Prophet* was translated by Richard Lawrence, Archbishop of Cashel (New Edition 1883). Another popular edition was done by R. H. Charles 1935. The second book, or Slavonic, known as the *Book of the Secrets of Enoch*, was translated by W. R. Morfill (edited by R. H. Charles) 1896.

The First Book or vision deals with the condemnation of transgressors and the blessings of the righteous. It continues with the descent of two hundred angels, their selection of wives, their offspring and the instruction of mankind in various scientific devices, including sorcery, astrology and divination. These are tales of the miraculous journey of Enoch in the company of an angel, from whom he learns the secrets of creation and the mysteries of Infinity. There is the second vision of wisdom, divided into three parables. The book of the revolutions of the luminaries of heaven, the sun, the moon; and the stars controlled in their movements by ministrations of angels. There is a vision of an allegorical forecast of the world's history up to the Messiah, followed by a series of prophecies and admonitions.

The Second Book deals with the cause of death as sin, the creation of men with freewill and the knowledge of good and evil, the Seraphim and the intercession of Saints, the Seven Heavens. The first Heaven contains a very great sea, greater than any earthly sea, and the elders and rulers of the orders of the stars. In the second heaven prisoners are suspended, reserved and awaiting eternal judgement. In the third heaven is described the Garden of Eden and the tree of life. In the fourth Heaven Enoch sees the course of the sun and moon and the wonderful ceatures which wait upon the sun. In the fifth Heaven are the watchers whose fallen brethren Enoch had already seen undergoing torments in the second Heaven. In the sixth Heaven are the seven bands of angels standing before the Lord in order of their rank. In the seventh heaven Enoch sees all the heavenly hosts, the ten great orders of angels standing before the Lord in the order of their rank, and the Lord sitting on His lofty throne.

To sum up in the words of Spence, "simultaneously with Christianity, these sects assumed a definite form, the eastern provinces of the Roman Empire being their sphere of operations at first. Their doctrines were an admixture of Indian, Babylonian and Christian creeds, astrology and magic with much of the Jewish Quabala also. From Alexandria, that centre of mystic learning, much of their distinctive beliefs and ritual were derived, while it seems certain that to some extent they became affiliated with mithraism to whose sheltering kindness occidental Christianity also owed much. Most of the sects had a priesthood of the mysteries, and these initiated priests practised magic arts, astrology, incantations, exorcisms, the fashioning of charms, talismans and amulets, of which many are extant at the present day. It is said that the Grecian mysteries, the Eleusinian, and Cabiric, for instance, were celebrated by the Gnostic sects down to a late date. They were looked upon as heretics by the Church, and were the victims of relentless persecution. In Persia also they were put to death, but some embraced Islamism, and transmitted their doctrines to the Dervish Sects, Manicheism, a later sect was founded by Manes, who belonged to the order of the Magi, and was famous for his skill in astrology, medicines and magic. This sect was anathema to the Church and, its later variants, Paulicians, Cathari, Albigensis, Lollards, and later still the Carbonari, never failed to arouse the persecuting fervour of the Church".

G. R. S. Mead. *Simon Magus*. 1892 T.P.S.
G. R. S. Mead. *Pistis Sophia*. 1896 T.P.S.
C. W. King. *The Gnostics and their Remains*. 1887 Nutt.
R. Lawrence. *The Book of Enoch the Prophet*. 1883 Kegan Paul.
W. R. Morfill. *The Book of Secrets of Enoch*. 1896 Clarendon.
R. H. Charles. *The Book of Enoch*. 1935 S.P.C.K.

Chapter 40. The Middle Pillar

In Chapter 13 was briefly described the centres or chakras through which the prana or vital force operates, along the Psychic nerves or channels (Nadi). The Ida to the left and the Pingala to the right coil around the centre column or Sushumna like the two serpents coiled around the caduceus carried by the messenger god Hermes or Mercury.

The Sushumna forms the great highway for the passage of the psychic forces of the human body. These forces are concentrated in the chakras which act like dynamos on which all the psycho-physical forces ultimately depend.

The first aim of the Practitioner of Yoga is to awaken what is known as Kundalini or the Serpent Power personified as the Goddess Kundalini. This mighty occult power lies coiled in the root chakra like a serpent asleep. Once awakened it is made to penetrate one by one the various centres, through which like a column of mercury it rises to the thousand petalled lotus in the brain. There it forms a fountain-like crest and falls as a shower of heavenly ambrosia to feed the physic body in all its parts. Thus the yogi becomes illuminated and filled with the supreme spiritual power.

Basically, therefore, one can determine a very close analogy between the eastern teachings and the western. In the caduceus symbolism we have a form of the Tree of Life. The Yoga method is worked with postures, concentration and a guru or teacher, and is so potent that it may be dangerous if done alone. When dealing with enormous voltages it is important to know how to switch them off. This can only be controlled in the eastern method by an experienced teacher under close personal supervision. It is, therefore, most unwise for westerners to attempt these techniques without adequate personal instruction.

The Western method is in the reverse direction and is easier to control; it consists of invoking or calling down the universal power. Used with care and some basic knowledge it can be employed gradually and therefore is always under some measure of control by reason. This is known as the Technique of the Middle Pillar.

The Glyph of the Tree, which you should now be familiar with in all its five colour scales as in the Minutum Mundum and four worlds, is the Key. The Western System calls down the power from above and is less liable to danger.

At this point we must reconsider the tree to describe what is sometimes considered as the eleventh Sephiroth, this is the mysterious point situated midway between 1 and 6 which is known as Daath or Knowledge and is usually represented as black in colour. If Chokmah is the active intelligent energy of Kether, and Binah the receptive quality of Kether then Daath is thought which created by Chokmah flows into Binah. This helps to clarify the idea of the Creative Trinity—Chokmah (the father), Binah (the mother or Holy Ghost) and Daath the word or knowledge by which the worlds were established.

The Middle Pillar exercise is based on the large figure of the Tree. Remember how that figure represents the microscosm as you face it. So place your back towards your large tree so that the pillar of severity is on your right side and the pillar of mercy is on your left. You make the Third pillar as you stand between them with the black column on your right and the white on your left. Imagine that you are in and part of the Tree. *In all cases where forces are invoked it is necessary to complete the four-fold breath and the banishing rituals first.*

Now imagine the universal energy all about you and extending in all directions to infinity, an enormous reservoir of power. Next imagine the Sephiroth Kether above your head revolving as a sphere of white iridescent light very bright and intense. Gradually as it revolves it attracts the energy from the universe. Next a shaft of white light is imagined to descend down to Daath (in the neck) which becomes bright, revolving and iridescent. When this is working well the Shaft then proceeds downwards to Tiphareth in the area of the heart. In turn the Shaft illuminates and activates Yesod in the region of the base of the spine and to Malkuth at the feet. After some practice this energy can be conveyed down the left side of the body and upwards again on the right. Further it can be made to circulate down the front and up the back. Eventually you will have your aura activated and resplendent, absorbing the universal energy and charging every organ and all parts of your body.

When you have reached some proficiency in this part of the exercise you can add sound to the proceedings by vibrating the respective Hebrew diety names as the shaft of light touches each of the Sephiroth on the Middle Pillar in turn.
The names are :

		Pronounced
1. Kether	EIEIEH	Eh-he-yeh
-. Daath	YHVH ALOHIM	Ye-hoh-voh E-loh-hem
6. Tiphareth	YHVH ALOAH Ve-DAAS	Ye-hoh-voh El-oah ve-Da-as
9. Yesod	SHADDAI AL CHAI	Shad-dai El Chai
10. Malkuth	ADNI HARTZ	Ah-doh-nai ha-Ah-retz

First you should practice vibrating these names seperately and memorizing their relative position on the Tree. The technique of vibrating these words syllable by syllable is easily mastered. They should be vibrated slowly on the beginning of a deep breath, so that they appear to make the whole body and eventually the whole room, resonate with the sound. This need not be loud, in fact it can just as well be practiced mentally. When you consider you have mastered this vibrating resonance you can then add the sounds one by one to the Sephiroth as the light shaft sets each one into activity. Thus you will add the creative power of sound to your visualization.

The next step in the exercise of the Middle Pillar is to add colour. For this purpose you work with the colours of the Minutum Mundum. This is a completely balanced scale which has the Sephiroth in the Queen's or negative scale and the paths in the King's or positive scale. And when you have become proficient in the Middle Pillar you can add the other Sephiroth in their various colours so that you are as one with the complete tree in sound and colour, in astral vision. Let your aura glow oval and clear pulsating with the fire of Tiphareth and giving energy to every part of your vital and physical body. It is wise at this stage to imagine that your aura is hardened at the outer surface like a skin of armour.

If you have to see anyone who has a depressing effect on you, or who is depressed or ill it is well to do this before seeing him so as to charge and harden your aura. You can then, if you require, give healing, and thus allow only what energy you wish to be transmitted and so prevent the depletion of your own aura and nervous system.

You have in this chapter the directions to attract unlimited energy for whatever purpose you wish. Guard this knowledge well and use it for good and not for evil. If you misuse it, surely it will short circuit, and recoil on you with devastating effect to your detriment.

Remember always that the mason was taught at his initiation to be cautious, remember also that Strength is in Silence. Those who know don't talk and those who talk don't know. Therefore do not talk about your exercises or abilities or powers to anyone who is not of at least the same stage of advancement as yourself. If you talk for personal glorification you will *not* benefit.

It is better for the beginner to keep his aura to himself and not allow it to flow freely towards others. When you feel that you have confidence and obtained some measure of control you can then apply the inner strength to healing if you do so desire.

This is probably the most important information in this present work. Use it well and it will be a source of strength to you.

As the tree with its ten Sephiroth represents the different principles in man Ceremonial Magic can thus be adapted to a system of expansion of the inner consciousness. When a room or a temple is set up with the various corresponding objects it can be used to dramatically formulate the whole tree or a particular part of it. In a ceremony performed by a number of individuals conversant with magical principles an enormous amount of power can be generated.

Israel Regardie. *The Art of True Healing.* 1964 Chicago.
W. E. Butler. *The Magician.* 1959 Aquarian.
W. E. Butler. *Apprenticed to Magic.* 1962 Aquarian.
S. L. McG. Mathers. *The Kabbalah Unveiled.* 1938 Kegan Paul.

Chapter 41. Pythagoras

Pythagoras was born about 582 B.C. at Samos, one of the Grecian Isles. As a young man and devoted to learning, he quitted his country having been initiated into all the Grecian mysteries. Accordingly, he went to Egypt, on which occasion Polycrates gave him a letter of introduction to the priest Amasis; he learned the Egyptian language, he associated with the Chaldaens and with the Magi.

Afterwards he went to Crete, and in company with Epemini-des, he descended into the Idaean cave (and in Egypt too, he entered into the holiest parts of their temples,) and learned all the most secret mysteries that relate to their Gods. Then he returned to Samos, and finding his country under the absolute dominion of Polycrates, he set sail and fled to Crotona in Italy. There, having given laws to the Italians, he gained a very high reputation, together with his scholars, who were about three hundred in number, and governed the republic in a most excellent manner.

He taught Geometry and arithmetic. He discovered the numerical relation of sounds on a string, and studied medicine. His dogmas included that the monad was the beginning of everything. From the monad proceeds an indefinite duad, which is subordinate to the monad as to its cause. That from the monad and the indefinite duad proceed numbers; from these numbers signs; from these last, lines of which plane figures consist. From plane figures are derived solid bodies. From solid bodies sensible bodies; of which last there are four elements, fire, water, earth and air. That the world is a sphere inhabited all over and results from a combination of these elements, and derives its motion from them.

Another of his theories was, that the air around the earth was immovable and pregnant with disease, and that everything was mortal; but that the upper air was in perpetual motion, pure and salubrious; that everything in that was immortal, and on that account divine. That the Sun and the Moon, and the stars were all gods; for in this the warm principle predominates which is the cause of life. That the Moon derives its light from the Sun. That there is a relationship between men and the gods, because men partake of the divine principle; on which account also, God exercises his providence for our advantage. Also that fate is the cause of the arrangement of the world both generally and particularly. Moreover that a ray from the sun penetrated both the cold aether and the dense aether; they call the air, the cold aether; the sea and moisture they call the dense aether. This ray descends into the depths and in this way vivifies everything. Everything that partakes of the principle of heat lives, on which account plants are also animated beings; but that all living things have not necessarily souls. That the soul is something torn off from the aether, both warm and cold, from the partaking of the cold aether. That the soul is something different from life. Also, that it is immortal, because that from which it is detached is immortal.

That animals are born from one another by seeds, that it is impossible for there to be any spontaneous production by the earth. That the seed is a drop from the brain which contains in itself a warm vapour; that when this is applied to the womb it transmits virtue, and moisture, and blood from the brain, from which flesh, sinews, bones, hair and the whole body are produced. From the vapour is produced the soul, also sensation. That the infant first becomes a solid body at the end of forty days, but according to the principles of harmony, it is not perfect until seven, or perhaps nine, or at the most ten lunar months, and then it is brought forth. Then it contains in itself all of the principles of life, which are connected together, and by their union and combination form a harmonious whole developing itself at the appointed time.

The senses in general, and especially the sight, are a vapour of excessive warmth, and on this account a man is said to see through air, and through water. For the hot principle is opposed by the cold one; since if the vapour in the eyes were cold, it would have the same temperature as the air, and so would be dissipated. In some passages he calls the eyes the gates of the sun. He speaks in a similar manner of hearing and of the other senses.

He also says that the soul of man is divided into three parts; intuition, reason, and mind, and that the first and last divisions are formed also in other animals, but that the middle one, reason, is only formed in man. That the chief abode of the soul is in those parts of the body which are between the heart and the brain. That portion of it which is in the heart is mind, but that deliberation and reason reside in the brain.

Moreover, that the senses are drops from them; and that the reasoning sense is immortal, but the others are mortal. The Soul is nourished by blood; and that reasons are the winds of the Soul. That it is invisible, and so are its reasons, since the aether itself is invisible. That the links of the soul are the veins, the arteries and the nerves. But that when it is vigorous, is by itself in a quiescent state, then its links are words and actions. That when it is cast forth upon the earth it wanders about, resembling the body. Moreover, that Mercury is the steward of Souls, and on that account he has the names of Conductor, and Infernal, since it is he who conducts the souls from their bodies, he conducts the pure soul to the highest region, and he does not allow the impure ones to approach them, nor to come near one another; but commits them to be bound in indissoluble fetters by the Furies. The Pythagoreans also assert that the whole air is full of Souls, and that these are accounted daemons, and heroes. It is by them that dreams are sent among men and also the tokens of disease and health; these last two, being sent not only to men, but to sheep also, and other cattle. That it is they who are concerned with purification, and expiations and all kind of divination, and oracular predictions, and things of that kind.

They also say, that the most important privilege in man is being able to persuade his soul to either good or bad. Men are happy when they have a good soul; yet they are never quiet, they never retain the same mind long. Virtue is harmony, and health, universal good, and God; on which account everything owes its existence and consistency to harmony. Also that friendship is a harmonious equality.

Most of his teachings have come down to us through other writers. Besides, his real work, or his most esoteric teaching was given by oral instruction. Fragments of this appear in the works of Lysis, Hierocles, Plato and others. His tests for pupils were severe. He first studied their activities in his gymnasium where he allowed them to react according to their nature without reprimand. Suddenly the student was imprisoned in a cell and given a problem "What means a triangle in a circle?", or something similar. Many hours were spent in solitude with a jug of water and a crust. Full of despondency he was then placed in front of the other novices who ridiculed him without mercy. If he reacted unfavourably he was not accepted as a pupil. It is said that Pythagoras made many enemies by this method, and in fact that one of these in later years brought about his downfall. The first two to five years were then spent in studies of mathematics and natural philosophy. After further tests the students were given the esoteric teachings which were based on all the Master had learned in his extensive travels.

Pythagoras can be credited with the discovery that there are only five symetrical solids, that is having an equal number of faces meeting at each of its angles, and these faces must be equal regular polygons i.e. figures whose sides and angles are all equal. These were the *Tetrahedron* having four equilateral triangles as faces, this being the simplest and lightest solid was taken to represent fire. The *Cube* with six squares, which when opened out represented the Cross was the most stable solid and represented earth. The *Octahedron* with eight equilateral triangles as faces being midway between fire and water represented air. The *Icosahedron* having twenty equilateral triangles represented water. *The Dodecahedron* was the most difficult to construct and consisted of twelve regular pentagons was the figure used by the Deity in tracing the Plan of the Universe. If the sides of a pentagon are extended the five pointed star is created. This was the sign used as the badge of the society and formed the basis of a great deal of the medieval magic lore. These figures made up of thin stiff cardboard and painted in the appropriate elemental colours can form interesting subjects for meditation or ornament. In Chapter 32 you were told how to draw a pentagon, there are two at the centre of your pentagram.

Finally however, Croton became engulfed in political turmoil and one of his old rejected pupils seized the opportunity for revenge. The result was that the college was destroyed and burned together with most of his books, and Pythagoras and his family perished in the flames. He was reputed to be nearly a hundred years old, but he had laid the foundation for the development of philosophy and culture of the western world.

Diogenes Laertius. *Lives of Eminent Philosophers*. 1891 Bell.
Edouard Schuré. *Pythagoras*. 1913 Rider.
H. Stanley Redgrove. *Bygone Beliefs*. 1920 Rider.
John Fellows. *The Mysteries of Freemasonry*. 1866 Reeves.

Chapter 42. Book "T"

Most of the information so far given about the Tarot has been condensed from Book T and other Golden Dawn manuscripts. This book according to the Rosicrucian mystical legend was found on the breast of Christian Rosenkrantz at the opening of his tomb in the fifteenth century. Certain words were said to have been written on the cover. They were "Ex Deomnascimur; In Christo (or Jehusuah) morimur; Per Spiritum Sanctum reviviscimus"—From God we are born; in Christ (or Jesus) do we die; through the Holy Spirit we rise again. That is the principle of the Gnostic Trinity—Father creator; Son or Solar Christ, the Logos or Serpent, the vivifying force; the Holy Spirit, the Great Mother which reproduces all things.

The awakening of the Kundalini is produced by ritual in the 5=6 ceremony of the G.D. The aspirant is led to the tomb wherein lies the Chief Adept in full regalia, representing Christian Rosencrantz; the tomb is opened and the aspirant demands; "out of the Darkness let Light arise". From the tomb a voice is heard: "Buried with that Light in a mystical death, rising again in a mystical resurrection, cleansed and purified through Him our Master, O Brother of the Rose and Cross. Seek thou the Stone of the Wise."

The following recondite cabalastic teaching was given to Mathers, one of the early chiefs of the G.D., by the "Hidden and Secret Chiefs", and was passed on to Dr. Felkin by the then Chief of Amen Ra Temple, Edinburgh. It is a curious description of the etheric links designated by the Tree and how the Tarot Cards can be applied to Pole and the Zodiac. This is another example of the principle of "as above so below" and is well worth serious study.

"The Law of the Convoluted Revolution of the Forces Symbolized by the Four Aces around the Northern Pole".

In the Book T. (the Tarot) it is written, 'Also the Dragon (i.e. Draco, the constellation of the Northern Pole of the Heavens) surroundeth the pole of Kether of the celestial Heavens'. It is furthermore laid down that the four Forces symbolized by the four Princesses or Amazons rule the celestial Heavens from the North Pole of the Zodiac unto 45 degrees of Latitude north of the ecliptic, and from the Throne of the Four Aces which rule in Kether. And again it is stated that the Throne of the

Ace of Cups	=	Head and first convolution of Draco.
Ace of Swords	=	Fore part of body and second convolution of Draco.
Ace of Pentacles	=	Hind part of body and third convolution of Draco.
Ace of wands	=	Tail and fourth convolution of Draco.

Regard thou therefore the form of this Constellation of Draco. It is convoluted in four places, answering to the rule of the Aces. For in the Four Forces of Yod, Heh, Vau, Heh (final), fire and water be contrary and also earth and air be contrary, and the throne of the elements will attract and seize, as it were the force of the element, so that herein be the forces of antipathy and sympathy, or what are known chemically as repulsion and attraction.

Recall also the allotments of the Triplicities :

Aries	Leo	Sagittarius	Fire	Wands
Cancer	Scorpio	Pisces	Water	Cups
Gemini	Libra	Aquarius	Air	Swords
Taurus	Virgo	Capricorn	Earth	Pentacles

It is said, Kether is in Malkuth and again that Malkuth is in Kether, but after another manner. For downwards through the four worlds the Malkuth of the less material will be linked into Kether of the more material. From the synthesis of the ten corruscations of the Aur (Light) proceedeth the influence unto EHEIEH, the Kether of Atziluth. And the connecting thread of the Ain Soph is extended through the worlds of the Ten Sephiroth and is in every direction. As the Ten Sephiroth operate in each Sephiroth, so there will be a Kether in every Malkuth, and a Malkuth in every Kether. Thus :

ADONAI MELEKH	will be the Malkuth of Atziluth
METATRON	will be the Kether of Briah
SANDOLPHON	
METATRON	will be the Malkuth of Briah
NEPHESCH LA MESSIAH	
CHAIOTH LA QADESH	will be the Kether of Yetzirah
ASCHIM	will be the Malkuth of Yetzirah
BASHITH LA GILGALIM	will be the Kether of Assiah

179

CHOLEM YESODOTH   will be the Malkuth of Assiah
THAUMIEL   will be the Kether of the Qlippoth

Now the symbol of the connection between the Malkuth of Yetzirah (mental) and the Kether of Assiah (material) will be of the form somewhat resembling an hour glass, the thread of the Ain Soph, before allude to traversing the centre thereof and forming the connection between the worlds. So that the symbol of the connection between the planes is this, and also the *modus operandi* of the translation of the force from one plane to another is this. And hence does not the title of the sphere of Kether of Assiah signify the commencement of the whirling motion.

From the diagram of the hour glass symbol it will be manifest that the Malkuth of Yetzirah will be the transmitter of the Yetziratic forces unto Kether of Assiah, that the latter will be the recipient thereof, and that the hour glass symbol or double cone will be the translator from one plane to the other. Hence, therefore let us consider the nomenclature of the tenth path (answering unto Malkuth) and of the first path (answering unto Kether).

The tenth path answering unto Malkuth : It is called the Resplendent Intelligence, and it is so called because it is exalted above every head and sitteth on the Throne of Binah, and it illumineth the splendour of all the lights and causeth the current of the influence to flow from the Prince of Countenances (i.e. Metatron or the Lord of Light).

The first path answering to Kether. It is called the wonderful or hidden intelligence (the highest Crown). For it is the Light to cause to understand the Primordial without commencement, and it is the Primal glory—for nothing created is worthy to follow out its essence.

Whence it is plain that Malkuth is as it were collector and synthesis of all the forces in its place or world : while Kether, being superior to all, also in its place and world, will be the recipient and arranger of the forces from the plane beyond, so as to distribute them into its subordinate sephiroth in a duly ordered manner.

And therefore any force of the multitudinous and innumerable forces in Malkuth may act through the upper cone of the hourglass symbol, and by means of the lower cone translate its operation into the Kether below, but its mode of transmission will be through its cones by the thread of Ain Soph or of the unformulated. So that in the transmission between the two worlds the formulate must first become the unformulate ere it can reformulate in new conditions (death and disintegration). For it must be plain that a force formulated in our world if translated into another will be unformulated according to the laws of a place different in nature, even as water in its fluid state will be subject to different laws to those governing it when in the conditions of either ice or steam.

And as before shown, there being a chief elemental division of the sephiroth Malkuth in the Minutum Mundum diagram, each of these will have its co-relative formula of transmission unto the succeeding Kether. Hence there is the dominion of the four Knaves or Princesses of the Tarot pack around the North Pole. Why then is it that the four Amazons or Knaves, answering unto the final Heh of YHVH, are here placed, rather than the four Kings, Queens, or Princes, or one of each nature?

We are taught that these are the Vice Regents of the name in the Four Worlds, and that they are thus attributed among the Sephiroth.

YOD	HEH	VAU	HEH (final)
CHOKMAH	BINAH	TIPHARETH	MALKUTH
KING	QUEEN	PRINCE	PRINCESS

"Now as Kether has to receive from Malkuth, it is necessary that in and about Kether there should be a force which partaketh of the nature of Malkuth though more subtle and refined in nature, and therefore is it that the final 'Heh' or Princess forces have their dominion placed above Kether, that so may attract from the malkuth of the higher and form a basis of action for the Aces. So that a refined matter may attract its like, and that the spiritual forces may not lose themselves in the void and so produce but a mistaken and whirling destruction for want of a settled basis, and herein is the mutual formulae in all things, of a spirit and of a body, seeing that each supplieth unto each that wherein the other is lacking. Yet herein also must there be a certain condition, otherwise the harmony will not be perfect, for unless the body be refined in nature it will hinder the action of the spirits cognate unto it; and unless the spirit be willing to ally itself to the body the latter will be injured thereby, and each will naturally react on the other.

Therefore, also, let the Adeptus Minor understand that there may be fault of the spirit as well as of the body, and that there is little difference between the material and sensuous person,

181

and the envious, malicious and self-righteous person—save that from their being more subtle and less evident, the sins of the latter are more insidious than those of the former, though both are alike evil. But it is as necessary to govern the spirit as to refine the body, and of what use is it to weaken the body by abstinence if at the same time uncharitableness and spiritual pride are encouraged. It is simply translating one sin into another.

And therefore are the final Heh forces necessary in Kether as it is said in the tenth path of Yetzirah: It is so called because it is exalted above every head and sitteth on the Throne of Binah. Now in the Tree the Sephiroth, Chokmah and Binah are referred to unto the Briatic world, which is called the Throne of the Atziluthic world, into which Kether is referred in the Tree, and referring unto the dominions of the Four Princesses, thou shalt find that in the sphere they include Chokmah and Binah as well as Kether.

Now there will be not one but four formulae of the application of the four forces of Malkuth into the revolution of the Ace in Kether, and these acting not singly but simultaneously and with a different degree of force, and seeing that while (were Malkuth and Kether in the same plane or world) the transmission of these forces from the one unto the other would proceed more or less in direct lines, in this case (seeing that Malkuth and Kether be in different planes and worlds) the lines of transmission of these forces are caught up and whirled about by the upper cone of the hour-glass symbol into the vortex, where and through passeth the thread of the unformulate—(i.e. Ain Soph. Etheric link). Hence they are projected in a whirling convolution (yet according to their nature) through the lower cone of the hour-glass symbol into Kether. Hence it resulteth that these formulae are of the nature of the Dragon or Serpent formulae (winged, air; finned, water; or footed, earthly).

Another action of the forces of Malkuth of Yetzirah transmitting into Kether of Assiah will be that of continued vibratory rays acting from the centre to the circumference, and that bringing into action the forces from the Tread of the unformulate (Ain Soph).

Recall that which is written in the chapter of the Chariots, Ezekiel 1 4–28, "a whirlwind came out of the north . . . also out of the midst thereof came the likeness of four living creatures" these creatures had the faces of a man, lion, ox and an eagle.

Chapter 43. Correspondences

Arthur Avalon states that "The Tantras say that it is in the power of man to accomplish all he wishes if he centres his will thereon . . . for man, they say, is in his essence one with the Supreme Lord (Universal Creative Principle), and the more he manifests spirit (Astral Light) the greater he is endowed with its powers. . . . The object of the Tantric Rituals is to raise these various forms of power to their fullest expression".

This quotation, although over-simplified, suggests that the centre and root of power in man lies in the Kundalini. We can understand why the god of the ancient and modern mysteries is the Universal Creative Principle and that Kundalini within man is called the "God within" or "hidden God" and how the finding and using of this astral light leads to illumination or initiation. That is why it is so necessary that exercises to awaken the force must be carried out in circumstances and environment which will enable the operator to maintain the fullest measure of control at all times. He must ensure that he does not at any time permit other persons or entities to invade his consciousness—or subconsciousness. These must be firmly banished.

The Kundalini is the sex force lying in three and a half coils at the base of the spinal column. It is that part of the Great Breath which is the mightiest manifestation of creative power in the human body. It is formed of three energies : Ida, on the left side of the spinal column, the Moon or feminine channel; Pingala, on the right side, the masculine or Sun channel; Sushumna, the channel of the uniting and dissolving fire, within the centre column itself. It is the serpent power, the creator, preserver and destroyer, the I.A.O. of Hermetic, Cabalistic and Gnostic sects. "She, the subtlest of the subtle, holds within herself the Mystery of Creation, and by her radiance, it is said, the universe is illumined, eternal knowledge awakened and liberation attained. . . . She maintains all beings of the world by means of inspiration and expiration."

The Kundalini must first be roused by powerful mind and will, along with suitable physical actions; certain modes of training and worship are prescribed, the use of images, emblems, symbols, pictures, mantras. Thus rendered active it is drawn to the cerebral centre to form a circuit, as in the case of ordinary positive and negative charges which are themselves but other manifestations of the universal polarity which affect the manifested world.

Pingala when roused goes upward from right to left, encircling the Lotuses or Chakras, these centre of physical and psychic force, reaching the pineal gland; at the root of the nose, between the eyebrows. These two, together with Sushumna, form a plaited knot at this same pineal gland. To be led up the "Middle Path" the vital force must be withdrawn from both the Pingala and the Ida, devitalizing the rest of the body for the time being, and made to enter the Sushumna piercing the Chakras on its upward path, absorbing the Tattwas of each Chakra, also the subtattwas with which each in turn is interchanged. Thus we have the earth tattwa of the chakra at the base of the spine; water, the spleen; fire, the navel or solar plexus; air, the heart; ether, the throat. Passing from the gross to the subtle the earth is dissolved in water; water absorbed by fire; fire is sublimed by air, and air by ether. This is called by some the transmutation of the sex force, leading to spiritual things. Having united with the universal in the cerebral centre (pituitary gland) it then descends, at the same time projecting back the tattwic forces into the various chakras, again taking up its latent potential position at the base of the spinal column, and the body resumes its vitality. The longer it can be retained in the cerebral centre, the seat of the Supreme Lord, the greater, it is said, will be the power and knowledge acquired by the Yogi.

Such is the "God within" of many and various sects. It is represented by the Caduceus of Hermes, with its twin serpents, negative and positive, twining round the central rod, the spinal column, surmounted at the pineal gland by the wings of what is called liberation; the ball at the top of the rod being the pituitary body, the seat of supreme power. Read again the Smaragdine tablet of Hermes in Chapter 5 and note how it ties up with this technique.

Heindel gives a diagram of the three paths taken by the Kundalini or unusued sex-power. He calls them, right of the spinal column, mystic; left, occultist; and central, adept. They all lead to illumination, that is clairvoyance, clairaudience, and impressional teaching. To each of these three processes are also attached the names: Jakin, Boaz and Macbenac or Mahabone, representing the Kundalini forces, the three pillars found in masonry, the cabalistic Pillars of Mercy, Severity and Mildness of the Tree of Life.

Beware then at all times of the Great danger of this Yoga practiced by unguided and immature students. This would not only be an intoxication of astral light, producing illusion and deception, even mania, but also the serious risk of a stronger entity working on and through the astral plane taking possession of a weaker and less informed mind and using it for its own ends, as is so often the case with so-called Masters of the various cults who are taken on trust because they appear to know more than the searcher. So bear in mind the warning of St. Paul which we gave in our introduction to "Prove all things, hold fast that which is good."

The Eastern teachings are from below to above, the Western method is from above to below—as demonstrated by the Middle Pillar exercise which has less likelihood of being contaminated by unwanted entities or forces. Preparation for the place for operation with the symbolism of the paths and sephiroth will create really desirable conditions. If you feel those conditions to be suitable proceed with your more advanced exercises. If not, postpone the attempt for a while. The correspondences already given will enable you to create on the material plane conditions and symbols which will guide your excursions; colour, sound, diagrams, objects, perfume all add their quota in producing the proper environment. A powerful, concentrated and positive will used with persistence should do the rest. Under no circumstances allow yourself to be swayed or persuaded by an external entity physical or astral. Prove and test at all times. If you meet a psychic force challenge it to produce its credentials. An antagonistic one will immediately become irritated and irrational or irresponsible. A good entity will prove itself. If in doubt Banish with the Pentagram ritual.

The correspondences which are most useful we have given you in these chapters. The three, seven and ten symbolized in the Tree of Life and the Tarot cards will form the basis for creating any desired background on which you wish to experiment. Call down the light which is from above and do not trust the serpent power from below. Remember that balance is the most important thing to acquire, balance in all things. That is why the Minutum Mundum is better for preliminary excursions as it is a balanced form of the Tree.

If you wish to extend your knowledge of correspondences study Astrology, particularly mundane astrology, as this deals with the qualities which operate on a certain situation at any given time. It can be very useful in considering the factors involved in any set of circumstances.

Extensive correspondences for the Sephiroth and the Paths are given in Crowleys *777* published in 1909, which was reprinted in 1955 with additions. His work on "Magic" also includes some of these tables. See also his *Book of Thoth*. For the advanced student at least one of these books is essential.

Westcott's *Numbers* is full of correspondences relating to the properties and use of numbers. Most books on the Tarot and Quabala are useful. But you must work out your own correspondences. Remember that each author selects and designates his correspondences which are thus coloured by his own personality and experience. Therefore take nothing for granted, work out your own by trial and test. Only in this manner will your mind become tuned to what is correct for you.

Books by Eliphas Levi or Papus are also worthy of close study. Gerald Massey gives profuse details of Egyptian and Christian Symbolism. The Rev. Robert Taylor deals with somewhat similar topics: he was imprisoned at Oakham gaol for his alleged anti-christian utterances and spent his time while incarcerated in writing the proof of his theories which were later published as *The Diegesis*.

Arthur Avalon (Sir John Woodroffe). *Serpent Power*. 1924 Madras.

Inquire Within. *Light Bearers of Darkness*. 1930 Boswell.

Inquire Within *The Trail of the Serpent*. 1936 Boswell.

Max Heindel. *Rosicrucian Cosmo-Conception*. 1934 California.

T. M. Stewart. *Symbolism of the Gods of the Egyptians*. 1927 Barkernille.

Anon. *Jacin and Boaz*. London.

Robert Taylor. *The Devil's Pulpit*. 1882 Freethought.

Robert Taylor. *The Diegesis*. 1829 Carlisle.

Chapter 44. Ritual

The object of ritual is to create atmosphere, help concentration and to build up a force for the production of a mental or magical effect. To aid this process you should have a room where you can be quiet and undisturbed. This need only be large enough to move about in freely say about 6 feet by 6 feet minimum. In the centre should be placed an altar in the shape of a double cube, this can be a small cupboard about 2 feet high and about 1 foot square or slightly larger, but in those proportions. It can have drawers or shelves for the storing of the magical instruments or weapons: the wand, incense burner or lamp representing fire; the cup representing water; the sword, dagger or fan representing air; and the pentacle or bread representing Earth. The altar should be covered with a clean cloth and the appropriate implements placed on top in their correct positions in relation to the compass.

To complete the setting the magician may wear a suitable gown in the appropriate colour to the purpose in hand. Until experience is gained a white dressing-gown kept especially for ceremonial would be suitable. This helps to set the scene, as to work in ordinary clothes would not tend to change the personality which is the basic reason for ritual.

First banish in all four quadrants as in Chapter 36. The Quabalistic Cross is now performed and is similar to movements of the Christian Cross but done with a purpose, as follows: Face the East, do the four-fold breathing; with the right hand:

1. Touch the forehead and vibrate the word ATEH (thou art).
2. Touch the breast and vibrate MALKUTH (the kingdom).
3. Touch the left shoulder vibrating the word VE-GEDULAH (and the Glory).
4. Touch the right shoulder vibrating the word VE-GEBURAH (and the Power).
5. Clasp the fingers over the breast vibrating LE-OLAM AMEN (forever Amen).

187

Whilst doing this imagine the white light of the universal energy coming down and forming a shining cross in and through your body, charging every organ and cell with vitality. The words are Hebrew and the names taken from the Sephiroth. Thus charged you are in a powerful condition to perform the lesser ritual of the pentagram.

6. Then go to the South and repeat the formula.
7. Once more facing West.
8. And North, as instructed performing the appropriate vibrations and returning to the East where you must be careful to complete the circle where you commenced.
9. Standing in the East with your arms outstretched say: "Before me stands Raphael"
10. "Behind me stands Gabriel"
11. "On my right hand stands Michael"
12. "On my left stands Auriel"
13. "Before me flames the Pentagram"
14. "Behind me shines the six-rayed star."

This should effectively eliminate any unwanted influences especially if your visualization of the figures of the pentagrams has been achieved. In addition to this barrier of astral fire around, you should build astral images of the Angelic figures in their several positions as you vibrate their names.

In the East Raphael is a vast angelic figure in the conventional style with robes of shimmering silk in bright yellow and mauve hues, which should flash and vibrate, the figure must be light and airy with a gentle breeze wafted from behind.

In the South the angelic form will have a predominance of flaming red relieved by vivid flashes of emerald green. In the hand of the figure is a sword of steel with the point upright, tongues of flame will lick the earth at the feet of Michael, and an intense heat should be felt.

In the West Gabriel will have the colours of blue contrasting with yellow. He holds aloft a chalice of water and stands in a stream of clear running water coming from a waterfall behind him.

In the North Auriel has a mixture of citrine, russet and black, he stands on very fertile ground, grass and wheat growing about his feet. Sheaves of corn are held in both his outstretched hands.

Finally the magician must feel the glowing pentagram on his

chest and the Star of David on his back. This latter has the ascending triangle in red and the descending triangle in blue.

This exercise may sound complex but with your previous experience of parts of it it should be fairly easy to memorize, and perform successfully. It sets the stage and prepares the mind for the next and last stage in the ritual. Then you imagine that you are backed onto the large figure of the Minutum Mundum in its brilliant colours and then you can perform the exercise of the Middle Pillar with renewed energy. (see Chapter 40.)

Now you have the full ritual comprising of the Cross, Pentagram and Pillar exercises. Repetition will bring about familiarity and perfection with the production of power and inner peace. The barbaric names suggested may appear strange and unnecessary, yet the ancients associated these vibratory mantras with the sound values or vibratory rates of the various parts of the body, physical and psychic and used them to acentuate and call into activity these centres. Their Hebrew origin is no detriment, they need not be associated with any religious or metaphysical bias. They are but key words and assist in the investigations of hidden knowledge and the secret side of man's nature.

Kether, the first Sephiroth, is the centre of light situated slightly above the crown of the head. There is situated the higher genius or that spirit which is not yet fully incarnate which must be called down as a source of inspiration, enlightenment and freedom. It is the very essence of life itself.

Daath, the shadowy Sephiroth, situated at the nape of the neck is the point at which we develop our mental and emotional propensities. It is the link in the subconscious between the higher Genius and the Ego or conscious self as the spirit makes descent into the group of properties around Tiphareth.

Tiphareth is the spiritual and emotional centre and is in the lower region of the heart, about the lower end of the sternum or breast bone.

Below at the base of the spine is Yesod and the seat of the lower emotions.

The aim of the visualization of the column of light descending is to analyse and recharge the vital points of the human organism. This light pure and unsullied can then be utilized for many techniques, one of which will now be given.

Do not employ this method until you are sure that you can do the full ritual and really feel and see the power. If you meet any danger, difficulty or disturbing entity be sure to project a flaming pentagram in the proper manner and return physically to the earth plane immediately. The exercise to be described is on the earth level.

Refer to the Tattwas (Chapter 15) take your earth symbol of the yellow square. Sit calmly and do the four-fold breath. Gaze at the card for about thirty seconds. Then by transferring the gaze to a white surface you should see, by a reflex action on the retina a similar shape in luminous lavender blue or mauve. When you have some degree of success with this you should visualize this square enlarged to about 6 feet high. When you can really visualize this clearly, go through as if it were a door, slowly and cautiously. If in difficulty banish without fear and return as you entered. Make a note of everything you perceive and record a brief description of your results.

This is only one method of clairvoyance, or entering into the spirit vision. There are many others. Yoga and the Western Wisdom are two ways of achieving the same end. The Tattwas may enable you to achieve astral projection. Proceed with caution and do not get too far in your first enthusiasm. Slow careful progress will enable you to gain confidence and familiarity with the new condition and will eliminate fear. With that confidence you can proceed later to venture further, but at all times maintain your psychic contact with the Tree of Life. Your large coloured drawing should be placed on the floor with Kether in the East.

When you feel competent to progress further each of the tattwas can be taken in turn. The pentagram for each element must be formulated starting at the appropriate angle (Chapter 32) and moving *always* clockwise when delineating the figure. Vibrate the word as you pinpoint the centre with a stabbing motion. Use the word also if you have occasion to banish with the pentagram on the astral plane. Memorize the ritual, practice the motions carefully, contact the power, avoid fear. Use the knowledge for good, do not abuse it, and go on your way rejoicing.

Aleister Crowley. *Magic*. 1929 London.
Yram. *Practical Astral Projection*. Rider
S. L. MacG. Mathers. *Book of the Sacred Magic of Abra-Melin the Mage*. 1898 Watkins.

Chapter 45. The Rosicrucians

For nearly three hundred years the very name Rosicrucian has been synonymous with Magus, consequently a source of mystery, and on numerous occasions the chief sales factor for many self-styled organizations, whose claims to authority were more imaginative than authentic. Very little was known about this supposed Brotherhood before the publication of A. E. Waite's book in 1887. Previously, Jenning's book had described practically everything in the form of farrago of the wildest absurdities except the Rosicrucians.

The name Rosicrucian was apparently unknown before 1598. The real history starts when, in 1614 in Cassel, in Germany, was published a document bearing the title "The Fama of the Fraternity of Meritorious Order of the Rosy Cross Addressed to the Learned in General and the Governors of Europe". This claimed to be a message from certain anonymous adepts who were deeply concerned for the condition of mankind, and greatly desired its moral renewal and perfection. It suggested that all learned men in the world should unite to establish a synthesis of the science, through which could be established the perfect method of the arts. The antiquated authorities of previous times were to be discredited, and the quarrellings and the squabblings of the literate were to cease. As the reformation had recently taken place in religion, so science was also to be cleansed. This was to be accomplished by the illuminated Brotherhood, the children of light who had been initiated into the mysteries of the Grand Orient, who lead the present age to perfection.

The Chief of the Movement, one Christian Rosen Creuze, a Teuton, a magical hierophant had learned the humanities in a convent where he had been placed at the age of five. After ten years he set out for the Holy Land with Brother P. A. L. who died at Cyprus. Continuing on alone he arrived at Damcar in Arabia where the Magi initiated him into all the secrets of the occult arts. He then went to Egypt and eventually to Spain, where he was told that they had learned the secrets of the Black Art from a much higher authority, namely Satan himself. At length he became a hermit in Germany where he decided after five years that he was designed for a greater purpose than rumination in solitude. He therefore collected a carefully chosen band about him and formed the Rosicrucian Society.

They erected a House of the Holy Ghost, healed the sick, invented a magical language, a cipher writing of magical potency, a large volume full of occult wisdom, and initiated other chosen members. The original members travelled in Europe to disseminate wisdom. These members died one by one and eventually also C.R.C. For one hundred and twenty years the secret of his burial place was to lie hidden.

During the third generation of adepts, the tomb of the illustrious founder was discovered during the rebuilding of one of their secret dwellings. The vault was discovered illuminated by an ever-burning lamp and the body was in a perfect state of preservation surrounded by a number of marvels which had been buried with him. This convinced the discoverers that it was now their duty to make these publicly known to the world. They therefore invited all worthy persons to apply for initiation. They did not publish their names and addresses, but asked that those who wished initiation to publish printed letters.

This caused tremendous excitement amongst the occultists of Europe, and a large number of publications for and against appeared. There was no such city as Damcar in Arabia, where was the House of the Holy Ghost which was alleged to have been seen by 100,000 persons. C.R.C., a boy of fifteen must have been exceptionally skilled to have impressed the Magi of Damcar. In spite of this controversy however, considerable credit was given to this first Rosicrucian publication.

About a year later appeared *The Confession of the Rosicrucian Fraternity*. This offered a gradual initiation to selected applicants, but indicated a protestant nature by execrating the Pope. In the following year 1616 was published *The Chymical Nuptials of Christian Rosencreutz*. This furnished details in the life of the founder of the organization. This publication makes C.R.C. an old man when he was initiated and contradicts the Fama. By this time many of the applicants for initiation had received no replies to their letters and it was generally considered that the whole matter was a hoax. Within about five years the Rosicrucians and their publications had fallen into complete obscurity. That does not rule out the possibility that the selected candidates did not talk, but remained to continue the work in secret. There is no doubt that the publications were sincerely in earnest and were essentially modern in their theosophical ideas.

In Nuremburg in the year 1598 a Rosicrucian Society was founded by a mystic and alchemist named Simon Studion, with the title "Militia Crucifera Evangelica", which held regular meetings. This was, in opinions and objects, identical with the Rosicrucian Body. In 1710 an adept named Sincereus Racatus (or Sigmund Richter) published *A Perfect and True Preparation of the Philosophical Stone according to the Secret Methods of the Brotherhood of the Golden and Rosy Cross*. With this was included the rules of the Society for the initiation of new members. This shows that a body was still holding meetings at Nuremburg. In 1783 at Altona was published *The Secret Symbols of the Rosicrucians of the Sixteenth and Seventeenth Centuries*. This was translated and reprinted in 1935.

About 1836 Godfrey Higgins in his "Anacalypsis" states "I have abstained from becoming a member of them, (Templars and Rosicrucians) that I might not have had my tongue tied or my pen restrained by the engagements I must have made on entering the chapter or encampment. But now I have reason to believe that they have become, in a very peculiar manner, what is called exclusively Christian Orders, and on this account are thought by many persons to be only a bastard kind of masons".

In 1866 a number of prominent masons formed a body known as the "Scietas Rosicruciana in Anglia" generally known as the Soc. Ros. These men were Robert Wentworth Little, Frederick Hockley, Kenneth McKenzie and Hargreave Jennings. In the Soc. Ros. membership was restricted to masons in good standing and several colleges exist today in both England and America. The main objects of the body is research into the more secret teachings of masonry, but judging from its transactions it does not appear to have reached a very high level of attainment.

About 1880 Dr. W. A. Woodman found certain manuscripts at an old bookshop in Farrington Street. These were the rites and rough diagrams for the five rituals of the outer order; ⓪ = 10 to ④ = 7 . He took these to Dr. Wynn Westcott a London coroner, and S. L. MacGregor Mathers both well known and prominent masons. With the manuscripts was a letter in German saying that the finder should communicate with Sapiens Dominantibur Astris, c/o Fräulein Anna Sprengal, at Hamburg, where they would receive interesting information. They were subsequently told to elaborate the rituals which was done by Mathers. From this was formed the first branch of "The Order of the Companions of the Rising Light of the Morning— the Golden Dawn in the Outer". In March 1888 a warrant was drawn up and the society formed with Isis—Urania Temple of the Hermetic Students of the Golden Dawn. The grades were Neophyte, Zelator, Theoreticus, Practicus and Philosophus; also a sub-grade the Portal leading from the Golden Dawn to the Rosae Rubae Aurea Crucis or the Inner Order.

In 1897 Dr. Westcott resigned from the Order because his employers had told him that magic was incompatible with his duties as coroner. About 1900 Mathers became involved with a Mr. and Mrs. Horos. Mrs. Horos through trickery persuaded Mathers that she had an inner knowledge of a very high order and he was completely fooled by her. In 1900 the Horos couple were the subject of a court action and imprisonment for immoral conduct. The G.D. was mentioned, at length, in Court which did it no good. There was also a great deal of inner unrest in the order which caused several members notably A. E. Waite, Aleister Crowley, Dion Fortune (Mrs. Evans) and others to break away and form their own orders.

In March 1910 Mathers took out a court order restraining the publication of Vol. I, No. 3 of Crowley's *Equinox*. A.C. had, in the previous issue, printed some of the G.D. rituals and had promised to print the remainder. This order was set aside later by the Court of Appeal and the volume was issued. Further public discussion naturally took place which was unfavourable publicity for the G.D. This eventually led to the disruption of the order and it became dormant. There were several lodges of the order in England and in America. The Golden Dawn, however, had the most complete and elaborate system of magic and hermeticism. In fact, as you have probably realized, this book is based on the elementary teachings of that order.

H. Spencer Lewis. *Rosicrucian Q & A*. 1929 California.
A. E. Waite. *Real History of the Rosicrucians*. 1887 Redway.
A. E. Waite. *The Brotherhood of the Rosy Cross*. 1924 Rider.

Geo. Von Welling. *Opus Magico-Cabalisticum.* 1735 Hamburg.
Israel Regardie. *My Rosicrucian Adventure.* 1936 Chicago.
Godfrey Higgins. *Anacalypsis.* 1836 London.
Hargreave Jennings. *The Rosicrucians.* 1870 London.
Anon. *The Secret Symbols of the Rosicrucians.* 1935 Chicago.

Chapter 46. Astro-theology

Many writers have, in the past, suggested that the parallelisms between the Ancient Egyptian and the Christian Scriptures, can be explained by no other than one conclusion, and that is, the Egyptian is the original from which the others have been taken, but amplified and written in a form better adapted for the Western Nations, which had been prepared for a clearer presentation of esoteric truth, by the teachings of those cultured men known to us Neo-Platonists. They formed the link between Osirianism and Christianity. If the latter had been developed into a well-established system, which the Catholic Fathers say it was, it is incredible that they have not noticed it. With the exception of Philo who is assumed to have lived about the commencement of the Christian era, there is not the slightest reference to either Christian or Jewish records and, what is not less strange, the Catholic Fathers make no reference to the Alexandrian School, until long after it had disappeared from history, which tends to confirm that these records have not the antiquity that is generally assigned to them, and the real character can only be understood by their astronomical application.

The best defined ancient Annual cycle is the Egyptian (which like the Indian and later the Greek) was divided into twelve months, with a sign for each month, and these form the signs of the Zodiac. The month was divided into three weeks, each containing 10 degrees (days of the week), or thirty degrees to each sign—360 degrees for the whole circle, which with the five intercallary days—or non-dies—correspond with the 365 days of the year. This Zodiac, with its signs, divisions and degrees, with corresponding pictorial figures and Star Charts, is the key which unlocks all Biblical Mysteries. The Science of Astronomy was well understood by cultured Egyptians from the most remote period of their history, for even the precessional cycle was known to them. They calculated it to contain 25,920 years, which is one degree for each 72 years. In this fact is formed the true meaning of the fable of the interpretation of the Hebrew Bible into Greek, called the Septuagint, by 72 men. It is only the mystic way of saying, that whoever knows the meaning of one sign, as representative, of the whole, understands the rest. A similar teaching is manifest in the Zodiac of the Temple of Dendera, in Upper Egypt where Harpocrates (representing the beginning of Spring) is seated on a lotus with his finger to his mouth. This might alternatively be the young divine child, the lotus being the symbol of his mother Isis. Harpocrates is also known as Horus the Child, hence he is frequently called the God of Silence; the mystic meaning when unfolded, is, that a solar lunar cycle is referred to; for Horus is the Young Sun, and Isis the Moon; intimating that all temple worship was regulated by and in accordance with Solar-lunar periods; but that this Knowledge was to be kept secret.

This young Child, or the commencement of a new yearly cycle, is the Hero Son of God, or Sun Saviour of all religions. In Egypt he is called Horus; in India, Krishna, and in Christendom, Jesus; but in the Astro-Masonic System he is Antinous, who became metamorphosed in Biblical narratives into Moses, David, Solomon, and many other names. This system was astro-theological long before it became astro-masonical, the latter of which is the most perfect and complete, and according to which the chief part of our Biblical narratives are compiled. That the Chaldean Nations were in possession of it is proved by the Assyrian Cuniform inscription, relating to the Deluge, discovered in the ruins of Nineveh by the late George Smith.

Another proof of the connections between these astral systems is found in the celebrated Turin Papyrus, from which is taken the Egyptian Ritual, or *Book of the Dead*. Bunsen (Vol. V, p. 89) was struck by the insertion of certain signs between what he supposed to have been the original text and scholia which read PTR-RE-SI. According to his idea they mean, "This is the interpretation", although he admits they may have another meaning. That meaning is supplied by Oxley. They read Petra or Peter, which according to the astral system, means the Pole Star, the highest and (apparently) the only immovable point in the heavens and mystically refers to the one basic truth of the system round which all others revolve. The New Testament gives it thus : "Thou art Peter, and upon this rock will I build my church, and the gates of Hell shall not prevail against it". The meaning of this is very apparent, by reference to the theological planisphere. The "church" is built upon a rock, and that rock, or foundation, is "Saint Peter", the Prince of the Apostles, and the Founder of the Catholic Church.

The discovery of the Astro-Masonic, or planispherical base of Biblical Narratives, is due to Henry Melville who spent 40 years on the work. (He died about 1880.) He studied it from a Masonic standpoint, intending to keep the secret of his discovery within the Masonic Fraternity and to which order it undoubtedly pertains, but the Heads of the Order regarded Melville's work as heretical, and declined to give it any official recognition. In consequence of this providential rejection on their part Melville determined to make it public, and as a result published *Veritas* a Revelation of the Mysteries, Biblical, Historical and Social, by means of the Median and Persian Laws. Without committing ourselves to all of Melville's deductions we can recommend *Veritas* as a most magnificent work and a reliable and scholarly production on the origin and meaning of the Biblical text. Melville took up the subject where it was left by such authors as Philo, Origen and Maimonides, and he has made public what they kept secret to the great advantage of every searcher for the pure truth. The system itself is abstruse, and requires application by the student, whose taste lies in the direction of mystic literature, but they who will take the trouble to master the science, will be abundantly assured of the truth. If you do happen to acquire a copy of *Veritas* make sure that the key, entitled "The Median and Persian Laws", is supplied too. This contains the tables of correspondences and without it the book is difficult to understand, it is usually in a pocket on the inside back cover.

The following example, is explanatory of the so-called Exodus of the Israelites from Egypt, which resolves itself into an account of the Sun's passage from the Winter Solstice, through one sign towards the Vernal Equinox; with the stars for people, constellations for tribes and the Sun for leader.

See Exodus XII., 39 : "and they baked unleavened cakes of the dough, which they brought forth out of Egypt, for it was not leavened; because they were thrust out of Egypt, and could not tarry, neither had they prepared themselves any victuals". When released from Egypt, a mixed multitude went up from Rameses to Succoth. The people escaped from Pharaoh, i.e. the Crocodile, our Scorpio, Lower Egypt. Rameses means thunder and Jove with his thunder is at R.A. 251. (R.A. means Right Ascension and refers to the numbered degrees around the planisphere starting at January with the *sign* Sagittarius). From thence they went to Succoth which is at R.A. 256, it being contrary to the Median Laws to take corn, Spica, the ear of corn, between the mill-stones at R.A. 256 and 251 (that is the five non-dies) and there it became their barley meal (i.e. the lactea). They procured water at R.A. 256, and the dough thus made, they took to Succoth, where one oven is seen, and they baked twelve cakes, a cake for each tribe i.e. the symbol of the Sun's disc for the twelve Signs of the Zodiac.

This argument suggests that these Bible Narratives are written on a basis not of personal history, but of stellar phenomena, which are of necessity infallibly true, as such; this taken along with the astral interpretation of the Creation, Deluge and the History of Israel, Birth and Death of Christ, together with the Revelation, sustains the statement Origen, that the places, cities and persons named therein are to be found in the stellar heavens and nowhere else. Up to that period of time in human development, it was needful to veil the truth in symbols, for none but the spiritually-minded Initiates could comprehend. Hence it is written (Matthew XIII, 34) "all these things spake Jesus to the multitudes in parables; and without a parable (allegory) spake he not unto them".

The Cross of Christ, as the symbol of the Sun God is formed by the vertical line between the Summer and Winter Solsticial points, and the horizontal line between the Vernal and Equi-noctial points; the divisions between the four arms form the four seasons of the year; and at these four points are stationed the four Evangelists, who record the history of the Sun Saviour, astro-masonically called Antinous, but biblically Jesus. All ancient civilized nations had this same cross, implied or expressed, for without it no sacred system could be concreted; there was not, and is not, a single so-called religious ceremonial, with its attendant worship, but that is in actual conformity with the Sun's path (apparent) through the heavens. The oldest Mother God known in history is the Egyptian Isis, and the youngest is the Greco-Latin Mary; both, along with others, are represented by our sign Virgo, or the Virgin, and the appearance of this constellation in company with Bootes (Joseph) at the left arm of the cross or the vernal equinox, is the prophecy of the birth of the Sun God in nine months i.e. nine signs, which brings the date to the winter solsticial point, our December 25th.

The *Bible* is a pure and simple astro-theologic, esoteric work composed and computed from the stellar phenomena as witnessed from the latitude of Egypt; and although conforming with the old Egyptian Hermetic Books, yet the Old Testament is compiled from the Chaldean or Aramaic Planisphere, modified for the New Testament, which is Greek. They were known to two orders; one represented by the modern Freemasons, whose rituals and ceremonies are essentially symbolic; the other by the state Churches, who use them for the regulation of their festivals, calendar, and external worship. As we know that Freemasonry is inimical to Papacy, it is but a continuation of the conflict which arose in the early stages of Church History, between the adherents of the Electic and Sacerdotal Schools. The Ecclesiastical part, for reasons which are well understood, never allowed the laity to be taught other than the literal and surface meaning; while the Mystic Brotherhoods were forbidden, by the rules of their order, to make public the real meaning of their symbols, of which only the highest degree Initiates were allowed to know. This part has always been held to be communicated orally and not by writings; and but for the boldness of Melville, who broke through this rule, the outside public would still be in ignorance concerning the true interpretation of all Hermetic Writings.

John Bentley. *A Historical View of Hindu Astronomy.* 1823 Calcutta.

E. M. Antoniadi. *L'Astronomie Egyptienne.* 1934 Paris.

Henry Melville. *Veritas.* 1874 Hall.

Gerald Massey. *Book of Beginning.* 1881 Williams & Norgate.

Gerald Massey. *The Natural Genesis.* 1883 Williams & Norgate.

Gerald Massey. *Ancient Egypt the Light of the World.* 1907 Fisher Unwin.

Church of Light. *Religion of the Stars Constellation Chart.* Los Angeles.

Chapter 47. The Gods

The iconoclast, with his weapons of ridicule and sarcasm, is a true ally to the dogmatic religious approach; both these with their dogma and preconceived ideas tend to reduce the value of symbolism in which the Gods of Egypt are so rich. Stewart defines a symbol as representing "an evolutionary stage in the life experience of one individual that can be reproduced in the life experience of another". Taking that as a starting point let us see if we can gain any constructive ideas from the varying types of the Egyptian and other Gods. There is no doubt that from the earliest known period the Egyptians were a very religious race, and that they reverenced one Great Divine Spirit, whom they adored under various manifestations. Ignorance and insufficient information has caused confusion; therefore, let us try to consider the known symbolism with reason.

To check and compare the qualities of the various groups of gods and mental concepts of the ancients and find a parallel in the system of correspondences you should make a small diagram of the Quaballa starting with a centre vertical line 6 inches high. Divide this into four sections $1\frac{1}{2}$ inches for your generating circles. The radius of the Sephiroth will then be $\frac{3}{8}$ inches. Ignore the paths. This figure should then be placed on a thin sheet of celluloid and the Sephiroth cut out neatly with a sharp pointed knife. This master pattern will allow you to draw any number of figures quickly on which you can place the names of the groups of gods, mental qualities or whatever else you wish to analyse. The diagram is of such a size that four can be drawn on one page of your looseleaf notebook for comparison.

Three of the groups you have already, namely the Sephiroth names, Keywords and astrological references in Chapter 16. We give hereunder several alternative attributions which you can place using one column on each figure.

Magical Weapon	Symbolisms	Mental Qualities	Alternative
1. Lamp	Spiritual Light, the Royal Self	Spirit	
2. Wand	Magical Will or Divine Wisdom	Wisdom	Receptive Mind
3. Cup	Intuition	Understanding	Cosmic space of mind
4. Sceptre and crown	Lordship and Divinity	Grace and Mercy	Discrimination
5. Sword	Reason and Capacity to disperse alien thoughts	Destruction and transition	Mental Concepts
6. Lamen	Intention to perform the Great Work	Ego	Eternal Life
7. Robe	Splendour and Glory	Emotion	Powers of Darkness
8. Book of Invocations	His Karmic Record the Magical Memory	Low grade thinking	Spiritual Intelligence
9. Altar and perfumes	His fixed will and aspiration	Astral flux	Motive
10. Temple, circle and pentacle	The Temple of the Holy Ghost		Method

The first column gives the magical weapons used in ceremonial magic, the second column gives their symbolism. The third column gives one aspect of the mental qualities as given by the G.D. The fourth column gives an alternative rendering. All these concepts when compared with the occult law of "as above so below" increase and amplifies the understanding of the various series of qualities and furnishes a yard-stick for interpretation.

Theosophy	Egyptian	Division of Soul		Chakra
1. Atma	Khabs	Yechidah	The Point or Monad	Sahasrara
2. Buddhi	Khu	Chiah	The Creative Self	Agna
3. Higher Manas	Ab	Neschama	The Intuitive Self	Visuddhi
4. ⎫ 5. ⎬ Manas 6. ⎭	⎫ ⎬ Sek-hem ⎭	⎫ ⎬ Ruach	⎫ ⎬ The Intellect	Anahata
7. Kama				Svaddisthana
8. Prana	⎫ ⎬ Ba	⎭	⎭	Marupura
9. Linga-Sarira	⎭	Nepesh	Sub-consciousness	Muladhara
10. Sthula-Sarira	Khat	Guph	Physical body	

Attribution of the Tarot Suits:

Pentacles	Swords	Cups	Wands
1. Root of the Powers of Earth	Root of the Powers of Air	Root of the powers of Water	Roof of the Powers of Fire
2. Lord of Harmonious Change	Lord of Peace Restored	Love	Dominion
3. Material Works	Sorrow	Abundance	Established Strength
4. Earthly Power	Rest from Strife	Pleasure	Perfected Work
5. Material Trouble	Defeat	Loss in Pleasure	Strife
6. Material Success	Earned success	Pleasure	Victory
7. Success unfulfilled	Unstable effort	Illusionary success	Valour
8. Prudence	Shortened force	Abandoned success	Swiftness
9. Material gain	Despair and Cruelty	Material Happiness	Great Strength
10. Wealth	Ruin	Perfected success	Oppression

These Key words should enable you to reconcile the various numbered cards of the Tarot suits to the Sephiroth on the tree, thus expanding your comprehension of the relative values of the cards.

The Gods of the ancients have many interpretations according to their contexts and relationship. The selection below will give some indication of their attributes (according to Crowley).

Roman	Greek	Egyptian	
1. Jupiter	Pan	Ptah	Ptah
2. Janus	Zeus, Iaccus	Isis	Amoun, Thoth
3. Juno, Cybele Hecate	Athenu, Uranus	Nephthys	Mant, Isis, Nephthys
4. Jupiter	Cybele, Demeter, Rhea, Here	Amoun	Amoun, Isis
5. Mars	Poseidon	Horus	Horus, Nephthys
6. Apollo	Ares, Hades	Ra	Asar, Ra
7. Venus	Iaccus, Apollo, Adonis	Hathoor	Hathoor
8. Mercury	Aphrodite, Nike	Thoth	Anubis
9. Diana	Hermes	Shu	Shu
10. Ceres	Zeus, Diana	Osiris	Seb. unwedded Isis and Nephthys

Many of the so-called names of the Deities are not really true names, but rather descriptive titles. Compound names represent complex energies, and such a god lacks the simplicity which is the first attribute of a Godhead. In many cases the uncertainty of primitive alphabets causes in the course of time forms which cannot easily be recognized. Except in the case of the Hebrews it is almost impossible to select satisfactory attributes for any given name. The use of form, legend or some predominant characteristic can aid in determining the placing of a name. A god of varying qualities may be placed in different compartments according to the attribute being considered. For example, Isis could be related to 3 as Mother, to 4 as Venus, to 6 as Harmony, to 7 as Love, to 9 as the Moon and to 10 as Virgin and so on. This makes an analysis of the Egyptian Gods very difficult; and the examples given must be considered with this in mind.

Scandinavian Gods	Officers in Masonic Lodge	G.D. Grades	Egyptian Regardie	Gods Nere Amsu
1. Wotan	—	Ipsisissimus	Ptah, amour	Osiris
2. Odin	P.M.	Magus	Tahuti	Tefnut
3. Frigga	—	Magister Templi	Isis	Shu
4. Wotan	W.M.	Adeptus Exemptus	Maat	Nut
5. Thor	S.W.	Adeptus Major	Horus	Seb
6.	J.W.	Adeptus Minor	Ra, Osiris	Osiris
7. Freya	S.D.	Philosophus	Hathor	Set, Sut
8. Odin, Loki	J.D.	Practicus	Anubis	Horus
9.	I.G.	Theoreticus	Shu, Pasht	Isis
10.	T. & Can	Zelator, Neophyte	Seb	Nephthys

The attribution given in the first three columns above are from Crowley's *777*. The officers of the Masonic Lodge are Past Master, Worshipped Master, Senior and Junior Wardens, Senior and Junior Deacons, Inner Guard, Tyler and Candidate. The fourth column is taken from Regardie's *Garden of Pomegranates*. The last column is from the Papyrus of Nere Amsu. (B.M.10.188 described in Archaelogia Vol. 52 London 1891).

E. A. W. Budge. *The Gods of the Egyptians*. 1904 London.
E. A. W. Budge. *Egyptian Religion*. 1900 London.
J. G. Wilkinson. *The Ancient Egyptian* (6 Vols.). 1837–41 Murray.
J. Van Stone. *The Pathway of the Soul*. 1912 Fowler.
E. A. W. Budge. *Egyptian Collection Guide*. 1930 Brit. Mus.

Chapter 48. Hermes

Hermes Trismegistus or Thrice Greatest Hermes was the name given to the Egyptian Thoth or Tehuti, the God of learning, wisdom and literature. He was the author of the books carried in the sacred processions of Egypt, which were records of ancient events and mysteries. These books described only by Clemens of Alexandria, a Christian writer of the second and third centuries, must be considered as of late concoction, and as chiefly of Greek manufacture. The two books of Hermes borne by the Chanter; the four astronomical books of Hermes, borne by the Horoscopus, who likewise carried a sundial and palm; another book, with ink and a reed borne by the Hierogrammatus; the ten books relating to the ceremonies of worship, borne by the Stolist, and the ten books concerning the Gods and the education of the priests, which the Prophet was bound to learn, cannot be regarded as genuine remains of remote Egyptian antiquity. These books are stated to be forty-two in number, thirty-six of which are learned by the ministers of religion; the remaining six, containing treatises on medicine, are learned by the Pastophori, or shrine-bearers.

Hermes Trismegistus was a fiction of the Neo-Platonic philosophy. He was the supposed mystical author of all wisdom and knowledge; the source of all intellectual light. He was the offspring of the amalgamation of Oriental and Hellenic philosophers; and much of the oriental spirit of mysticism and of exaggeration is visible in the circle of ideas in which he moved. Iamblicus attributes to him 20,000 books, upon the authority of Seleucus; but he adds that Manetho has assigned to him 36,525 books; as this last number coincides with the total number of years of the Egyptian chronology in the Ancient Chronicles, where it is obtained by multiplying the 1461 years of the Canicular cycle by 25, we perceive that this mystical mode of computing the number of books of Hermes of late date.

In conclusion, we direct your attention to the *Discourse on Initiation* addressed by Hermes to his son Tatian, as a final reminder of the object of contemplation as a means of revealing the inner life.

"I address this discourse to thee, O Tatian! that thou mayest be initiated into the name of the Supreme God. If thou canst understand it, that which seems to thee for the most part to be invisible will become manifest, but the Invisible ever exists without having occasion to manifest itself. It ever exists, and it makes all things visible. Invisible because eternal, it makes all things become apparent without manifesting itself. Uncreated, it makes all things manifest by rendering them visible. Visibility belongs to things created, it is Genesis. He, therefore, who alone is Uncreate is for that very reason unrevealed and invisible; but by making all things manifest He reveals Himself in them and by them, more especially to those to whom He is willing to reveal Himself.

"Therefore, O my son, first pray to the Lord and Father of all, to the Only God, to the God from whom Unity has proceeded, that He may be favourable to thee, and that thou mayest be able to understand Him. Meditation alone can understand the Invisible, because it is itself invisible. If thou art able, thou wilt see Him, O Tatian, by the eyes of thine understanding, for the Lord does not hide Himself, He reveals Himself throughout the Universe. Thou canst understand Him, lay hold of Him with thine hands, and contemplate the image of God. But how could He manifest Himself to thee if that which is in thee is invisible to thyself? If thou wilt see him, think of the Sun, think of the Moon in her course, think of the stars in ordered array. Who sustains that order? For order is caused by number and by place. The Sun is the greatest of the gods of heaven : all the celestial gods recognize him as their King and their ruler; and this Star, greater than both earth and sea together, permits other stars much smaller than himself to revolve about him. What reverence, what awe is it that compels him to do so? The course of each of these other stars in the heavens is various and unequal. Who has appointed to each of them the direction and length of its course? The Great Bear revolves upon its own axis, and causes the universe to revolve with it. Who uses it as an instrument? Who has put limits to the sea? Who has laid the foundation of the earth?

"There is then O Tatian! a Creator and a Ruler of all this universe. Place, number and order could not be maintained without a Creator. Order cannot exist without place, and without

limits; there must therefore be a Ruler, O my son. Disorder must
have a Ruler that it may attain unto Order. If thou hadst wings,
couldst rise in the air, and there, hovering between earth and
heaven, couldst behold the solid earth, the languid seas, the flowing rivers, the light air, fire with its subtle nature, the courses of
the stars, and the heaven which envelopes them, what a magnificent spectacle thou wouldst behold, O my son. How thou wouldst
see in a moment the immovable moving, and the invisible becoming manifest in the order and beauty of the universe.

"If thou wouldst contemplate the Creator even in perishable
things, in things which are on earth, or in the deep, reflect, O my
son, on the formation of man in his mother's womb; contemplate
carefully the skill of the Workman; learn to know Him according
to the divine beauty of the work Who formed the orb of the eye?
Who pierced the openings of the nostrils and of the ears? Who
made the mouth to open? Who traced out the channels of the
veins? Who made the bones hard? Who covered the flesh with
skin? Who separated the fingers and the toes? Who made the feet
broad? Who hollowed out the pores? Who spread out the spleen?
Who formed the heart like a pyramid? Who made the sides wide?
Who formed the caverns of the lungs? Who made the honourable
parts of the body conspicuous, and concealed the others? See
how much skill is bestowed on one species of matter, how much
labour on one single work; everywhere there is beauty, everywhere perfection, everywhere variety. Who made all these things?
Who is the mother, who is the father, if it be not the only and
invisible God, who has created all these things by his will?

"No one pretends that a statue or a picture can exist without
a sculptor or a painter; and shall this creation not have a Creator?
O blindness. O impiety. O ignorance. Beware, O my son Tat.
How thou deprivest the work of the Workman. Rather give to
God, the name which suits him best. Call him the Father of all
things, for he is the only God, and it is his nature to be a Father,
and, if I may be permitted to use so bold an expression, it is his
nature to engender and to create. And as nothing can exist without a Creator, God himself could not exist if he were not incessantly creating in the air, on the earth, in the deep, in the universe
which is not God. He is that which is, and that which is not, for
he has made manifest that which is, and that which is not he
retains in himself.

"Such is the God who is superior to his name, the God invisible and visible, who reveals himself to the mind and to the sight, who has no body, and yet many bodies, or rather all bodies, for there is nothing which is not God. This is why all names are His, for He is the only Father, and this is why He has no name, for He is the Father of all. What can I say of thee? What can I say to Thee? Where shall I look that I may bless Thee? Above, below, within or without? There is no path, no place eternal to Thee. There are no beings but Thee. All is in Thee, all proceeds from thee. Thou givest all and receivest nothing which does not belong to Thee.

"When shall I praise Thee, O Father. For no one can know thy time or thine hour? For what should I praise Thee? for that which thou hast revealed, or for that which thou hast concealed? How shall I praise Thee, as belonging to me, and possessing Thee as mine own? Or as a Being who is distinct from me? For thou art all that I can be, all that I can do, all that I can say; for Thou art all, and there is nothing which is not Thee. Thou art all that is born, and all that is not born; Thou art wisdom in thought, the creating Father, the God who acts, the Supreme Deity, and the Author of all things. The subtlest thing in matter is air, in the air the soul, in the soul wisdom, in wisdom God."

Francis Barrett says "He was called Ter Maximus, as having a perfect knowledge of all things contained in the world (as his Aureus, or Golden Tractate, and his Divine Pymander show) which things he divided into three Kingdoms, e.g. animal, vegetable and mineral, in the knowledge and comprehension of which three he excelled and transmitted to posterity, in enigmas and symbols, the profound secrets of nature, likewise a true description of the Philosophers Quintessence, or Universal Elixir, which he made as the receptacle of all celestial and terrestial virtues. The great Secret of the philosophers he discoursed on, which was found engraved upon a Smaragdine table, in the valley of Ebron".